FUTURE
English for Results

1

Marjorie Fuchs

Lisa Johnson

Sarah Lynn

Irene Schoenberg

Series Consultants

Beatriz B. Díaz

Ronna Magy

Federico Salas-Isnardi

Future 1
English for Results

Pearson Education, 221 River Street, Hoboken, NJ 07030 USA

Staff credits: The people who made up the *Future* team, representing editorial, production, design, manufacturing, and marketing, are Pietro Alongi, Rhea Banker, Peter Benson, Nancy Blodget, Elizabeth Carlson, Jennifer Castro, Tracey Munz Cataldo, Natalia Cebulska, Aerin Csigay, Mindy DePalma, Dave Dickey, Gina DiLillo, Warren Fischbach, Pam Fishman, Nancy Flaggman, Irene Frankel, Shelley Gazes, Gosia Jaros-White, Mike Kemper, Niki Lee, Melissa Leyva, Stefan Machura, Amy McCormick, Linda Moser, Liza Pleva, Joan Poole, Sherry Preiss, Stella Reilly, Mary Rich, Lindsay Richman, Barbara Sabella, Katarzyna Starzynska-Kosciuszko, Loretta Steeves, Kim Steiner, Alexandra Suarez, Katherine Sullivan, Paula Van Ells, and Marian Wassner.

Cover design: Rhea Banker
Cover photo: Kathy Lamm/Getty Images
Text design: Elizabeth Carlson
Text composition: Word and Image Design Studio Inc.
Text font: Minion Pro

Library of Congress Cataloging-in-Publication Data
A catalog record for the print edition is available from the Library of Congress.

Printed in the United States of America
ISBN 13: 9780134696140 (Student Book with MyEnglishLab)
ISBN 10: 013469614X (Student Book with MyEnglishLab)
1 17

ISBN 13: 9780134659558 (Student Book with Essential Online Resources)
ISBN 10: 0134659554 (Student Book with Essential Online Resources)
3 17

The authors wish to thank **Irene Frankel** for managing a very complex project with great skill, intelligence, insight, and equanimity, and **Nancy Blodgett** for her enormous amount of hard work, dedication, support, and enthusiasm.

Marjorie Fuchs, Irene Schoenberg, Lisa Johnson, Sarah Lynn,
authors of Student Book 1

Contents

To the Teacher

Welcome to *Future*
English for Results

Future is a six-level, four-skills course for adults and young adults correlated to state and national standards. *Future* supports Workforce Innovation and Opportunity Act (WIOA) goals and prepares adults for College and Career Readiness (CCRS), English Language Proficiencies (ELP), job skills, standardized tests, and EL-Civics. It incorporates research-based teaching strategies, corpus-informed language, and the best of modern technology.

KEY FEATURES

Future provides everything your students need in one integrated program.

In developing the course, we listened to what teachers asked for and we responded, providing six levels, more meaningful content, a thorough treatment of grammar, explicit skills development, abundant practice, multiple options for state-of-the-art assessment, and innovative components.

Future serves students' real-life needs.

We began constructing the instructional syllabus for *Future* by identifying what is most critical to students' success in their personal and family lives, in the workplace, as members of a community, and in their academic pursuits. *Future* provides outstanding coverage of life-skills competencies, basing language teaching on actual situations that students are likely to encounter and equipping them with the skills they need to achieve their goals. The grammar and other language elements taught in each lesson grow out of these situations and thus are practiced in realistic contexts, enabling students to use language meaningfully, from the beginning.

Future grows with your students.

Future takes students from absolute beginner level through low-advanced proficiency in English, addressing students' abilities and learning priorities at each level. As the levels progress, the curricular content and unit structure change accordingly, with the upper levels incorporating more academic skills, more advanced content standards, and more content-rich texts.

Future is fun!

Humor is built into each unit of *Future*. Many of the conversations, and especially the listenings, are designed to have an amusing twist at the end, giving students an extra reason to listen—something to anticipate with pleasure and to then take great satisfaction in once it is understood. In addition, many activities have students interacting in pairs and groups. Not only does this make classroom time more enjoyable, it also creates an atmosphere conducive to learning in which learners are relaxed, highly motivated, and at their most receptive.

Future puts the best of 21st-century technology in the hands of students and teachers.

In addition to its expertly developed print materials and audio components, *Future* goes a step further.

- Every **Student Book** comes with **Essential Online Resources** and optional **MyEnglishLab** for use at home, in the lab, or wherever students have access to a computer. The online resources can be assigned by teachers and used both by students who wish to extend their practice beyond the classroom and by those who need to "make up" what they missed in class.
- The **Tests and Test Prep** book comes with the *Future* Exam*View*® *Assessment Suite*, enabling teachers to print ready-made tests, customize these tests, or create their own tests for life skills, grammar, vocabulary, listening, and reading.
- The **Companion Website** provides a variety of teaching support, including a PDF of the Teacher's Edition and Lesson Planner notes for each unit in the Student Book.

Future provides all the assessment tools you need.

- The **Placement Test** evaluates students' proficiency in all skill areas, allowing teachers and program administrators to easily assign students to the right classes.
- The **Tests and Test Prep** book for each level provides:
  - **Printed unit tests** with accompanying audio CD. These unit tests use standardized testing formats, giving students practice "bubbling-in" responses as required for CASAS and other standardized tests. In addition, reproducible test prep worksheets and practice tests (in the online resources) provide invaluable help to students unfamiliar with such test formats.
  - The *Future* Exam*View*® *Assessment Suite* is a powerful program that allows teachers to create their own unique tests or to print or customize already prepared tests at three levels: pre-level, at-level, and above-level.
- **Performance-based assessment:** Lessons in the Student Book end with a "practical assessment" activity such as Role Play, Make It Personal, or Show What You Know. Each unit culminates with both a role-play activity and a problem-solving activity, which require students to demonstrate their oral competence in a holistic way. The **Teacher's Edition and Lesson Planner** provides speaking rubrics to make it easy for teachers to evaluate students' oral proficiency.
- **Self-assessment:** For optimal learning to take place, students need to be involved in setting goals and in

monitoring their own progress. *Future* has addressed this in numerous ways. In the Student Book, checkboxes at the end of lessons invite students to evaluate their mastery of the material. End-of-unit reviews allow students to see their progress in grammar and writing. After completing each unit, students go back to the goals for the unit and reflect on their achievement. In addition, the Essential Online Resources and MyEnglishLab provide students with continuous feedback (and opportunities for self-correction) as they work through each lesson. The Workbook contains the answer keys, so that students can check their own work outside of class.

Future addresses multilevel classes and diverse learning styles.

Using research-based teaching strategies, *Future* provides teachers with creative solutions for all stages of lesson planning and implementation, allowing them to meet the needs of all their students.

- The **Multilevel Communicative Activities Book** provides an array of reproducible activities and games that engage students through different modalities. Teachers' notes provide multilevel options for pre-level and above-level students, as well as extension activities for additional speaking and writing practice.
- The **Teacher's Edition and Lesson Planner** offers pre-level and above-level variations for every lesson plan, as well as numerous optional and extension activities designed to reach students at all levels.
- The **Transparencies and Reproducible Vocabulary Cards** include picture and word cards that will help kinesthetic and visual learners acquire and learn new vocabulary. Teachers' notes include ideas for multilevel classes.
- The **Essential Online Resources** included with the Student Book have extraordinary tools for individualizing instruction, as well as providing immediate feedback. All new reading and writing printable activities support College and Career Readiness goals (for levels 1–5). Multiple life-skills and listening activities with listen, record, and compare functions allow students to practice these skills outside of class. In addition, the audio files for the book are available in the Essential Online Resources, enabling students to listen to any of the material that accompanies the text.
- The **MyEnglishLab** option includes everything in the Essential Online Resources and much more. Readings with interactive activities and feedback (for all units in levels 1–5) support College and Career Readiness skills. Grammar Coach video presentations and additional online interactive activities for all of the grammar lessons give students extra grammar practice.

- The **Workbook with Audio**, similarly, allows students to devote their time to the lessons and specific skill areas that they need to work on most. In addition, students can replay the audio portions they want to listen to as many times as necessary, choosing to focus on the connections between the written and spoken word, listening for grammar, pronunciation, and/or listening for general comprehension.

Future's persistence curriculum motivates students to continue their education.

Recent research about persistence has given us insights into how to keep students coming to class and how to keep them learning when they can't attend. Recognizing that there are many forces operating in students' lives—family, jobs, childcare, health—that may make it difficult for them to come to class, programs need to help students:
- Identify their educational goals.
- Believe that they can successfully achieve them.
- Develop a commitment to their own education.
- Identify forces that can interfere with school attendance.
- Develop strategies that will help them try to stay in school in spite of obstacles.

Future addresses all of these areas with its persistence curriculum. Activities found throughout the book and specific persistence activities in the back of the book help students build community, set goals, develop better study skills, and feel a sense of achievement. In addition, the Essential Online Resources and MyEnglishLab are unique in their ability to ensure that even those students unable to attend class are able to make up what they missed and thus persist in their studies.

Future supports busy teachers by providing all the materials teachers need, plus teacher support.

The **Student Book**, **Workbook with Audio**, **online resources**, **Multilevel Communicative Activities Book**, and **Transparencies and Reproducible Vocabulary Cards** were designed to provide teachers with everything they need in the way of ready-to-use classroom and homework materials so they can concentrate on responding to their students' needs.

Future provides ample practice with flexible options to best fit the needs of each class.

The Student Book provides 60–100 hours of instruction. It can be supplemented in class by using:
- Teacher's Edition and Lesson Planner expansion ideas
- Transparencies and Reproducible Vocabulary Cards
- Workbook exercises
- Multilevel Communicative Activities

- Tests
- Essential Online Resources activities, as well as Student Book audio
- MyEnglishLab activities
- Activities on the Companion Website (futureenglishforresults.com)

TEACHING MULTILEVEL CLASSES

Teaching tips for pair and group work

Using pair and group work in an ESL classroom has many proven benefits. It creates an atmosphere of liveliness, builds community, and allows students to practice speaking in a low-risk environment. Many of the activities in *Future* are pair and small-group activities. Here are some tips for managing these activities:

- Limit small groups to three or four students per group (unless an activity specifically calls for larger groups). This maximizes student participation.
- Change partners for different activities. This gives students a chance to work with many others in the class and keeps them from feeling "stuck."
- If possible, give students a place to put their coats when they enter the classroom. This allows them to move around freely without worrying about returning to their own seats.
- Move around the classroom as students are working to make sure they are on task and to monitor their work.
- As you walk around, try to remain unobtrusive, so students continue to participate actively, without feeling they are being evaluated.
- Keep track of language points students are having difficulty with. After the activity, teach a mini-lesson to the entire class addressing those issues. This helps students who are having trouble without singling them out.

Pairs and groups in the multilevel classroom

Adult education ESL classrooms are by nature multilevel. This is true even if students have been given a placement test. Many factors—including a student's age, educational background, and literacy level—contribute to his or her ability level. Also, the same student may be at level in one skill, but pre-level or above-level in another.

When grouping students for a task, keep the following points in mind:

- *Like-ability* groups (in which students have the same ability level) help ensure that all students participate equally, without one student dominating the activity.
- *Cross-ability* groups (in which students have different ability levels) are beneficial to pre-level students who need the support of their at- or above-level classmates. The higher-level students benefit from "teaching" their lower-level classmates.

For example, when students are practicing a straightforward conversation substitution exercise, like-ability pairings are helpful. The activity can be tailored to different ability levels, and both students can participate equally. When students are completing the more complex task of creating their own conversations, cross-ability pairings are helpful. The higher-level student can support and give ideas to the lower-level student.

The *Future* Teacher's Edition and Lesson Planner, the Teacher's Notes in the Multilevel Communicative Activities Book, and the Teacher's Notes in the Transparencies and Reproducible Vocabulary Cards all provide specific suggestions for when to put students in like-ability versus cross-ability groups, and how to tailor activities to different ability levels.

Level	Description	CASAS Scale Scores
Intro	True Beginning	Below 180
1	Low Beginning	181–190
2	High Beginning	191–200
3	Low Intermediate	201–210
4	High Intermediate	211–220
5	Low Advanced	221–235

Unit Tour

Unit Opener

Each unit starts with a full-page photo that introduces the themes and vocabulary of the unit.

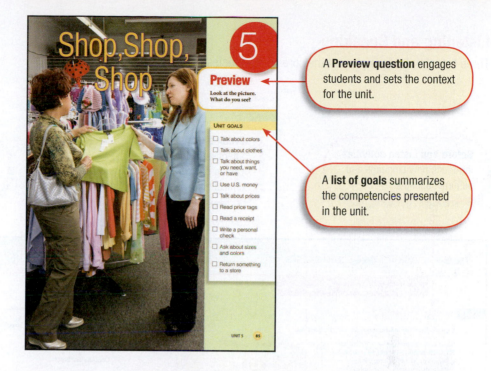

A **Preview question** engages students and sets the context for the unit.

A **list of goals** summarizes the competencies presented in the unit.

Vocabulary

Theme-setting vocabulary is presented in picture dictionary format.

Oral and written activities provide abundant vocabulary practice.

Show what you know activities allow students to use new words in conversation and provide an assessment opportunity for the teacher.

Vocabulary learning strategies give students the tools to continue learning outside of class.

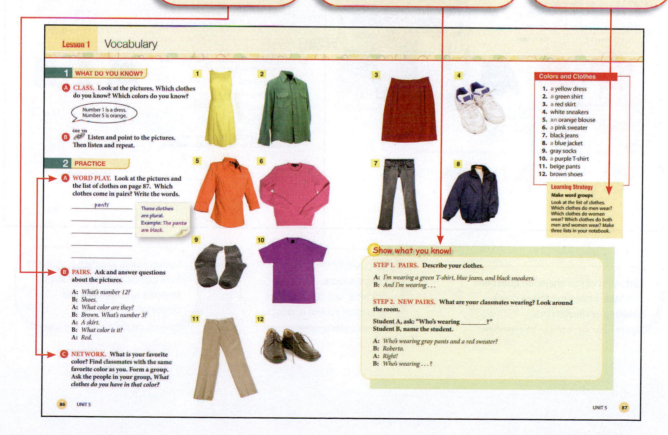

Listening and Speaking

Three listening lessons present the core competencies and language of the unit.

Before You Listen activities introduce new language and cultural concepts.

Prediction questions focus attention on the context-setting photo and encourage critical thinking.

The **Pronunciation Watch** and exercises focus on the sound patterns, stress, and intonation of English.

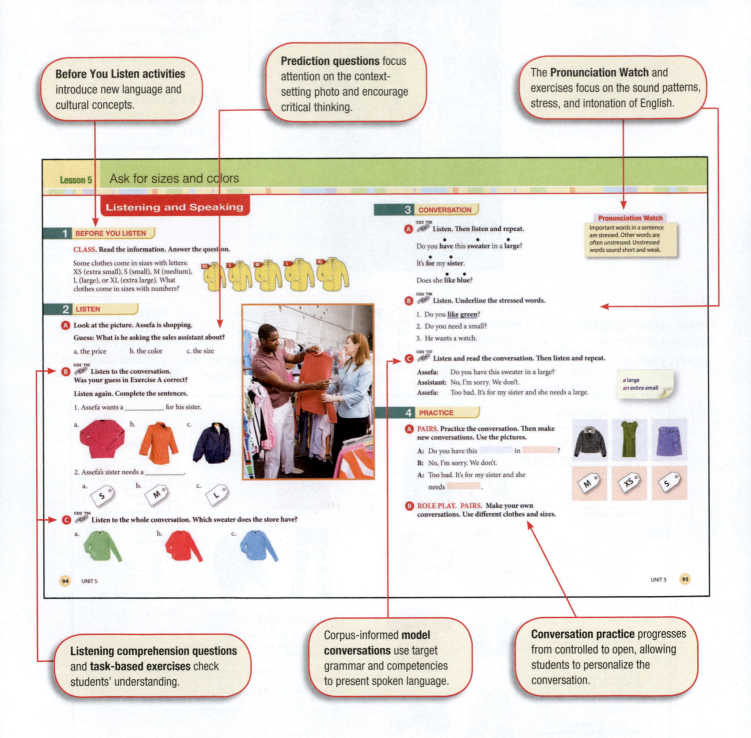

Listening comprehension questions and **task-based exercises** check students' understanding.

Corpus-informed **model conversations** use target grammar and competencies to present spoken language.

Conversation practice progresses from controlled to open, allowing students to personalize the conversation.

Grammar

Each unit presents three grammar points in a logical, systematic grammar syllabus.

Grammar charts present the target grammar point with minimal metalanguage.

Grammar Watch notes call attention to specific aspects of the grammar point.

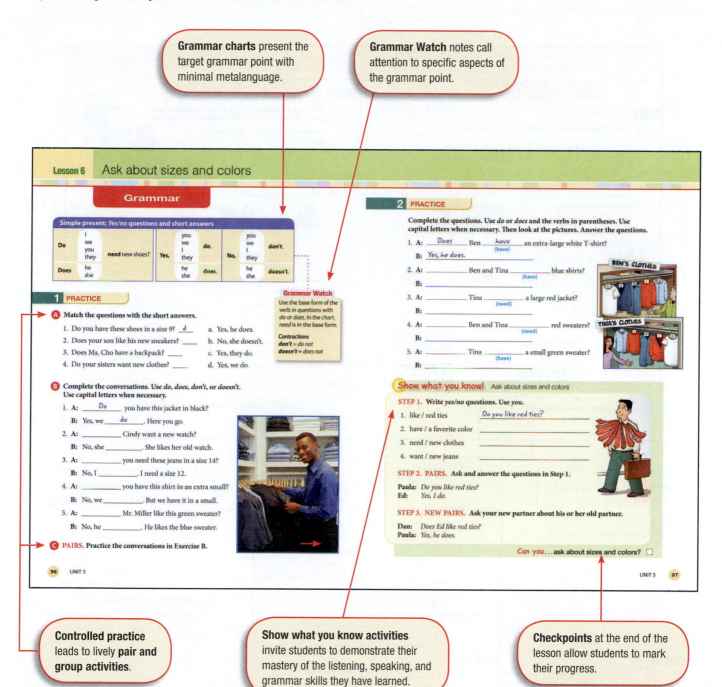

Controlled practice leads to lively **pair and group activities**.

Show what you know activities invite students to demonstrate their mastery of the listening, speaking, and grammar skills they have learned.

Checkpoints at the end of the lesson allow students to mark their progress.

Life Skills

The Life Skills lesson in each unit focuses on functional language, practical skills, and authentic printed materials, such as schedules, labels, and signs.

Short conversations model functional language related to the Life Skills topic.

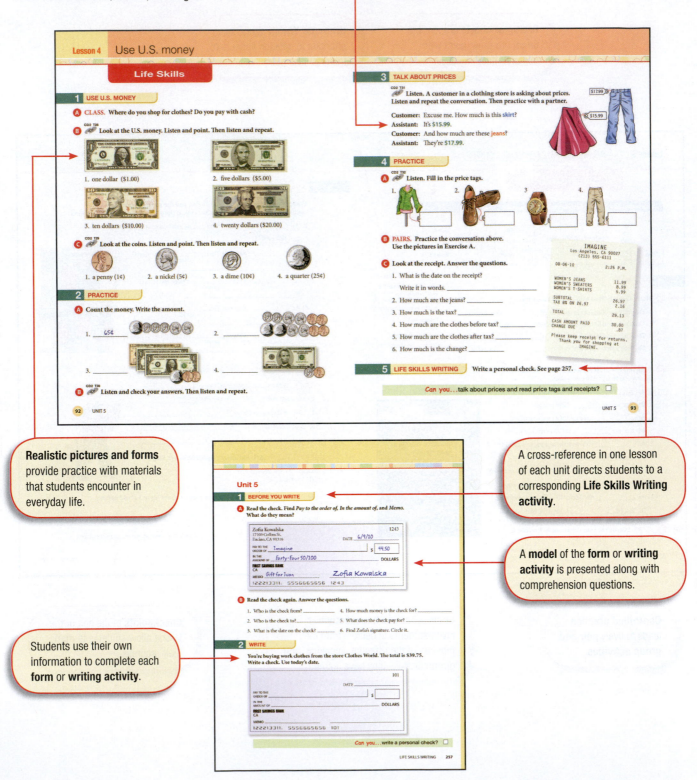

Realistic pictures and forms provide practice with materials that students encounter in everyday life.

A cross-reference in one lesson of each unit directs students to a corresponding **Life Skills Writing activity**.

A **model** of the **form** or **writing activity** is presented along with comprehension questions.

Students use their own information to complete each **form** or **writing activity**.

Reading

High-interest articles introduce students to cultural concepts and useful, topical information. Students read to learn while learning to read in English.

Pre-reading questions accompanied by pictures pre-teach vocabulary and activate students' background knowledge.

The **article** recycles language that students have learned.

Reading

1 BEFORE YOU READ

A CLASS. Look at the $5 bill. Who is the man in the picture?

B Look at other bills you have. Who are the people on the bills?

C Look at the U.S. presidents on the coins. Which presidents do you know?

1. GEORGE WASHINGTON
2. JOHN ADAMS
3. THOMAS JEFFERSON
4. JAMES MADISON

D GROUPS OF 3. Look at the coins again. Answer the questions in the chart.

	Which president is on the coin?	When was he president?	Which president was he?
1	George Washington	1789–1797	first
2			
3			
4			

2 READ

CD2 T38

Listen. Read the article.

The New One-Dollar Coin

Many Americans don't know the names of the U.S. presidents. But now people can learn their names. How? With money! The U.S. government is making four new $1 coins every year. Each coin shows a different U.S. president.

The front of each coin has a lot of information about the president. It has the president's picture, his name, the dates he was president, and which president he was. For example, the George Washington coin says that he

The new George Washington $1 coin

was the president from 1789 to 1797. It also says he was the first president.

The back of the coin shows the Statue of Liberty. The date of the coin is on the edge.

Some people like the new coins. But other people don't like them. In the past, the U.S. government made other $1 coins. Those coins were not popular. Will the U.S. president $1 coins be popular? We'll have to wait and see.

3 CHECK YOUR UNDERSTANDING

A Read the article again. What is the main idea? Complete the sentence.

The U.S. government is making new _____.

B Read the sentences. Circle *True* or *False*.

1. Most Americans know all the U.S. presidents.   True   (False)
2. The new $1 coins show different U.S. presidents.   True   False
3. On the front of the coin, you see the Statue of Liberty.   True   False
4. The old $1 coins were not popular   True   False

Show what you know!

PAIRS. Talk about it. Do you have any $1 coins? What is on them? Do you use them? Do you like them?

Comprehension questions check understanding of the article and build reading skills.

Show what you know activities allow students to internalize, personalize, and apply the information they have learned.

Review

The Review page synthesizes the unit grammar through contextualized cloze or dictation activities.

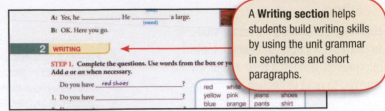

A **Writing section** helps students build writing skills by using the unit grammar in sentences and short paragraphs.

Expand

The final page of the unit allows students to review and expand on the language, themes, and competencies they have worked with throughout the unit.

Lively **role-play activities** motivate students, allowing them to feel successful. Teachers can use these activities to assess students' mastery of the material.

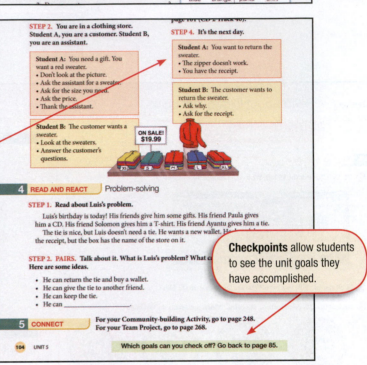

Cross-references direct students to the **Persistence Activity** and **Team Project** for that unit.

Checkpoints allow students to see the unit goals they have accomplished.

Persistence Activities

Persistence activities build community in the classroom, help students set personal and language goals, and encourage students to develop good study skills and habits.

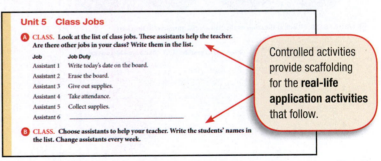

Controlled activities provide scaffolding for the **real-life application activities** that follow.

Team Projects

Each unit includes a collaborative project that integrates all of the unit themes, language, and competencies in a community-building activity.

A **graphic organizer** helps students collect the information they need for the task.

Students work in teams to create a **poster**, **chart**, **graph**, or **booklet** that relates to the unit theme.

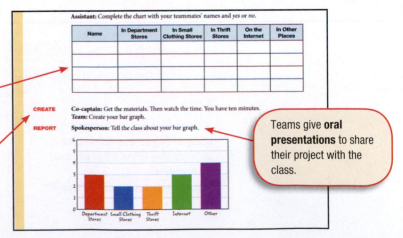

Teams give **oral presentations** to share their project with the class.

MyEnglishLab

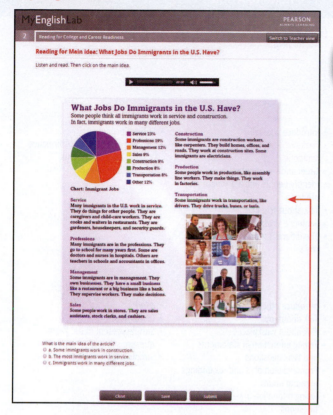

MyEnglishLab delivers rich online content to engage and motivate **students**.

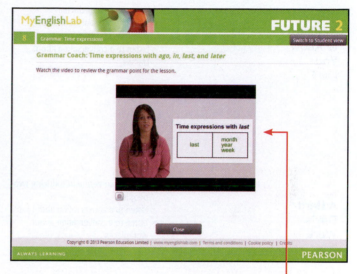

Grammar Coach videos give additional grammar presentations and practice.

MyEnglishLab also provides students with:
- rich interactive practice in listening, speaking, vocabulary building, and life skills
- immediate and meaningful feedback on wrong answers
- grade reports that display performance and time on task

Reading and writing lessons, based on College and Career Readiness Standards (CCRS), develop essential skills for academic and career readiness.

MyEnglishLab delivers innovative teaching tools and useful resources to **teachers**.

With **MyEnglishLab**, teachers can:
- view student scores by unit and activity
- monitor student progress on any activity or test
- analyze class data to determine steps for remediation and support

Scope and Sequence

UNIT	VOCABULARY	LISTENING	SPEAKING AND PRONUNCIATION	GRAMMAR	
Pre-Unit **Getting Started** *page 2*	Classroom instructions; Asking for help	• Listen to classroom instructions • Listen to ways of asking for help	• Follow classroom instructions • Ask for help	• Introduction to imperatives	
1 **Getting to Know You** *page 5*	Countries	• Listen to an introduction • Listen to a conversation about countries of origin • Listen to a conversation about classes	• Introduce yourself • Shake hands when you meet someone • Greet and say goodbye • Identify people and ask where they are from • Talk about school • Sentence stress • The different sounds in *he's* and *she's*	• Subject pronouns • Simple present of *be*: Affirmative and negative statements • Contractions with *be*	
2 **A Hard Day's Work** *page 25*	Jobs; Workplaces	• Listen to someone introducing two people • Listen to a conversation about jobs • Listen to a conversation about workplaces	• Introduce others • Talk about jobs • Talk about workplaces • Falling intonation in statements and *Wh-* questions • Pronunciation of *-s* and *-es* endings in plural nouns • Rising intonation in *yes/no* questions	• *A/an* • Plural nouns • Simple present of *be*: *Yes/no* questions and short answers • Simple present of *work* and *live*	
3 **Time for Class** *page 45*	Things in a classroom; People and places at school	• Listen to a teacher giving instructions for a test • Listen to a conversation about things in the classroom • Listen to a conversation about people and places at school	• Give and follow classroom commands • Talk about things in the classroom • Identify people at school • Get someone's attention and ask for information • Voiced *th* sound • Word stress	• Imperatives • *This, that, these, those* • Object pronouns	
4 **Family Ties** *page 65*	Family members; Physical descriptions	• Listen to a conversation about family members • Listen to a conversation about what someone looks like • Listen to a conversation about children's ages and grades in school	• Talk about family members • Describe people • Give age and child's grade in school • Understand the U.S. school system • Understand cultural appropriateness of asking about age • Pronunciation of possessive *'s* • Linking words together: consonant to vowel	• Possessive adjectives and *'s* with names • *Be* and *have* with descriptions • *How old is/are . . . ?*	

LIFE SKILLS	READING	WRITING	NUMERACY	PERSISTENCE
• Learn the letters of the alphabet • Learn numbers	• Locate the U.S. map in your book	• Identify capital and lowercase letters	• Learn numbers	• Learn about your book • Learn about working in pairs and groups
• Give first and last name • Give spellings • Use appropriate titles • Complete a personal information form	• Read a paragraph about class attendance • Read an article about immigrants in the U.S. • Problem-solving: Read a paragraph about class placement	• Write sentences about your name and marital status • Write sentences about yourself, a classmate, or your teacher • Start country names with capital letters • Start people's names with capital letters • Start sentences with capital letters • End sentences with a period	• Interpret a pie chart • Take a class survey	• Talk about attendance • Persistence Activity: Name game • Project: Make a poster about your classmates
• Use cardinal numbers 0–9 • Give phone number and area code • Read a telephone directory • Listen to a message and write a phone number • Complete a form at work • Project: Create a Venn diagram of jobs and workplaces	• Read an introduction of two people • Read an article about talking to a job counselor • Problem-solving: Read a paragraph about work schedules	• Write a sentence about someone's job • Write sentences about your job and workplace • End questions with a question mark	• Learn cardinal numbers 0–9	• Network Activity: Find classmates with the same job as you. • Persistence Activity: Goal setting: Why learn English?
• Use cardinal numbers 10–100 • Give locations of places around school • Complete a school registration form	• Read a paragraph about arriving late to class • Read a letter of advice about good study habits • Problem-solving: Read a paragraph about test-taking	• Write sentences about things in your classroom • Write tips for learning English	• Count classroom items • Learn cardinal numbers 10–100	• Understand classroom rules • Learn good study habits • Set study goals • Network Activity: Find classmates who want to practice the same study skill as you. • Identify learning strategies • Project: Make a booklet about your school • Persistence Activity: School supplies
• Use ordinal numbers 1st–31st • Identify day, date, and month • Read calendars • Write dates in numbers and words • Give date of birth and birthday • Complete an emergency contact form • Project: Make a calendar of holidays	• Read an article about blended families • Read a paragraph about the physical characteristics of family members • Problem-solving: Read a paragraph about personal phone calls at work	• Write sentences about yourself and your family • Start months with capital letters	• Interpret a calendar • Learn ordinal numbers 1st–31st • Count students and categorize by physical description • Interpret a pie chart • Understand percentages • Calculate age based on date of birth	• Network Activity: Find classmates with the same birthday month as you. • Persistence Activity: My friends and family

Text in red = Civics and American culture

UNIT	VOCABULARY	LISTENING	SPEAKING AND PRONUNCIATION	GRAMMAR	
5 **Shop, Shop, Shop** *page 85*	Colors and clothes	• Listen to a conversation about shopping for a gift • Listen to a customer asking about sizes and colors • Listen to interviews with people returning clothing to a store	• Talk about needs and wants • Ask about sizes • Read size labels • Talk about likes and dislikes • Return something to a store • Sentence rhythm (weak words)	• Simple present affirmative • Simple present: *Yes/no* questions and short answers • Simple present negative	
6 **Home, Sweet Home** *page 105*	Rooms of a house, furniture, and appliances	• Listen to a conversation about a house for rent • Listen to a conversation with a building manager about features of an apartment • Listen to directions on an automated telephone recording	• Describe a house or apartment • Ask about apartment and house rentals • Give directions • Stress in compound nouns	• *There is/There are* • *There is/There are: Yes/no* questions • Prepositions of direction and location	
7 **Day After Day** *page 125*	Daily routines and leisure activities; Clock times	• Listen to a conversation about schedules • Listen to a conversation about weekend activities • Listen to a radio show about ways of relaxing	• Talk about daily routines • Ask when something happens • Talk about leisure activities • Talk about frequency of activities • The weak pronunciation of *do you* in questions • Pronunciation of *-s* and *-es* endings in third-person singular present tense verbs	• *Wh-* questions and prepositions of time • Adverbs of frequency • *How often?* and expressions of frequency	
8 **From Soup to Nuts** *page 145*	Common foods	• Listen to two friends talking about food they like and dislike • Listen to someone ordering a meal in a restaurant • Listen to a call-in radio show about nutrition	• Talk about likes and dislikes • Read a menu • Order meals in a restaurant • Talk about the nutritional value of common foods • Talk about different ways to prepare food • Pronunciation of *I like* and *I'd like* • Intonation of choice questions with *or*	• Count and non-count nouns • Choice questions with *or* • *How much/How many*	

LIFE SKILLS	READING	WRITING	NUMERACY	PERSISTENCE
• Use U.S. money • Talk about prices • Read a receipt • Understand sales tax • Write a personal check • Project: Talk about where classmates shop for clothes	• Read a paragraph about a birthday gift • Read about clothing sizes • Read an article about presidential dollar coins • Identify presidents • Problem-solving: Read a paragraph about returning gifts	• Write sentences about problems with clothing • Write sentences about things people need, want, or have • Use hyphens in amounts on personal checks	• Learn values of U.S. money • Count U.S. money • Understand prices • Understand a shopping receipt • Make a bar graph about where classmates shop	• Network Activity: Find classmates with the same favorite color as you. • Persistence Activity: Class jobs
• Read addresses • Give addresses • Read an Apartment for Rent ad • Understand how to rent an apartment • Address an envelope • Project: Make a floor plan for your dream house	• Read an article about smoke alarms and fire safety at home • Read a paragraph about furnished apartments • Problem-solving: Read a paragraph about rent increases	• Write sentences about houses and things in them • Write directions to a place • Use abbreviations in addresses	• Talk about numbers of rooms in a home • Compare rents of two homes	• Network Activity: Find classmates who live in your neighborhood. • Persistence Activity: My vocabulary learning startegies
• Identify abbreviations for days of the week • Interpret a work schedule • Read and complete a time sheet • Understand Social Security numbers • Write a note to request time off	• Read about weekly schedules • Read an article about how Americans spend their free time • Problem-solving: Read a paragraph about busy schedules	• Write sentences about your schedule and free-time activities • Use capital letters for days of the week • Use abbreviations for days of the week	• Tell time • Count hours worked in a day or week • Interpret bar graphs • Conduct a survey about classmates' free time and make a bar graph • Project: Create a schedule	• Network Activity: Find classmates with the same free-time activity as you. • Persistence Activity: Daily planner
• Read store flyers and compare prices for food • Read food labels • Understand U.S. measurements of weight • Write a note listing things to buy • Project: Create a menu	• Read a paragraph about what someone eats for lunch • Read an article about expiration dates on food • Problem-solving: Read a paragraph about healthy eating habits	• Write a shopping list • Write a sentence about the nutritional value of foods • Write sentences about food your classmates want • Use commas between things in a list	• Learn weights of food • Compare prices • Understand nutritional information on food labels	• Network Activity: Find classmates who shop for food near your home. • Persistence Activity: Getting-to-know-you tea

Text in red = Civics and American culture

UNIT	VOCABULARY	LISTENING	SPEAKING AND PRONUNCIATION	GRAMMAR	
9 **Rain or Shine** *page 165*	Weather, seasons, and temperature	• Listen to a conversation about weather and current activities • Listen to a conversation about preparing for a storm • Listen to a weather report for different U.S. cities • Understand temperatures in degrees Fahrenheit	• Talk about activities taking place now • Talk about the weather • Pronunciation of *–ing* ending • Project: Give a weather report	• Present continuous: Affirmative and negative statements • Present continuous: *Yes/no* questions and answers • Adverbs of degree: *Really, very, pretty*	
10 **Around Town** *page 185*	Places in the community	• Listen to a conversation about the location of a place • Listen to someone giving directions by bus • Listen to a radio show about weekend events • Learn how to get information about events in your community	• Ask where places are • Ask about bus routes, schedules, and fares • Talk about activities in the immediate future • Word stress • Sentence stress	• Prepositions of place • Simple present: Questions with *how, how much,* and *where* • Present continuous for the future	
11 **Health Matters** *page 205*	Parts of the body; Symptoms and illnesses	• Listen to a mother calling school about a sick child • Understand and follow procedures for a child missing school • Listen to a conversation with someone who missed work • Identify appropriate reasons to miss work • Listen to a call-in radio show about remedies for illnesses	• Call to explain absence • Describe symptoms • Call in sick to work • Talk about past activities • Give advice • Pronunciation of *was/were* and *wasn't/weren't*	• Review: Simple present statements and questions • *Be* simple past: Statements • *Should*: Statements	
12 **Help Wanted** *page 225*	Job duties	• Listen to someone asking about a job and talking about his skills • Listen to a conversation about availability • Listen to an interview with the owners of a new business	• Respond to a Help Wanted sign • Talk about ability and inability • Ask a co-worker to work your shift • Respond to personal information questions in a simple job interview • Ask and answer questions about past experience • Sentence stress: *Can* and *can't* in statements • Sentence stress: *Can* and *can't* in short answers	• *Can* for ability: Affirmative and negative statements • *Can* for ability: Questions and short answers • *Be* simple past: *Yes/no* and *Wh-* questions	

LIFE SKILLS	READING	WRITING	NUMERACY	PERSISTENCE
• Talk about weather conditions • Respond to weather emergencies • Create an emergency plan for your family • Write a postcard to a friend	• Read a paragraph about the weather in two cities • Read an article about small talk • Understand how to make small talk • Problem-solving: Read a paragraph about weather emergencies	• Write sentences about activities you or others are doing currently • Write sentences about today's weather • Use the degree mark for temperatures	• Read a thermometer in degrees Fahrenheit	• Network Activity: Find classmates who spend their day off the same way as you. • Persistence Activity: Important dates in school
• Identify forms of transportation • Identify traffic signs • Interpret destination signs on buses • Read bus schedules • Write directions to get to a place	• Read a paragraph about the location of a new supermarket • Read an article about resources available at the public library • Get a library card • Problem-solving: Read a paragraph about items left on a bus	• Write sentences about your weekend plans • Write sentences about your classmates' weekend plans	• Understand a bus schedule	• Network Activity: Find classmates who get to school the same way as you. • Persistence Activity: Things I read in English • Project: Make a booklet about places in your community
• Make a doctor's appointment • Read an appointment card • Follow instructions during a medical exam • Interpret medicine labels • Complete a medical information form • Project: Make a poster about healthy habits	• Read a paragraph about illnesses • Read an article about the health benefits of walking • Problem-solving: Read a paragraph about a sick child	• Write sentences comparing two pictures • Write suggestions for health problems	• Read medicine labels and understand correct dosages	• Talk about attendance • Persistence Activity: Individual barriers, group support
• Read want ads • Identify different ways to find a job • Complete a job application • Project: Make a list of skills needed for your dream job	• Read a paragraph about a busy day at a clothing store • Read an article about appropriate body language for a job interview • Problem-solving: Read a paragraph about recommending someone for a job	• Write a want ad for a job you want • Write sentences about your job experience and skills • Use commas in short answers to *yes/no* questions	• Calculate weekly earnings based on hourly wages	• Network Activity: Find classmates with the same work shift as you. • Persistence Activity: Now I can

Text in red = Civics and American culture

Correlations

UNIT	CASAS Reading Basic Skill Content Standards	CASAS Listening Basic Skill Content Standards	
1	**U1:** R1.2; 1.3; 1.4; 2.2; 2.4; 2.5; 3.1; 3.3; 3.8; 6.1; **L3:** R1.1; 2.6; 2.4; **L4:** 1.4; **L5:** 2.5; **L6:** 3.10; 3.12; **L7:** 3.1; 3.2; **L8:** 3.10; SWYK Review: 3.10	**U1:** L1.1; 1.2; 1.4; 2.1; 3.1; **L1:** L1.2; 2.3; **L3:** 3.4; **L4:** 1.3; **L5:** 3.2; **L6:** 3.3; **L7:** 1.2; 1.4; 3.1; 3.4; 4.2; 4.10; SWYK Expand: L3.3; 3.4; 4.1; L4.2	
2	**U2:** R1.2; 1.3; 1.4; 2.2; 2.4; 2.5; 3.1; 3.3; 3.8; 6.1; **L2:** R3.12; **L3:** 6.1; **L4:** 4.1; **L7:** 3.2; 3.3; SWYK Expand: 3.3; 3.10	**U2:** L1.1; 1.2; 1.4; 2.1; 3.1; **L1:** L1.1; 3.1; 3.4; 4.1; **L2:** 1.2; 1.4; **L3:** 3.1; **L4:** 3.6; **L5:** 3.3	
3	**U3:** R1.2; 1.3; 1.4; 2.2; 2.4; 2.5; 3.1; 3.1; 3.3; 3.8; 6.1; **L1:** R3.12; **L2:** 3.3; 3.6; 3.10; **L3:** 3.6; 3.12; **L4:** 3.3; 3.6; 3.12; 7.1; 7.8; **L6:** 3.10; 3.12; **L7:** 4.1; 4.9; **L9:** 3.10; SWYK Review: 3.10; SWYK Expand: 7.1; 7.8	**U3:** L1.1; 12; 1.4; 2.1; 3.1; **L1:** L1.1; 1.2; **L2:** 2.1; 2.5; 4.1; **L4:** 3.4; **L7:** 1.1; 1.2; 2.3; **L8:** 2.1; 3.3; 3.4; SWYK Expand: 5.2	
4	**U4:** R1.2; 1.3; 1.4; 2.2; 2.4; 2.5; 3.1; 3.1; 3.3; 3.8; 6.1; **L1:** R3.10; **L2:** 3.10; **L3:** 3.10; **L4:** 2.2; 4.9; **L5:** 3.11; **L7:** 4.1; 4.3; **L9:** 3.12; SWYK Review: 3.12; SWYK Expand: 3.11	**U4:** L1.1; 12; 1.4; 2.1; 3.1; **L1:** L3.4; **L2:** 3.4; **L3:** 1.3; **L5:** 3.3; 3.4; **L7:** 3.4; **L8:** 3.4; 4.2; **L9:** 3.4; SWYK Expand: 3.4	
5	**U5:** R1.2; 1.3; 1.4; 2.2; 2.4; 2.5; 2.12; 3.1; 3.1; 3.3; 3.8; 4.1; 4.4; 6.1; **L3:** R6.1; **L4:** 4.6; 5.1; **L5:** 6.1; **L6:** 2.5; 6.1; **L7:** 6.3; SWYK Expand: 3.11; 4.9	**U5:** L1.1; 12; 1.4; 2.1; 3.1; **L1:** L3.4; **L2:** 5.1; **L4:** 3.5; **L5:** 3.3; **L7:** 3.3; 3.11; **L8:** 5.2; 6.1; SWYK Review: 3.4; SWYK Expand: 3.3	
6	**U6:** R1.2; 1.3; 1.4; 2.2; 2.4; 2.5; 3.1; 3.1; 3.3; 3.8; 6.1; **L1:** R3.12; **L2:** 2.7; 3.12; 4.1; 6.2; **L3:** 2.7; 3.12; 6.2; **L4:** 3.3; 3.11; 3.12; 4.1; **L5:** 3.3; 3.12; **L6:** 3.12; **L7:** 2.7; 4.1; 6.2; **L8:** 4.9; **L9:** 3.12; SWYK Review: 3.12; SWYK Expand: 3.3	**U6:** L1.1; 12; 1.4; 2.1; 3.1; **L1:** L3.3; **L2:** 5.1; 5.2; **L3:** 3.4; **L5:** 3.2; 3.3; 3.4; 4.3; 6.5; **L6:** 3.2; 3.3; **L7:** 3.1; 3.4; **L8:** 3.4; 4.3; 5.1; SWYK Review: 3.3; 3.4; SWYK Expand: 3.3; 3.4	
7	**U7:** R1.2; 1.3; 1.4; 2.2; 2.4; 2.5; 3.1; 3.1; 3.3; 3.8; 6.1; **L1:** R2.7; 4.1; **L2:** 4.2; **L3:** 4.2; 4.6; **L4:** 4.2; 4.6; **L5:** 4.6; **L6:** 4.2; 4.6; **L7:** 3.3; 3.11; **L9:** 4.6; SWYK Review: 4.6; SWYK Expand: 3.3; 3.11	**U7:** L1.1; 12; 1.4; 2.1; 3.1; **L1:** L1.1; 3.1; **L2:** 3.3; 3.4; **L3:** 3.4; **L4:** 3.4; **L5:** 3.1; 3.4; 4.1; 4.2; **L7:** 3.1; **L8:** 3.1; 5.1; 5.2; **L9:** 3.4; SWYK Review: 3.43.1; 5.1; 5.23.1; 3.4; 4.1; 4.2	
8	**U8:** R1.2; 1.3; 1.4; 2.2; 2.4; 2.5; 3.1; 3.1; 3.3; 3.8; 6.1; **L1:** R4.1; 4.8; **L2:** 3.3; 4.2; **L3:** 4.1; **L4:** 3.3; 3.11; 4.1; 4.3; 4.9; 6.2; **L5:** 4.1; 4.4; **L7:** 3.11; 4.1; 6.2; 7.8; **L8:** 4.1; 4.8; SWYK Review: 4.1; SWYK Expand: 3.3; 3.11; 4.4	**U8:** L1.1; 12; 1.4; 2.1; 3.1; **L1:** L1.1; 3.1; **L2:** 3.4; **L3:** 1.3; **L5:** 1.3; 3.3; 5.1; **L6:** 3.4; **L8:** 5.1; SWYK Review: 1.3; SWYK Expand: 3.3	
9	**U9:** R1.2; 1.3; 1.4; 2.2; 2.4; 2.5; 3.1; 3.1; 3.3; 3.8; 6.1; **L1:** R4.8; **L2:** 3.12; 4.9; 6.1; **L3:** 7.13; **L4:** 2.12; **L5:** 6.1; **L7:** 6.1; 7.7; 7.8; **L8:** 6.1; SWYK Expand: 7.8	**U9:** L1.1; 12; 1.4; 2.1; 3.1; **L1:** 1.1; 3.4; **L2:** 5.1; **L4:** 1.1; **L5:** 3.1; **L7:** 3.4; **L8:** 1.1; 5.1; SWYK Expand: 5.2	
10	**U10:** R1.2; 1.3; 1.4; 2.2; 2.4; 2.5; 3.1; 3.1; 3.3; 3.8; 6.1; **L1:** R3.13; **L2:** 3.3; 4.9; 6.1; **L3:** 4.9; 6.1; **L4:** 2.1; 4.8; **L5:** 4.8; **L6:** 3.12; **L7:** 3.12; 6.2; SWYK Review: 2.5; 4.6; SWYK Expand: 4.9	**U10:** L1.1; 12; 1.4; 2.1; 3.1; **L1:** L1.1; **L2:** 3.4; 4.1; 5.1; **L4:** 2.4; 3.4; **L5:** 3.4; 3.5; **L6:** 3.4; 3.5; **L8:** 5.1; **L9:** 3.4; SWYK Review: 3.4; SWYK Expand: 3.4	
11	**U11:** R1.2; 1.3; 1.4; 2.2; 2.4; 2.5; 3.1; 3.1; 3.3; 3.8; 6.1; **L1:** R2.12; **L2:** 2.12; **L4:** 3.6; 3.7; 3.11; 4.6; 6.2; **L5:** 3.14; 7.4; **L6:** 7.4; **L7:** 6.1; 6.2; 7.8; **L8:** 6.1; **L9:** 2.1; SWYK Review: 3.14; 7.4; SWYK Expand: 3.14	**U11:** L1.1; 12; 1.4; 2.1; 3.1; **L1:** L1.1; 2.1; **L2:** 5.11; **L4:** 1.3; 3.7; 3.8; 5.1; **L5:** 1.3; 3.7; 3.8; **L7:** 3.3; **L8:** 5.1; **L9:** 2.5; SWYK Expand: 2.5; 3.4	
12	**U12:** R1.2; 1.3; 1.4; 2.2; 2.4; 2.5; 3.1; 3.1; 3.3; 3.8; 6.1; **L1:** R3.2; 3.3; **L2:** 6.1; **L4:** 2.7; 2.12; 4.6; **L5:** 3.12; 3.14; **L6:** 3.14; **L7:** 3.11; 7.1; **L9:** 4.6; SWYK Review: 4.6; SWYK Expand: 4.6	**U12:** L1.1; 12; 1.4; 2.1; 3.1; **L1:** L1.1; 3.4; **L2:** 5.1; **L3:** 3.8; **L5:** 5.1; 7.1; **L6:** 3.4; **L8:** 5.1; **L9:** 3.4; 3.5; SWYK Review: 3.4; 3.5; SWYK Expand: 3.4; 3.5	

CASAS Competencies	Unit CCR Standards
U1: 0.1.4, 0.1.5; **L1:** 0.1.6, 0.1.7, 0.2.1; **L2:** 0.1.1, 0.1.6, 0.1.7, 0.2.1; **L3:** 0.1.7, 0.2.2, 0.2.3; **L4:** 0.1.2, 0.2.1; **L5:** 0.1.2, 0.2.1; **L6:** 2.7.2, 2.7.3, 6.4.2, 6.7.4; **L7:** 0.1.2, 0.1.7, 0.2.1; **L8:** 0.1.2, 0.1.7, 0.2.3; **SWYK Review:** 0.1.1, 0.1.2, 0.1.7, 0.2.1, 0.2.3, 7.3.1; **SWYK Expand:** 0.1.2, 0.1.7, 0.2.1, 0.2.3, 0.2.4	RI/RL.1.1, RI.1.2, RI.1.3, RI.1.4, RI.1.7, RI.1.8, W.1.3, W.1.5, W.1.8, SL.1.1, SL.K.2, SL.K.3, SL.1.4, SL.K.6, SL.1.6, L.1.1.d, L.1.1.e, L.1.1.f, L.1.1.g, L.1.1.l, L.1.2.a, L.1.2.b, L.1.2.c, L.1.2.d, L.1. 4.a, L.1.5.a, L.1.5.b, L.1.5.c, L.1.6
U2: 0.1.4, 0.1.5, 0.1.7, 4.1.8; **L1:** 0.2.1, 0.2.4, 7.4.1; **L2:** 0.2.1, 0.2.4; **L3:** 0.2.1, 0.2.4; **L4:** 0.2.2, 2.1.7, 6.0.1, 6.0.2; **L5:** 0.2.1, 0.2.4; **L6:** 0.2.1, 0.2.4; **L7:** 0.2.1, 0.2.4, 4.4.1; **L8:** 0.2.1, 0.2.4, 4.4.1; **L9:** 0.1.2, 0.2.1, 0.2.4, 7.4.3; **SWYK Review:** 0.1.2, 0.2.1, 0.2.3; **SWYK Expand:** 0.1.2, 0.2.1, 0.2.3, 0.2.4, 6.6.5, 7.1.1, 7.3.1, 7.3.2	RI/RL.1.1, RI.1.2, RI.1.3, RI.1.4, RI.1.7, RI.1.8, W.1.3, W.1.5, W.1.8, SL.1.1, SL.K.2, SL.K.3, SL.1.4, SL.K.6, SL.1.6, L.1.1.b, L.1.1.c, L.1.1.e, L.1.1.g, L.1.1.i, L.1.1.l, L.1.2.c, L.1.2.d, L.1.2.g, L.1.2.h, L.1.2.i, L.1. 4.a, L.1.5.a, L.1.5.b, L.1.5.c, L.1.6
U3: 0.1.2, 0.1.4, 0.1.5, 0.1.7, 0.2.1, 0.2.4; **L1:** 7.4.1; **L3:** 0.2.3, 2.8.5; **L4:** 0.2.3, 7.1.1, 7.4.1; **L7:** 2.8.3, 6.0.1, 6.0.2; **L8:** 2.8.3; **SWYK Review:** 0.2.3; **SWYK Expand:** 0.2.3, 2.8.2, 2.8.3, 7.1.1, 7.3.1, 7.3.2	RI/RL.1.1, RI.1.2, RI.1.3, RI.1.4, RI.1.7, RI.1.8, W.1.2, W.1.5, W.1.8, SL.1.1, SL.K.2, SL.K.3, SL.1.4, SL.K.6, SL.1.6, L.1.1.d, L.1.1.e, L.1.1.g, L.1.1.i, L.1.1.l, L.1. 4.a, L.1.5.a, L.1.5.b, L.1.5.c, L.1.6
U4: 0.1.2, 0.1.4, 0.1.5, 0.1.7; **L1:** 0.2.1, 0.2.4, 6.7.3, 7.4.1; **L2:** 0.2.1, 0.2.4, 6.7.3; **L3:** 0.2.1, 0.2.4; **L4:** 0.2.1, 0.2.4, 2.7.3, 6.4.2, 6.7.4; **L5:** 0.2.1, 0.2.4; **L6:** 0.2.1, 0.2.4; **L7:** 0.2.1, 0.2.4, 2.3.2, 2.3.4, 6.0.1, 6.0.2; **L8:** 0.2.1, 0.2.4, 2.1.2, 2.5.1, 2.8.1; **SWYK Review:** 0.2.1, 0.2.3, 0.2.4; **SWYK Expand:** 0.2.1, 0.2.3, 0.2.4, 2.3.2, 2.3.4, 2.7.1, 7.1.1, 7.3.1, 7.3.2	RI/RL.1.1, RI.1.2, RI.1.3, RI.1.4, RI.1.7, RI.1.8, W.1.3, W.1.5, W.1.8, SL.1.1, SL.K.2, SL.K.3, SL.1.4, SL.K.6, SL.1.6, L.1.1.b, L.1.1.e, L.1.1.f, L.1.1.g, L.1.1.l, L.1.2.b, L.1. 4.a, L.1.5.a, L.1.5.b, L.1.5.c, L.1.6
U5: 0.1.2, 0.1.4, 0.1.5, 0.1.7, 0.2.1, 0.2.4; **L1:** 1.2.9, 7.4.1; **L2:** 1.2.9; **L3:** 1.2.9, 7.4.3; **L4:** 1.1.6, 1.2.1, 1.2.4, 1.2.9, 1.6.4, 1.8.1, 5.4.2, 6.1.5; **L5:** 1.2.9; **L6:** 1.2.9; **L7:** 1.1.6, 5.2.1; **L8:** 1.3.3, 1.6.4; **L9:** 0.2.3, 1.2.9; **SWYK Review:** 0.2.3, 1.2.9; **SWYK Expand:** 0.2.3, 1.2.1, 1.2.2, 1.2.5, 1.2.6, 1.2.9, 1.3.1, 1.3.3, 7.3.1, 7.3.2	RI/RL.1.1, RI.1.2, RI.1.3, RI.1.4, RI.1.5, RI.1.7, RI.1.8, RI.1.9, W.1.2, W.1.5, W.1.8, SL.1.1, SL.K.2, SL.K.3, SL.1.4, SL.K.6, SL.1.6, L.1.1.e, L.1.1.g, L.1.1.l, L.1. 4.a, L.1.5.a, L.1.5.b, L.1.5.c, L.1.6
U6: 0.1.2, 0.1.4, 0.1.5, 0.1.7, 0.2.1, 0.2.4; **L1:** 0.2.3, 1.4.1, 7.4.1; **L2:** 1.4.1, 1.4.2; **L3:** 0.2.3, 1.4.1, 1.4.2; **L4:** 1.4.1, 1.4.8, 6.4.2, 6.7.4; **L5:** 1.4.1; **L6:** 1.4.1, 1.4.8; **L7:** 0.2.3, 1.4.2, 2.4.1; **L8:** 2.1.7, 2.1.8, 2.2.1; **L9:** 2.2.1; **SWYK Review:** 0.2.3, 1.4.1, 1.4.2, 2.2.1, 7.1.1, 7.4.1; **SWYK Expand:** 0.2.3, 7.3.1, 7.3.2	RI/RL.1.1, RI.1.2, RI.1.3, RI.1.4, RI.1.5, RI.1.7, RI.1.8, W.1.2, W.1.5, W.1.8, SL.1.1, SL.K.2, SL.K.3, SL.1.4, SL.K.6, SL.1.6, L.1.1.e, L.1.1.j, L.1.1.l, L.1. 4.a, L.1.5.a, L.1.5.b, L.1.5.c, L.1.6
U7: 0.1.2, 0.1.4, 0.1.5, 0.1.7, 0.2.1, 0.2.4; **L1:** 2.3.1, 7.4.1; **L2:** 2.3.1, 2.3.2, 2.6.1; **L3:** 0.2.3, 2.3.1, 2.3.2; **L4:** 0.2.3, 4.2.1, 3.1, 2.3.2, 4.4.3, 4.6.2; **L5:** 2.3.1, 2.6.1; **L6:** 2.3.2; **L7:** 6.7.2; **L8:** 0.1.8, 2.6.1; **SWYK Review:** 0.2.3; **SWYK Expand:** 0.2.3, 2.3.1, 7.1.1, 7.3.1, 7.3.2	RI/RL.1.1, RI.1.2, RI.1.3, RI.1.4, RI.1.5, RI.1.7, RI.1.8, W.1.2, W.1.5, W.1.8, SL.1.1, SL.K.2, SL.K.3, SL.1.4, SL.K.6, SL.1.6, L.1.1.e, L.1.1.j, L.1.1.l, L.1.2.b, L.1. 4.a, L.1.5.a, L.1.5.b, L.1.5.c, L.1.6
U8: 0.1.2, 0.1.4, 0.1.5, 0.1.7, 0.2.1, 0.2.4; **L1:** 1.2.8, 3.5.1, 3.5.2, 7.4.1; **L2:** 0.1.8, 1.2.8, 2.3.1; **L3:** 0.1.8, 0.2.3, 1.2.8; **L4:** 1.2.8, 1.4.1, 1.6.1; **L5:** 1.2.8, 2.6.4, 3.5.1; **L6:** 1.2.8, 2.6.4; **L7:** 0.2.3, 1.2.2, 1.2.4, 1.6.1, 1.6.5, 3.5.1, 3.5.2; **L8:** 1.2.4, 1.6.1, 3.5.1, 3.5.2; **L9:** 1.2.4; **SWYK Review:** 0.2.3, 1.2.4; **SWYK Expand:** 0.2.3, 2.6.4, 7.3.1, 7.3.2	RI/RL.1.1, RI.1.2, RI.1.3, RI.1.4, RI.1.7, RI.1.8, W.1.2, W.1.5, W.1.8, SL.1.1, SL.K.2, SL.K.3, SL.1.4, SL.K.6, SL.1.6, L.1.1.b, L.1.1.e, L.1.1.h, L.1.1.l, L.1.2.e, L.1. 4.a, L.1.5.a, L.1.5.b, L.1.5.c, L.1.6
U9: 0.1.2, 0.1.4, 0.1.5, 0.1.7, 0.2.1, 0.2.4; **L1:** 2.3.3, 7.4.1; **L2:** 0.1.8, 2.1.8, 2.3.3; **L3:** 0.2.3, 7.4.3; **L4:** 0.2.3, 2.1.2, 2.3.3, 2.5.1, 3.4.8; **L5:** 2.3.3, 2.5.1, 3.4.8; **L6:** 1.2.9; **L7:** 0.1.8, 0.2.3, 2.3.3; **L8:** 1.2.9, 2.3.3; **L9:** 0.2.3, 2.3.3; **SWYK Review:** 0.2.3; **SWYK Expand:** 0.2.3, 1.2.8, 2.3.2, 2.3.3, 3.4.8, 7.3.1, 7.3.2	RI/RL.1.1, RI.1.2, RI.1.3, RI.1.4, RI.1.7, RI.1.8, W.1.2, W.1.5, W.1.8, SL.1.1, SL.K.2, SL.K.3, SL.1.4, SL.K.6, SL.1.6, L.1.1.e, L.1.1.f, L.1.1.g, L.1.1.l, L.1.2.g, L.1.2.h, L.1.2.i, L.1. 4.a, L.1. 4.c, L.1.5.a, L.1.5.b, L.1.5.c, L.1.6
U10: 0.1.2, 0.1.4, 0.1.5, 0.1.7, 0.2.1, 0.2.4; **L1:** 0.1.6, 1.2.6, 1.2.7, 2.2.1, 2.5.1, 7.4.1; **L2:** 1.2.6, 1.2.7, 2.2.1; **L3:** 1.2.6, 1.2.7; **L4:** 1.9.1, 2.2.2, 2.2.3, 2.2.4; **L5:** 1.1.6, 2.2.2, 2.2.3, 2.2.4; **L6:** 1.3.1, 2.2.1; **L7:** 0.2.3, 2.5.6; **L8:** 2.6.1, 2.6.3; **SWYK Review:** 0.2.3, 2.6.3; **SWYK Expand:** 0.2.3, 2.6.3, 7.3.1, 7.3.2, 7.4.1	RI/RL.1.1, RI.1.2, RI.1.3, RI.1.4, RI.1.7, RI.1.8, W.1.3, W.1.5, W.1.8, SL.1.1, SL.K.2, SL.K.3, SL.1.4, SL.K.6, SL.1.6, L.1.1.e, L.1.1.g, L.1.1.j, L.1.1.l, L.1. 4.a, L.1.5.a, L.1.5.b, L.1.5.c, L.1.6
U11: 0.1.2, 0.1.4, 0.1.5, 0.1.7, 0.1.8, 0.2.1, 0.2.4; **L1:** 3.6.1, 7.4.1; **L2:** 3.6.1, 3.6.3, 3.6.4, 3.6.5; **L3:** 3.1.3, 3.6.3, 3.6.4; **L4:** 0.1.6, 0.2.3, 3.1.2, 3.2.1, 3.3.1, 3.3.2, 3.3.4, 3.6.3, 3.6.4; **L5:** 2.3.2, 3.1.2, 3.6.3, 3.6.4, 3.6.5; **L6:** 3.6.3; **L7:** 3.4.2, 3.5.2, 3.5.9; **L8:** 3.4.2, 3.5.4, 3.5.9, 3.6.3; **L9:** 0.1.3, 3.3.2, 3.4.1; **SWYK Review:** 0.1.3; **SWYK Expand:** 0.1.3, 3.5.2, 3.5.4, 3.5.8, 3.5.9, 7.1.1, 7.3.1, 7.3.2	RI/RL.1.1, RI.1.2, RI.1.3, RI.1.4, RI.1.7, RI.1.8, W.1.5, W.1.8, SL.1.1, SL.K.2, SL.K.3, SL.1.4, SL.K.6, SL.1.6, L.1.1.e, L.1.1.g, L.1.1.l, L.1. 4.a, L.1.5.a, L.1.5.b, L.1.5.c, L.1.6
U12: 0.1.2, 0.1.4, 0.1.5, 0.1.7, 0.2.1, 0.2.4; **L1:** 0.2.3, 4.1.6, 4.1.8, 7.4.3; **L2:** 4.1.2, 4.1.3, 4.1.6, 4.1.8, 4.1.9; **L3:** 4.1.2, 4.1.3, 4.1.6, 4.1.8; **L4:** 0.2.3, 4.1.2, 4.1.3, 4.1.6, 4.1.8; **L5:** 4.1.6, 4.1.8, 4.8.3; **L6:** 0.2.3, 4.1.2, 4.1.3, 4.1.6, 4.1.8, 4.1.9, 4.8.3; **L7:** 0.1.8, 4.1.2, 4.1.5, 4.1.6, 4.4.1; **L8:** 0.1.8; **L9:** 0.1.6, 0.1.8, 4.1.2, 4.1.5, 4.1.6, 4.1.8; **SWYK Review:** 0.1.6, 4.1.2, 4.1.5, 4.1.6, 4.1.7, 4.1.8; **SWYK Expand:** 0.1.6, 4.1.2, 4.1.5, 4.1.6, 4.1.7, 4.1.8, 7.1.1, 7.3.1, 7.3.2	RI/RL.1.1, RI.1.2, RI.1.3, RI.1.4, RI.1.7, RI.1.8, W.1.3, W.1.5, W.1.8, SL.1.1, SL.K.2, SL.K.3, SL.1.4, SL.K.6, SL.1.6, L.1.1.e, L.1.1.g, L.1.1.l, L.1. 4.a, L.1.5.a, L.1.5.b, L.1.5.c, L.1.6

About the Series Consultants and Authors

SERIES CONSULTANTS

Dr. Beatriz B. Díaz has taught ESL for more than three decades in Miami. She has a master's degree in TESOL and a doctorate in education from Nova Southeastern University. She has given trainings and numerous presentations at international, national, state, and local conferences throughout the United States, the Caribbean, and South America. Dr. Díaz is the district supervisor for the Miami-Dade County Public Schools Adult ESOL Program, one of the largest in the United States.

Ronna Magy has worked as an ESL classroom teacher and teacher-trainer for nearly three decades. Most recently, she has worked as the ESL Teacher Adviser in charge of site-based professional development for the Division of Adult and Career Education of the Los Angeles Unified School District. She has trained teachers of adult English language learners in many areas, including lesson planning, learner persistence and goal setting, and cooperative learning. A frequent presenter at local, state and national, and international conferences, Ms. Magy is the author of adult ESL publications on life skills and test preparation, U.S. citizenship, reading and writing, and workplace English. She holds a master's degree in social welfare from the University of California at Berkeley.

Federico Salas-Isnardi has worked for 20 years in the field of adult education as an ESL and GED instructor, professional development specialist, curriculum writer, and program administrator. He has trained teachers of adult English language learners for over 15 years on topics ranging from language acquisition and communicative competence to classroom management and individualized professional development planning. Mr. Salas-Isnardi has been a contributing writer or consultant for a number of ESL publications, and he has co-authored curriculum for site-based workforce ESL and Spanish classes. He holds a master's degree in applied linguistics from the University of Houston and has completed a number of certificates in educational leadership.

AUTHORS

Marjorie Fuchs has taught ESL at New York City Technical College and LaGuardia Community College of the City University of New York and EFL at the Sprach Studio Lingua Nova in Munich, Germany. She has a master's degree in applied English linguistics and a certificate in TESOL from the University of Wisconsin–Madison. She has authored or co-authored many widely used books and multimedia materials, notably *Focus on Grammar: An Integrated Skills Approach* (levels 3 and 4), *Longman English Interactive 3* and *4*, *Grammar Express* (*Basic and Intermediate*), and workbooks to the *Oxford Picture Dictionary*.

Lisa Johnson has taught ESL and EFL for 20 years in the United States, Taiwan, and Russia, and is currently an instructor at City College of San Francisco. Based on her experience teaching VESL courses, she co-authored *Apply Yourself: English for Job Search Success*. She also co-authored or edited the Communication Companions for the *Longman English Interactive* series and contributed to *Talking Business Intermediate*: *Mastering the Language of Business*. In addition, she co-authored a large-scale curriculum for health care professionals. Ms. Johnson holds a master's degree in TESOL from the University of Northern Iowa.

Sarah Lynn has taught ESL and EFL for 20 years in the United States and abroad, and she currently teaches ESL at the Harvard Bridge to Learning and Literacy Program in Cambridge, Massachusetts. Ms. Lynn holds a master's degree in TESOL from Teachers College, Columbia University. She has trained volunteers and given workshops on the teaching of reading, kinesthetic techniques in the classroom, and cross-cultural communication. She has developed curricula for adult education programs in the areas of reading, life skills, and civics, and she is the co-author of *Business Across Cultures*. She has also contributed to numerous teacher resource materials, including those for *Side by Side*, *Foundations*, and *Word by Word*.

Irene E. Schoenberg has taught ESL for more than two decades at Hunter College's International English Language Institute and at Columbia University's American Language Program. Ms. Schoenberg holds a master's degree in TESOL from Teachers College, Columbia University. She has trained teachers at Hunter College, Columbia University, and the New School University, and she has given workshops and academic presentations at ESL programs and conferences throughout the world. Ms. Schoenberg is the author or co-author of numerous publications, including *True Colors*; *Speaking of Values 1*; *Topics from A to Z*, Books 1 and 2; and *Focus on Grammar: An Integrated Skills Approach* (levels 1 and 2).

Acknowledgments

The authors and publisher would like to extend special thanks to our Series Consultants whose insights, experience, and expertise shaped the course and guided us throughout its development.

Beatriz B. Díaz Miami-Dade County Public Schools, Miami, FL
Ronna Magy Los Angeles Unified School District, Los Angles, CA
Federico Salas-Isnardi Texas A & M University—TCALL, College Station, TX

We would also like to express our gratitude to the following individuals. Their kind assistance was indispensable to the creation of this program.

Consultants

Wendy J. Allison Seminole Community College, Sanford, FL
Claudia Carco Westchester Community College, Valhalla, NY
Maria J. Cesnik Ysleta Community Learning Center, El Paso, TX
Edwidge Crevecoeur-Bryant University of Florida, Gainesville, FL
Ann Marie Holzknecht Damrau San Diego Community College, San Diego, CA
Peggy Datz Berkeley Adult School, Berkeley, CA
MaryAnn Florez D.C. Learns, Washington, D.C.
Portia LaFerla Torrance Adult School, Torrance, CA
Eileen McKee Westchester Community College, Valhalla, NY
Julie Meuret Downey Adult School, Downey, CA
Sue Pace Santa Ana College School of Continuing Education, Santa Ana, CA
Howard Pomann Union County College, Elizabeth, NY
Mary Ray Fairfax County Public Schools, Falls Church, VA
Gema Santos Miami-Dade County Public Schools, Miami, FL
Edith Uber Santa Clara Adult Education, Santa Clara, CA
Theresa Warren East Side Adult Education, San Jose, CA

Piloters

MariCarmen Acosta American High School, Adult ESOL, Hialeah, FL
Resurrección Ángeles Metropolitan Skills Center, Los Angeles, CA
Linda Bolognesi Fairfax County Public Schools, Adult and Community Education, Falls Church, VA
Patricia Boquiren Metropolitan Skills Center, Los Angeles, CA
Paul Buczko Pacoima Skills Center, Pacoima, CA
Matthew Horowitz Metropolitan Skills Center, Los Angeles, CA
Gabriel de la Hoz The English Center, Miami, FL
Cam-Tu Huynh Los Angeles Unified School District, Los Angeles, CA
Jorge Islas Whitewater Unified School District, Adult Education, Whitewater, WI
Lisa Johnson City College of San Francisco, San Francisco, CA
Loreto Kaplan Collier County Public Schools Adult ESOL Program, Naples, FL
Teressa Kitchen Collier County Public Schools Adult ESOL Program, Naples, FL
Anjie Martin Whitewater Unified School District, Adult Education, Whitewater, WI
Elida Matthews College of the Mainland, Texas City, TX
Penny Negron College of the Mainland, Texas City, TX
Manuel Pando Coral Park High School, Miami, FL
Susan Ritter Evans Community Adult School, Los Angeles, CA
Susan Ross Torrance Adult School, Torrance, CA
Beatrice Shields Fairfax County Public Schools, Adult and Community Education, Falls Church, VA
Oscar Solís Coral Park High School, Miami, FL
Wanda W. Weaver Literacy Council of Prince George's County, Hyattsville, MD

Reviewers

Lisa Agao Fresno Adult School, Fresno, CA
Carol Antuñano The English Center, Miami, FL
Euphronia Awakuni Evans Community Adult School, Los Angeles, CA
Jack Bailey Santa Barbara Adult Education, Santa Barbara, CA
Robert Breitbard District School Board of Collier County, Naples, FL
Diane Burke Evans Community Adult School, Los Angeles, CA
José A. Carmona Embry-Riddle Aeronautical University, Daytona Beach, FL
Veronique Colas Los Angeles Technology Center, Los Angles, CA
Carolyn Corrie Metropolitan Skills Center, Los Angeles, CA
Marti Estrin Santa Rosa Junior College, Sebastopol, CA
Sheila Friedman Metropolitan Skills Center, Los Angeles, CA
José Gonzalez Spanish Education Development Center, Washington, D.C.
Allene G. Grognet Vice President (Emeritus), Center for Applied Linguistics
J. Quinn Harmon-Kelley Venice Community Adult School, Los Angeles, CA
Edwina Hoffman Miami-Dade County Public Schools, Coral Gables, FL
Eduardo Honold Far West Project GREAT, El Paso, TX
Leigh Jacoby Los Angeles Community Adult School, Los Angeles, CA
Fayne Johnson Broward County Public Schools, Ft. Lauderdale, FL
Loreto Kaplan, Collier County Public Schools Adult ESOL Program, Naples, FL
Synthia LaFontaine Collier County Public Schools, Naples, FL
Gretchen Lammers-Ghereben Martinez Adult Education, Martinez, CA
Susan Lanzano Editorial Consultant, Briarcliff Manor, NY
Karen Mauer ESL Express, Euless, TX
Rita McSorley North East Independent School District, San Antonio, TX
Alice-Ann Menjivar Carlos Rosario International Public Charter School, Washington, D.C.
Sue Pace Santa Ana College School of Continuing Education, Santa Ana, CA
Isabel Perez American High School, Hialeah, FL
Howard Pomann Union County College, Elizabeth, NJ
Lesly Prudent Miami-Dade County Public Schools, Miami, FL
Valentina Purtell North Orange County Community College District, Anaheim, CA
Mary Ray Fairfax County Adult ESOL, Falls Church, VA
Laurie Shapero Miami-Dade Community College, Miami, FL
Felissa Taylor Nause Austin, TX
Meintje Westerbeek Baltimore City Community College, Baltimore, MD

Thanks also to the following teachers, who contributed their ideas for the Persistence Activities:

Dave Coleman Los Angeles Unified School District, Los Angeles, CA
Renee Collins Elk Grove Adult and Community Education, Elk Grove, CA
Elaine Klapman Venice Community Adult School, Venice, CA (retired)
Yvonne Wong Nishio Evans Community Adult School, Los Angeles, CA (retired)
Daniel S. Pittaway North Orange County Community College District, Anaheim, CA
Laurel Pollard Educational Consultant, Tucson, AZ
Eden Quimzon Santiago Canyon College, Division of Continuing Education, Orange, CA

Getting Started

Welcome to Class

1 USE THE ALPHABET

CD1 T2

A 🔘 Look at the letters. Listen and point. Then listen and repeat.

> • Letters can be *capital letters.*
>   Examples: *A, B, C*
> • Letters can also be *small letters.*
>   Examples: *a, b, c*

Aa	Bb	Cc	Dd	Ee	Ff	Gg	Hh	Ii	Jj	Kk	Ll	Mm
Nn	Oo	Pp	Qq	Rr	Ss	Tt	Uu	Vv	Ww	Xx	Yy	Zz

B **PAIRS.** Look at the letters again. Student A, say a letter. Student B, point to the letter.

CD1 T3

C 🔘 Listen. Circle the letter you hear.

1. (A) E 2. F S 3. I Y 4. B V

5. K Q 6. C Z 7. H A 8. G J

CD1 T4

D 🔘 Listen. Write the letter.

1. __A__ 2. _____ 3. _____ 4. _____ 5. _____

> These letters are *vowels.* Other letters are *consonants.*

2 USE NUMBERS

CD1 T5

A 🔘 Look at the numbers. Listen and point. Then listen and repeat.

1	2	3	4	5	6	7	8	9
10	20	30	40	50	60	70	80	90

B **PAIRS.** Look at the numbers again. Student A, say a number. Student B, point to the number.

CD1 T6

C 🔘 Listen. Write the number you hear.

1. __5__ 2. _____ 3. _____ 4. _____ 5. _____

6. _____ 7. _____ 8. _____ 9. _____ 10. _____

3 FOLLOW INSTRUCTIONS

Look at the pictures. Listen to your teacher. Repeat the sentences.

Take out your book.

Point to the picture.

Read the information.

Put away your book.

Look at the board.

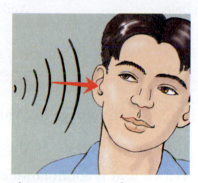
Listen to your teacher.

Open your notebook.

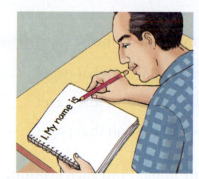
Write sentences.

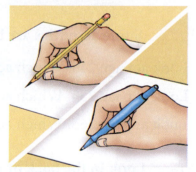
Use a pencil./Use a pen.

4 ASK FOR HELP

Read the questions. Listen to your teacher and repeat.

Can you repeat that, please?

How do you say _____ in English?

5 WORK WITH YOUR CLASS

Look at the pictures. Listen to your teacher. Repeat the sentences.

Work in pairs.

Work in groups.

Work as a class.

6 LEARN ABOUT YOUR BOOK

A **CLASS.** Turn to page iii. Answer the questions.

1. How many units are in this book?
2. Which unit is about families?
3. Which unit is about health?

B **CLASS.** Some activities are in the back of the book. Answer the questions.

1. Look at page 245. Which activities start on that page?
2. Look at page 253. Which activities start on that page?
3. Look at page 265. Which activities start on that page?

C **PAIRS.** Look in the back of your book. Find each section.
Write the page number.

Map of the World _____   Postal Abbreviations _____

Grammar Reference _____   Word List _____

Map of the U.S. and Canada _____   Audio Script _____

Getting to Know You

1

Preview

Look at the picture.
Where are the people?
Who are they?

UNIT GOALS

- [ ] Read a world map
- [ ] Introduce yourself
- [ ] Talk about where you are from
- [ ] Say and spell your first name and last name
- [ ] Use titles
- [ ] Complete a form with your personal information
- [ ] Talk about people in your class
- [ ] Talk about school

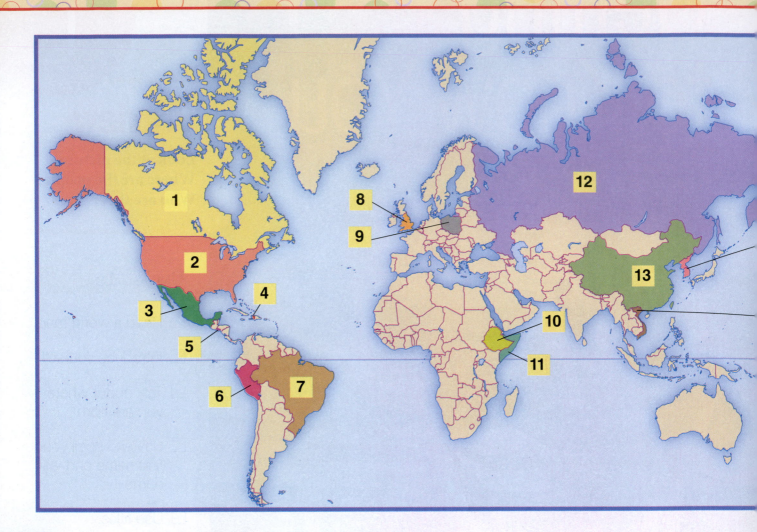

1 WHAT DO YOU KNOW?

A CLASS. Look at the map. Which countries do you know?

> Number 3 is Mexico.

CD1 T7

B Listen and point to the countries.
Then listen and repeat.

2 PRACTICE

A PAIRS. Student A, look at the list of countries on page 7.
Say a country. Student B, point to the country on the map.

> Vietnam.

B Look at the map. Find your country.

Write the name of your country.

_____

C PAIRS. What country are you from? Point to the map. Tell your partner.

A: *I'm from Ecuador. What about you?*
B: *I'm from Sudan.*

D GROUPS OF 3. Meet your classmates.

A: *Hi. I'm Monica Cruz. I'm from Mexico.*
B: *Hi. I'm Loc Tran. I'm from Vietnam.*
C: *Hi. I'm Joseph Duval. I'm from Haiti.*

Countries

1. Canada
2. the United States
3. Mexico
4. Haiti
5. El Salvador
6. Peru
7. Brazil
8. England
9. Poland
10. Ethiopia
11. Somalia
12. Russia
13. China
14. Korea
15. Vietnam

Learning Strategy

Write personal sentences

Write three sentences in your notebook about people from different countries.

My teacher is from Canada.

Show what you know!

STEP 1. SAME GROUPS. Write the names of your classmates from Exercise D and their countries.

_____*Monica*_____ is from _____*Mexico*_____.

1. _____ is from _____.

2. _____ is from _____.

For help, ask:
"Can you write it for me, please?"

STEP 2. Tell your class about one classmate from your group in Exercise D.

Monica is from Mexico.

Listening and Speaking

1 BEFORE YOU LISTEN

CLASS. Look at the picture. Read the information.

In the United States and Canada, people shake hands when they meet for the first time. What about in your country?

2 LISTEN

A Look at the picture. Luisa and Ilya are new students.

Guess: What are they saying?

CD1 T8

B Listen to the conversation. Was your guess in Exercise A correct?

Listen again. Choose the correct picture.

a.

b.

CD1 T9

C Listen to the whole conversation. Complete the sentences.

1. Ilya is from ____.   a. Russia   b. Poland

2. Luisa is from ____.   a. Mexico   b. Peru

3 CONVERSATION

A Listen and read. Look at the pictures.

Hi. I'm Hong Li.
Hi. I'm Hong Li.

I'm from China.
I'm from China.

Nice to meet you.
Nice to meet you.

Nice to meet you, too!

CD1 T11

B Listen. Then listen and repeat.

Nice to **meet** you.

Nice to meet **you, too**.

Where are you **from**?

What about **you**?

Pronunciation Watch

In English, important words in a sentence are stressed. Stressed words sound long and strong.

4 PRACTICE

A **PAIRS.** Practice the conversation. Use your own information.

A: Hi. I'm _____.

B: Hi. I'm _____.

A: Nice to meet you.

B: Nice to meet you, too.

A: Where are you from?

B: I'm from _____. What about you?

A: I'm from _____.

B **MAKE IT PERSONAL. CLASS.** Walk around the room. Meet other classmates.

Life Skills

1 SAY AND SPELL YOUR NAME

A Review the alphabet on page 2.

CD1 T12

B Listen to two students talking. Read the conversation. Then listen and repeat.

A: What's your first name?
B: My first name is Loc.
A: How do you spell that?
B: L-O-C.
A: L-O-C?
B: Right.
A: And what's your last name?
B: Tran.
A: OK. Thanks.

last name = family name

2 PRACTICE

CLASS. Practice the conversation again. Walk around the room. Talk to three classmates. Write their names.

First Name	Last Name
Loc	Tran

Writing Watch

Start names with capital letters. Example: *Loc*

3 USE TITLES

CD1 T13

Listen and point to the pictures. Then listen and repeat.

Mr. Johnson

Miss Chan (Ms. Chan)

Mrs. Brown (Ms. Brown)

Can you… say and spell your first name and last name? ☐

4 PRACTICE

Use titles with last names, not first names.
Example: *John Smith* = *Mr. Smith*, not ~~Mr. John~~
• Say Mr. for both married and single men.
• Say Ms. for both married and single women.

A Look at the pictures. Check (✓) the correct title.

1.

2.

3.

1.
☐ Mr. Lopez
☐ Mrs. Lopez

2.
☐ Miss Parker
☐ Mrs. Parker

3.
☐ Ms. Lee
☐ Mr. Lee

CD1 T14

B Listen. Some students are signing up for classes. Write the first or last name. Circle the correct title.

1. (Mr.) Mrs. Ms. Miss
First Name: _____
Last Name: ____Chen____

2. Mr. Mrs. Ms. Miss
First Name: ____Darya____
Last Name: _____

3. Mr. Mrs. Ms. Miss
First Name: ____Ana____
Last Name: _____

C READ AND WRITE. Read about Elsa Medina. Then write about yourself in your notebook.

> My first name is Elsa. My last name is Medina. I'm from Ecuador. I'm married.

Writing Watch

Start sentences with a capital letter. End sentences with a period.

5 LIFE SKILLS WRITING

Complete a personal information form. See page 253.

Can you...use titles? ☐

Listening and Speaking

1 BEFORE YOU LISTEN

A **READ.** **Look at the pictures. Read and answer the questions.**

It's time for class. Ana is at her desk. But two students are not there. Jae Yong is absent. Artur is late.

Ana.   Here.   Jae Yong.   He's absent.   Artur.   Oh, no. I'm late.

1. Who is absent? _____

2. Who is late? _____

B **CLASS.** **What about *your* class? Who is absent today?**

2 LISTEN

A **Look at the picture. Luisa and Sen are classmates.**

Guess: What is Luisa's question?

a. What's that?   b. Who's that?

CD1 T15

B **Listen to the conversation. Was your guess in Exercise A correct?**

Listen again. Complete the sentences.

1. _____ is the man in the picture.
   a. Nikolai   b. Ilya

2. Nikolai is from _____.
   a. Russia   b. Poland

CD1 T16

C **Listen to the whole conversation. Choose the correct picture of Ilya.**

a.    b.

3 CONVERSATION

CD1 T17

A 💿 Listen. Notice the different sounds in *he's* and *she's*. Then listen and repeat.

He's from Mexico.   She's absent.

> he = 🚹   she = 🚺
> he's = he is   she's = she is

CD1 T18

B 💿 Listen. Which word do you hear?

1. a. He's   (b.) She's

2. a. He's   b. She's

3. a. He's   b. She's

CD1 T19

C 💿 Listen and read the conversation. Then listen and repeat.

Luisa: Who's that?
Sen: That's Ilya.
Luisa: No, that's not Ilya.
Sen: Oh, you're right. That's Nikolai.
Luisa: Nikolai? Where's he from?
Sen: He's from Russia.

4 PRACTICE

A **PAIRS.** Practice the conversation. Then make new conversations. Use the information in the boxes.

A: Who's that?
B: That's the teacher.
A: No, that's not the teacher.
B: Oh, you're right. That's _____.
A: _____? Where's _____ from?
B: _____'s from _____.

	he	Korea
Jin Su		
	she	Mexico
Laura		
	she	Somalia
Ubah		

B **MAKE IT PERSONAL. PAIRS.** Make your own conversations. Use the conversation in Exercise A. Ask about a classmate.

Talk about people in your class

Grammar

Affirmative of *be* with *I, he,* and *she*		
I	**am**	from Russia.
He		a student.
She	**is**	in level 1.
Nikolai		

Grammar Watch

We usually use contractions in conversation.

Contractions
I am = **I'm**
he is = **he's**
she is = **she's**

1 PRACTICE

A **Change the underlined words to contractions.**

1. My name is Luisa Flores. <u>I am</u> in level 1. *I'm*

   <u>I am</u> from Peru.

2. That's Emilio. <u>He is</u> in my class.

3. Ms. Reed is the teacher. <u>She is</u> from Canada.

4. Carlos is a new student. <u>He is</u> from Mexico.

5. Gabriela is from Mexico, too. <u>She is</u> in level 3.

CD1 T20

B **Listen and check your answers.**

C **Look at the pictures. Complete the sentences. Use capital letters and contractions.**

I'm
from Mexico.

1. ___*I'm*___ from Mexico.

2. ___*She's*___ from Vietnam.

3. _____ from El Salvador.

_____
from Peru.

4. _____ from Peru.

5. _____ from Korea.

6. _____ from China.

Negative of *be* with *I, he,* and *she*			
I	am		from Mexico.
He She Luisa	is	not	the teacher. in level 3.

········· **Grammar Watch**

Contractions

I am not = **I'm not**
he is not = **he's not** OR **he isn't**
she is not = **she's not** OR **she isn't**

2 PRACTICE

A Look at the identification cards. Underline the correct word.

Greenville Adult School
Dora Moreno
Level 1
Peru
Identification Card

Greenville Adult School
Dawit Solomon
Level 1
Ethiopia
Identification Card

1. Dora **is** / **isn't** from Peru.

2. She **is** / **isn't** from Ethiopia.

3. Assefa **is** / **isn't** in Level 3.

4. He **is** / **isn't** in Level 1.

B PAIRS. Look at the chart. Student A, choose a person. Make sentences about the person. Student B, guess the person.

A: *She's from Peru. She's absent.*
B: *Luisa?*
A: *No! Dora.*

Level 1 Attendance				Monday
Name	**Country**	**Here**	**Absent**	**Late**
Mr. Carlos Delgado	Mexico			✓
Ms. Luisa Flores	Peru	✓		
Ms. Hae-Jin Lee	Korea	✓		
Ms. Eun Young Lim	Korea		✓	
Ms. Dora Moreno	Peru		✓	
Mr. Emilio Vargas	Mexico	✓		

Show what you know! Talk about people in your class

GROUPS OF 3. Student A, say a true or false sentence about yourself. Use *I'm* or *My name is.* Students B and C, guess *True* or *False.*

A: *My last name is Garcia.*
B: *True.*
C: *I think it's false.*
A: *It's true. I'm Carmen Garcia.*

Can you... talk about people in your class? ☐

Read about immigrants in the U.S.

Reading

1 BEFORE YOU READ

CD1 T21

A 🔘 **Listen and read. Point to the pictures.**

1. Mr. Addis is in the U.S. to be safe. His country isn't safe.

2. Mrs. Sarit is in the U.S. for work. Her job here is good.

3. Mrs. Medina is in the U.S. to be with her family. Her brother and his family are here.

B PAIRS. Talk about it. Why are *you* here?

C CLASS. Some people are happy to be in the U.S. 🙂

Some people are not happy to be in the U.S. 🙁

What are some reasons people are not happy to be in the U.S.?

CD1 T22

Listen. Read the article.

Immigrants in the United States

Many immigrants come to the United States. Why?
- Some people come for work. They get jobs here.
- Some people come to be safe. They are not safe in their countries.
- Some people come to be with their family. For example, a man comes first. His wife comes later to be with him.

Are immigrants happy to be in the U.S.? It is difficult to come to a new country. But 80% of immigrants say they are happy to be here.

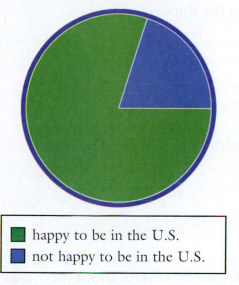

■ happy to be in the U.S.
■ not happy to be in the U.S.

Source: U.S. Census Bureau

Read the article again. Then read the sentences. Circle *True* or *False*.

1. Some immigrants come to the U.S. for work.   (**True**)   **False**

2. Families always come to the U.S. together.   **True**   **False**

3. Most immigrants are happy to be in the U.S.   **True**   **False**

Show what you know!

CLASS. Take a survey. Ask your classmates, "Are you happy to be here?" You can answer *yes, no,* or *sometimes*. Make a pie chart for your class. Use the pie chart in the article as a model.

Listening and Speaking

1   BEFORE YOU LISTEN

A Look at the words in the box.
Then look at the pictures.
Match. Write the words
on the lines.

| boring | easy | ~~good~~ |
| great | hard | interesting |

1. ___good___   2. _____   3. _____

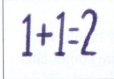
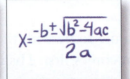

$$1+1=2$$

$$x = \frac{-b \pm \sqrt{b^2 - 4ac}}{2a}$$

4. _____   5. _____   6. _____

B **PAIRS.** Compare answers.

2   LISTEN

A Look at the picture. Min Jung is asking
Ilya and Kamaria about their class.

Guess: How is the class?

a. hard   b. good

B CD1 T23

Listen to the conversation.
Was your guess in Exercise A correct?

Listen again. Complete the sentences.

1. Ilya and Kamaria are in _____.
   a. level 1   b. level 2

2. The students are _____.
   a. good   b. great

C CD1 T24

Listen to the whole conversation.
Complete the sentence.

Ilya says: "English is _____."

3 CONVERSATION

CD1 T25

Listen and read the conversation. Then listen and repeat.

Min Jung: Hi! So, what class are you in?
Ilya: We're in level 1.
Min Jung: Oh. How is it?
Kamaria: It's good. The teacher is great.
Min Jung: What about the students?
Ilya: They're great, too.

4 PRACTICE

A GROUPS OF 3. **Practice the conversation.
Then make new conversations. Use the words in the boxes.**

A: Hi. What class are you in?

B: We're in level 1.

A: Oh. How is it?

C: It's   . The teacher is   .

A: What about the students?

B: They're   , too.

| easy | great | interesting |
| helpful | smart | friendly |

B MAKE IT PERSONAL. GROUPS OF 3. **Make your own conversations.
Use the conversation in Exercise A. Talk about your English class.**

Talk about school

Grammar

Affirmative of *be* with *we*, *you*, *they*, and *it*

We Luisa and I You They Sen and Ilya	are	in level 1. friendly.

It The book	is	interesting.

Contractions
we are = **we're**
you are = **you're**
they are = **they're**
it is = **it's**

you   you

1 PRACTICE

A Look at the pictures of some new students at Greenville Adult School.

Complete the sentences. Use the correct form of *be*.

1. **Mr. Salas:** You ___*are*___ in level 1.
   Tai-Ling: Thanks.

2. **Mr. Salas:** Here. You _____ in level 2.
   Paulo: Thank you.
   Ai-Lun: Thanks. Bye.
   Paulo: Goodbye, Mr. Salas.

3. **Paulo:** So, you and Meseret are in level 1.
   Tai-Ling: Yes. We _____ in level 1.

4. **Paulo:** So, how is your class?
   Tai-Ling: It _____ interesting.
   Ai-Lun: And how are the students?
   Meseret: They _____ great.

B **ROLE PLAY. GROUPS OF 5.** Practice the conversations in Exercise A. Student A, you are Mr. Salas. Students B, C, D, and E, you are the new students. Remember: Use contractions in conversation.

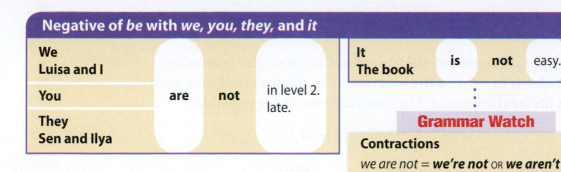

Negative of be with we, you, they, and it

We Luisa and I			in level 2.
You	are	not	late.
They Sen and Ilya			

It The book	is	not	easy.

Grammar Watch

Contractions

*we are not = **we're not** OR **we aren't**
*you are not = **you're not** OR **you aren't**
*they are not = **they're not** OR **they aren't**
*it is not = **it's not** OR **it isn't**

2 PRACTICE

A Read the conversations.
Underline the correct words.

1. **André and Li:**   Oh no. **We're** / **We're not** late.
   Teacher: It's OK. You're on time. **You're** / **You're not** late.

2. **Teacher:**   Where are Maria and Carmen? **They're** / **They're not** here.
   Maria and Carmen: Oh. **We're** / **We're not** here. Sorry we're late.

3. **Solomon:**   My class is good. **It's** / **It's not** interesting. How is your class?
   Irina: My class **is** / **is not** interesting, too.

4. **Solomon:**   How are the students?
   Irina: They're great. **They're** / **They're not** friendly.

B **PAIRS.** Practice the conversations.

Show what you know! Talk about school

PAIRS. Look at the picture of Jin-Hee and Antonio.
Student A, you are Jin-Hee. Student B, you are Antonio.
Talk about school. Use words from the box.

boring	easy	friendly	good	great	hard	helpful	interesting	smart

A: *How is your class?*
B: *It isn't good . . .*

Can you… talk about school? ☐

1 GRAMMAR

A Some students are talking about their classes. Complete the sentences with the correct form of *be*. Use the affirmative in the first sentence and the negative in the next sentence. Use contractions where possible.

1. **Claude:** I _'m_____ in level 2. I _'m not___ in level 1.

2. **Sook:** The book _____ hard. It _____ easy.

3. **Paula:** My teacher _____ from the U.S. He _____ from Canada.

4. **Santiago:** Paula and I _____ from Mexico. We _____ from El Salvador.

5. **Lei:** I _____ in level 1. I _____ in level 2.

6. **Tamar:** My classmates _____ helpful. My class _____ hard.

B **PAIRS.** Look at the pictures. Complete the conversations. There is more than one correct answer. Remember, start sentences with a capital letter. End sentences with a period.

1.

2.

3.

4.

C **SAME PAIRS.** Practice the conversations.

D 🔘 **DICTATION. Listen. Complete the conversation. Use capital letters when necessary.**

Luisa: This is Bao and Hanh. ___They're___ from Vietnam.

Ilya: Nice to _____ _____. _____ Ilya Petrov.

Luisa and I are students at the Greenville Adult School.

_____ in level 1.

Hanh: Nice to meet you, Ilya. Where _____ you _____?

Ilya: _____ _____ Russia.

Luisa: Bao and Hanh _____ students at Greenville, too.

_____ in level 5, and _____ in level 6.

Ilya: Really? That's great.

2 WRITING

STEP 1. Complete the sentences. Choose the correct word.

1. My name ____is____ Ilya Petrov. I _____ from Russia.
             (is / are)   (is / am)

2. Luisa is my classmate. _____ _____ from Peru.
                           (They / She) (is / are)

   _____ are in level 1.
   (We / She)

3. Ms. Reed _____ the teacher. _____ _____
               (is / are)   (He / She) (are not / is not)

   from my country. _____ _____ from Canada.
                     (He / She) (is / are)

STEP 2. Write two or three sentences about yourself, a classmate, or your teacher. Use the sentences in Step 1 as examples.

_____

_____

_____

3 ACT IT OUT · What do you say?

STEP 1. Review the Lesson 2 conversation between Luisa and Ilya (CD 1 Track 9).

STEP 2. PAIRS. You are at a party. Say hello and introduce yourselves. Shake hands. Talk about where you are from.

4 READ AND REACT · Problem-solving

STEP 1. Read about Roberto's problem.

Roberto Cruz is a new student at the Riverside Adult School. He is in a level 1 class. He thinks the other students in his class are friendly. He thinks the teacher is great. But there's one problem. The class is too easy. He thinks he needs level 2.

STEP 2. PAIRS. Talk about it. What is Roberto's problem? What can Roberto do? Here are some ideas.

- He can talk to the teacher.
- He can go to a different school.
- He can stay in level 1.
- He can _____.

5 CONNECT

For your Community-building Activity, go to page 245.
For your Team Project, go to page 265.

Which goals can you check off? Go back to page 5.

A Hard Day's Work

Preview

Look at the picture.
Who are the people?

UNIT GOALS

- ☐ Introduce someone
- ☐ Talk about jobs
- ☐ Use numbers 0–9
- ☐ Give phone numbers
- ☐ Complete a form at work
- ☐ Ask about jobs
- ☐ Talk about where you work

1 WHAT DO YOU KNOW?

A **CLASS.** Look at the pictures. Which jobs do you know?

> Number 3 is a doctor.

B CD1 T27

Listen and point to the pictures. Then listen and repeat.

2 PRACTICE

A **PAIRS.** Student A, look at the list of jobs on page 27. Name a job. Student B, point to the picture.

> A cashier.

B **WORD PLAY. GROUPS OF 3.** Student A, act out a job. Students B and C, guess the job.

B: *You're a homemaker.*
A: *No.*
C: *You're a gardener.*
A: *Right!*

C Write your job. Use true or made-up information.

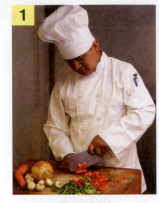

3

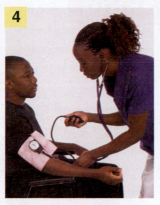

4

5

6

9

10

Jobs

1. **a** cook
2. **a** waiter / **a** waitress
3. **a** doctor
4. **a** nurse
5. **a** gardener
6. **a** driver
7. **a** cashier
8. **a** sales assistant
9. **an** accountant
10. **an** office assistant
11. **a** homemaker
12. **a** child-care worker
13. **a** housekeeper
14. **an** artist
15. **a** painter
16. **an** electrician

Learning Strategy

Use your language

Look at the list of jobs. Make cards for three or four words. On one side, write the word in English. On the other side, write the word in your language.

Show what you know!

STEP 1. Walk around the room. Ask three classmates about their jobs. Complete the chart.

Soo-Jin: *What do you do?*
Antonio: *I'm a cook.*

STEP 2. Introduce one classmate to your class.

Soo-Jin: *This is Antonio. He's a cook.*
Class: *Nice to meet you, Antonio.*

Name	Job
Antonio	a cook

Listening and Speaking

1   BEFORE YOU LISTEN

CD1 T28

A   **READ.**   Look at the picture. Emilio, Gabriela, and Pierre are at a party.

Listen and read the conversation.

B   **GROUPS OF 3.**   Introduce two classmates.

A: _____, this is _____.
    _____, this is _____.
B: Hi, _____. Nice to meet you.
C: Hi, _____. Nice to meet you, too.

> Pierre, this is Gabriela. Gabriela, this is Pierre.

> Hi, Pierre. Nice to meet you.

> Hi, Gabriela. Nice to meet you, too.

2   LISTEN

A   Look at the picture again. After the introduction, Gabriela asks Pierre a question.

Guess: What is Gabriela's question?

a. What do you do?   b. How is your class?

CD1 T29

B   Listen to the conversation. Was your guess in Exercise A correct?

Listen again. Complete the sentences.

1. Pierre is a gardener and _____.
    a. a driver   b. a student

2. Gabriela is a student and _____.
    a. an artist   b. a nurse

CD1 T30

C   Listen to the whole conversation. What is Emilio's job?

a.    b.

3 CONVERSATION

A CD1 T31 💿 **Listen. Then listen and repeat.**

A: What do you do?

B: I'm a student.

> **Pronunciation Watch**
>
> In *Wh-* questions and in statements, the voice goes down at the end.

B CD1 T32 💿 **Listen and read the conversation. Then listen and repeat.**

Gabriela: So, what do you do?

Pierre: I'm a gardener. And I'm a student at Greenville Adult School.

Gabriela: Really? I'm a student there, too. And I'm an artist.

Pierre: Oh, that's interesting.

4 PRACTICE

A **PAIRS.** Practice the conversation. Then make new conversations. Use the pictures.

A: What do you do?

B: I'm _____.

A: Really? I'm _____, too. And I'm _____.

B: Oh, that's interesting.

B **MAKE IT PERSONAL. PAIRS.** Make your own conversations. Use the conversation in Exercise A. Use true or made-up information.

Talk about jobs

Grammar

Grammar Watch

A/An		
Pierre is Paula is	**a**	gardener. driver.

Gabriela is Tal is	**an**	artist. electrician.

Grammar Watch

- Use **a** before consonant sounds.
- Use **an** before vowel sounds.

1 PRACTICE

A Underline the correct word.

1. **A:** That's Lily. She's **a** / **an** office assistant.

   B: Oh, really? I'm **a** / **an** office assistant, too.

2. **A:** Paul is **a** / **an** teacher, right?

   B: No. He's not **a** / **an** teacher. He's **a** / **an** nurse.

3. **A:** I'm **a** / **an** gardener. What about you?

   B: I'm **a** / **an** electrician.

4. **A:** This is Dr. and Mrs. Silver. He's **a** / **an** doctor and she's **a** / **an** accountant.

   B: Nice to meet you. I'm Teresa Castro. I'm **a** / **an** child-care worker.

5. **A:** What do you do?

   B: I'm **a** / **an** homemaker. I'm also **a** / **an** artist.

CD1 T33

B 💿 Listen and check your answers.

C PAIRS. Practice the conversations in Exercise A.

D WRITE. Complete the sentences. Use *a* or *an*. Then write a sentence about someone you know.

1. Bob is ___a___ cashier.

2. Lucia is _____ electrician.

3. Kevin is _____ driver.

4. John is _____ cook.

5. Sarah is _____ office assistant.

6. Hai is _____ accountant.

7. Genet is _____ student.

8. _____

Singular and plural nouns

John is	**a cook**.	John and Linda are	**cooks**.
Amy is	**a waitress**.	Amy, Ana, and Luz are	**waitresses**.

2 PRACTICE

A Write the plural form of these words: *nurse, gardener, cashier, waitress,* and *driver.*

_____nurses_____   _____   _____   _____   _____

CD1 T34

B Listen and check your answers. Notice the pronunciation of the –s and –es endings. Listen again and repeat.

C Look at the pictures. Complete the sentences.

1. They're _____drivers_____.

2. Rosa is _____.

3. Jill, Mei, and I are _____.

4. Bob is _____.

Show what you know!   Talk about jobs

STEP 1. Look at the jobs. These jobs are the five most common jobs in the U.S. Guess: Which job is number 1, 2, 3, 4, and 5? Write a number next to each job. (The answers are given in Step 3.)

____ driver   ____ teacher   ____ cashier   ____ sales assistant   ____ office assistant

STEP 2. GROUPS OF 3. Talk about your answers.

A: *I think cashiers are number 1.*
B: *No, I think . . .*

CD1 T35

STEP 3. Listen and check your answers in Step 1.

Can you...talk about jobs? ☐

Life Skills

1　USE NUMBERS 0–9

A **CLASS.** Think about numbers in your life. When do you use numbers? Do you use numbers at work?

CD1 T36

B Look at the numbers. Listen and point. Then listen and repeat.

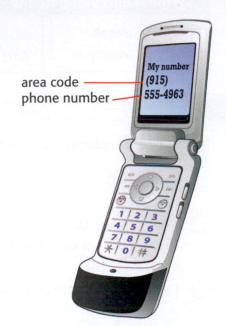

area code
phone number

My number
(915)
555-4963

0 zero	1 one	2 two	3 three	4 four
5 five	6 six	7 seven	8 eight	9 nine

2　PRACTICE

CD1 T37

A Listen. Circle the area code you hear.

1. 212　(512)　　3. 305　315　　5. 919　915
2. 713　714　　4. 408　708　　6. 786　706

We often say
oh for O.

B **PAIRS.** Look at the pictures. Which places do you know? Write the words from the box on the lines.

| ~~a hospital~~　　an office　　a restaurant　　a child-care center |

1. ___a hospital___　　　　2. _____

3. _____　　　　4. _____

3 GIVE PHONE NUMBERS

CD1 T38

Listen to the messages on the answering machines.
Write the missing numbers.

1. Call Mr. Fernandez at Center Hospital about the gardener job.

(562) 555-1_____

2. Call Grace Simms at Grace's Office Supplies about the cashier job.

(___8) 555-7_____

3. Call Jin Heng Wu at Riverside Child Care about the child-care worker job.

(___) 555-_____2

4. Call Ms. Rodriguez at Carla's Restaurant about the waiter job.

(___) ___-_____

4 PRACTICE

CD1 T39

A Listen and read the conversation. Then listen and repeat.

Elena: What's your phone number?
Asad: 555-4963.
Elena: And what's the area code?
Asad: 915.

B **CLASS.** Walk around the room. Ask two classmates for their phone number and area code. Write the numbers. Use true or made-up information.

	Name	(Area Code) Phone Number
	Asad	(915) 555-4963
1.		
2.		

5 LIFE SKILLS WRITING

Complete a form at work. See page 254.

Can you... use numbers 0–9 and give your phone number? ☐

Listening and Speaking

1 LISTEN

A Look at the picture. Ilya and Claudia are at a party. They're talking about Sara.

Guess: What does Sara do?

a. Sara is a student.

b. Sara is a teacher.

CD1 T40

B Listen to the conversation. Was your guess in Exercise A correct?

Listen again. Complete the sentences.

1. Sara is _____.
   a.   b.

2. Ilya is _____.
   a.   b.

CD1 T41

C Listen to the whole conversation. Complete the sentences.

1. Claudia says, "I'm _____." (Check (✔) all the correct answers.)

   ☐ an electrician   ☐ a cook   ☐ a waitress

   ☐ a child-care worker   ☐ a cashier   ☐ a doctor

2. Claudia is _____. (Check (✔) one answer.)

   ☐ a homemaker   ☐ a gardener   ☐ a housekeeper

2 CONVERSATION

A CD1 T42
Listen. Then listen and repeat.

Are you a student?   Is he a cook?

B CD1 T43
Listen to the sentences. Does the voice go up or down at the end?

	1.	2.	3.	4.
Up	☑	☐	☐	☐
Down	☐	☐	☐	☐

C CD1 T44
Listen and read the conversation. Then listen and repeat.

Claudia: Who's that? Is she a teacher?
Ilya: No, she's not. She's a student.
And she's a cashier at Al's Restaurant.
Claudia: Oh, that's interesting. And what do you do?
Ilya: I'm a cook.

3 PRACTICE

A PAIRS. Practice the conversation. Then make new conversations. Use the words in the boxes.

A: Who's that? Is _____ a teacher?
B: No, _____ 's not. _____ 's a student.
And _____ 's _____ .
A: Oh, that's interesting. And what do you do?
B: I'm _____ .

she	a cashier	a sales assistant
he	an electrician	a painter
she	a nurse	an accountant

B MAKE IT PERSONAL. PAIRS. Make your own conversations. Use the conversation in Exercise A. Student A, ask about a classmate. Student B, give true answers.

Ask about jobs

Grammar

Be: *Yes/no* questions and short answers

Are	you	a teacher?	**Yes,**	I **am**.	**No,**	I'**m not**	OR	
Is	he	a teacher?	**Yes,**	he **is**.	**No,**	he'**s not**	OR	he **isn't**.
Is	she	a teacher?	**Yes,**	she **is**.	**No,**	she'**s not**	OR	she **isn't**.
Is	Sara	a teacher?						
Are	you	teachers?	**Yes,**	we **are**.	**No,**	we'**re not**	OR	we **aren't**.
Are	they	teachers?	**Yes,**	they **are**.	**No,**	they'**re not**	OR	they **aren't**.
Is	your job	hard?	**Yes,**	it **is**.	**No,**	it'**s not**	OR	it **isn't**.
Is	it	hard?						

Writing Watch

End questions with a question mark.

1 PRACTICE

A **Write *yes/no* questions about jobs.**

1. cook / she / a / Is   Is she a cook?
2. they / Are / sales assistants ____________
3. a / Are / waitress / you ____________
4. Is / painter / he / a ____________
5. John / a / gardener / Is ____________
6. the job / easy / Is ____________

B **Complete the conversations. Use capital letters when necessary.**

1. **A:** Are they waiters?
   B: No, they're not. (OR they aren't.)
2. **A:** ____________ she a cook?
   B: Yes, ____________.
3. **A:** ____________ Marta and Kim office assistants?
   B: Yes, ____________.
4. **A:** ____________ you an electrician?
   B: No, ____________.
5. **A:** ____________ he an accountant?
   B: No, ____________.
6. **A:** ____________ Mr. Garcia a painter?
   B: Yes, ____________.

Look at the pictures. Complete the conversations. Add *a* or *an* when necessary.
Use capital letters and periods when necessary.

1. **A:** <u>Is she an</u> accountant?

   B: <u>Yes, she is.</u>

2. **A:** _____ artists?

   B: _____

3. **A:** _____ electrician?

   B: _____

4. **A:** _____ nurse?

   B: _____

5. **A:** _____ gardeners?

   B: _____

6. **A:** _____ waitress?

   B: _____

Show what you know! Ask about jobs

GROUPS OF 3. Student A, think of a famous singer, athlete, or actor.
Students B and C, ask *yes/no* questions and guess the famous person.

B: *Is it a woman?*
A: *No, it isn't.*
C: *Is the man an athlete?*
A: *Yes, he is.*
B: *Is he from Brazil?*
A: *Yes, he is.*
C: *Pele?*
A: *Yes!*

Can you... ask about jobs? ☐

Reading

1   BEFORE YOU READ

A   Look at the pictures. Read the sentences about job skills.
Check (✓) the sentences that are true for you.

☐ I use a computer.

☐ I take care of children.

☐ I cook.

☐ I clean.

☐ I pay the bills.

☐ I'm organized.

B   **GROUPS OF 4.**   Talk about your answers. Who has the same job skills?

A: *I cook and clean, and I'm organized. What about you, Ken?*
B: *I'm organized, too. And I . . .*

2 READ

CD1 T45

Listen. Read the article.

Homemaker Finds a Job

Li Chen looks at job information in a job counselor's office.

Li Chen is a homemaker. Now her children are in school. She wants a job. But she's a homemaker. What kind of job can she do? She talks to a job counselor.

The job counselor asks Li, "What do you do at home every day?"

"Well," Li says, "I take care of the children. I cook. I clean. I pay the bills online."

The counselor says, "You can do a lot of things! You're good with children. You're organized. You're good with numbers. You use a computer!" She helps Li find a job.

3 CHECK YOUR UNDERSTANDING

A Read the article again. Answer the questions.

1. What does Li do at home every day? Underline four activities in the article.

2. What does the counselor think?
   a. Li can do many things.   b. Li can be a cook.   c. Li can't get a job.

3. What are Li's job skills?

   She is _____, _____, and _____.

   She can use _____.

B What is the main idea of the article? Complete the sentence.

Your skills at home are also good _____ skills.

> The *main idea* is the most important idea in an article.

C PAIRS. What do you think? What is Li's new job?

Show what you know!

PAIRS. Talk about it. What are your job skills? What jobs can you do now? What job do you want in five years?

UNIT 2   **39**

Talk about where you work

Listening and Speaking

1 BEFORE YOU LISTEN

CLASS. Look at the picture. For some jobs, like security guards, people need uniforms. What other jobs need uniforms?

2 LISTEN

A Look at Miriam's uniform. What is her job?

_____

CD1 T46

B Look at the picture. Dora is at a party. She is talking to Miriam and Pierre.

Listen to the conversation. Was your answer in Exercise A correct?

CD1 T46

C Listen again. Where does Miriam work?

a.

b.

CD1 T47

D Listen to the whole conversation. Complete the sentences.

1. Pierre is a _____.
   a. nurse   b. teacher   c. student

2. Pierre says, "It's _____."
   a. an interesting job   b. a hard job   c. a great job

E **CLASS.** Read and discuss.

Miriam says, "That's not a job." Pierre says, "Yes, it is."
Who is right, Miriam or Pierre?

3 CONVERSATION

CD1 T48

Listen and read the conversation. Then listen and repeat.

Dora: What do you do?
Miriam: I'm a nurse.
Dora: Really? Where do you work?
Miriam: I work at a school on Main Street. I'm a school nurse.
Dora: Oh. That's interesting.

4 PRACTICE

A **PAIRS.** Practice the conversation.
Then make new conversations.
Use the information in the boxes.

A: What do you do?
B: I'm _____ .
A: Really? Where do you work?
B: I work at _____ on Main Street.
A: Oh. That's interesting.

B **MAKE IT PERSONAL. PAIRS.**
Make your own conversations.
Talk about your jobs and workplaces.

A: *Where do you work?*
B: *I work at a store. I'm a cashier.*
A: *Oh. That's nice.*

C **NETWORK.** Find classmates with
the same job as you. Form a group.
Ask the people in your group,
Where do you work?

a carpenter

a caregiver

a construction site

a nursing home

an assembly line worker

a stock clerk

a factory

a store

Talk about where you work

Grammar

Simple present affirmative: *Work* and *live*

| I
You
We
They | **work** | at a school. |
| | **live** | in Texas. |

| He
She
Miriam | **works** | at a school. |
| | **lives** | in California. |

Grammar Watch

• With *he, she,* and the name of a person, the simple present verb ends in **-s**: *work**s**, live**s***

• For spelling rules for the simple present tense with *he, she,* and *it,* see page 273.

PRACTICE

A Alex is talking about himself and some friends. Underline the correct word.

1. That's my friend George. He **work** / <u>**works**</u> at a store.

2. George **live** / **lives** in New York. My wife and I **live** / **lives** in New York, too.

3. I **work** / **works** at a store, too! I'm a cashier.

4. This is Gloria. She **live** / **lives** in Florida. She **work** / **works** at a hospital.

5. Olga and Marcos **work** / **works** at a hospital, too. They're security guards.

B Look at the ID cards. Complete the sentences. Use the verbs in parentheses.

1. Helen Lam (be) _____ *is* _____ a nurse.

   She (live) _____ in Los Angeles.

   She (work) _____ at General Hospital.

2. Luis Mendoza and Nadif Fall (be) _____ accountants. They (live) _____ in Tampa.

   They (work) _____ for Andrews Accounting.

C **GROUPS OF 5.** Play the Memory Game. Talk about what you do and where you work. Use true or made-up information.

Tal: *I'm a cook. I work at a restaurant.*
Sahra: *Tal is a cook. He works at a restaurant. I'm a sales assistant. I work at a store.*

1 GRAMMAR

Complete the conversation. Use the words in the box.

a   an   waiters   is   Is   ~~Is~~   work   work   works

A: _____*Is*_____ that Raul?

B: No. That's Pablo Gomez. He _____ with Maria

and Helena Peres. They _____ at Rico's Diner.

A: Oh. What do they do?

B: They're _____.

A: Really? I _____ at a restaurant, too. I'm _____ cook

at Paul's Restaurant. What about you? What do you do?

B: I'm _____ electrician.

A: How's your job? _____ it hard?

B: Yes, it _____. But it's interesting, too.

2 WRITING

STEP 1. **Read the information about Helena Peres.**
Answer these questions: What does Helena do?
Where does she work? Where does she live?

Helena _*is a waitress.*_____

She _____

She _____

Name: Helena Peres
Job: Waitress
Place of work: Rico's Diner
Home: Queens, New York

STEP 2. **Answer the questions about yourself.**
What do you do? Where do you work? Where do you live?

Write complete sentences.

_____

_____

_____

Show what you know!

3 ACT IT OUT — What do you say?

STEP 1. CD1 T49 🔘 Listen to the conversation.

STEP 2. PAIRS. You are at school. Student A, introduce Students B and C. Students B and C, continue the conversation. Talk about your jobs and workplaces.

4 READ AND REACT — Problem-solving

STEP 1. Read about Karine's problem.

Karine lives in Riverside. She is a nurse's assistant. She works at Riverside General Hospital. She works days. At night, Karine takes English classes at the Learning Center. She wants to be a nurse.

One day, Karine goes to work. Her manager says, "Karine, I need you to work nights." But Karine has classes at night.

STEP 2. PAIRS. Talk about it. What is Karine's problem? What can Karine do? Here are some ideas.

- She can say, "I can't work nights."
- She can find another English class.
- She can call her teacher.
- She can _____.

5 CONNECT

For your Goal-setting Activity, go to page 246.
For your Team Project, go to page 266.

Which goals can you check off? Go back to page 25.

Time for Class

Preview

Look at the picture. Where are the people? Does this place look like your school?

UNIT GOALS

- [ ] Give and follow classroom instructions
- [ ] Complete a school registration form
- [ ] Talk about things in the classroom
- [ ] Use numbers 10–100
- [ ] Talk about places at school
- [ ] Talk about people and places at school

1   WHAT DO YOU KNOW?

A   **CLASS.** Look at the pictures. Which things do you know?

> Number 7 is *chalk*.

CD1 T50

B   Listen and point to the pictures. Then listen and repeat.

2   PRACTICE

A   **PAIRS.** Look at the pictures. Student A, choose one thing. Say, "Point to the _____." Student B, point to the correct picture.

> Point to the notebook.

B   **WORD PLAY.** Look at the list of things in the classroom on page 47. Complete the chart with the correct words.

Things you write with	Things you can read	Furniture
chalk		

C   **PAIRS.** Compare answers.

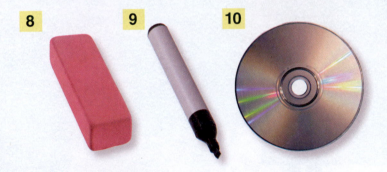

2

3

Things in the Classroom

1. desk	9. marker
2. chair	10. CD
3. computer	11. notebook
4. book	12. piece of paper
5. dictionary	13. folder
6. board	14. three-ring binder
7. chalk	15. backpack
8. eraser	16. cell phone

Learning Strategy

Use pictures

Look at the list of things in the classroom. Make cards for three or four words. On one side, write the word in English. On the other side, draw a picture of the word.

6

7

11 **12** **13** **14**

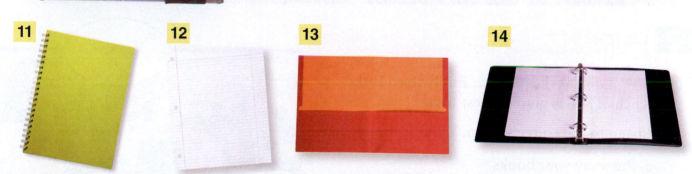

Show what you know!

GROUPS OF 5. Look at the list of things in the classroom. What things do you have with you today? Make a list.

3 _____ dictionaries _____   ____ _____

____ _____   ____ _____

____ _____   ____ _____

____ _____

Give and follow classroom instructions

Listening and Speaking

1 BEFORE YOU LISTEN

A **READ.** Ramiro and Kamila go to English class after work. Read the sentences.

1. Ramiro and Kamila try to bring their books and notebooks to class.
2. Sometimes they borrow some paper.
3. When Ramiro and Kamila are late, they don't interrupt the class.
4. They sit down and turn off their cell phones.

B Look at the pictures. Read the sentences again. Match.

2 LISTEN

CD1 T51

A Look at the picture. Emily Reed is the teacher. She is giving a test today.

Listen to the conversation. What is she saying?

a. Put away your books.
b. Open your dictionaries.
c. Please bring your notebooks.

CD1 T51

B Listen again. Read the sentences. Circle *True* or *False*.

1. Ms. Reed says, "Take out a pencil."   **True   False**

2. Aram says, "Can I borrow a pencil?"   **True   False**

CD1 T52

C Listen to the whole conversation. Complete the sentence.

_____ cell phone is ringing.

a. Aram's   b. Chan's   c. Ms. Reed's

3 CONVERSATION

CD1 T53

Listen and read the conversation. Then listen and repeat.

Ms. Reed: OK, everyone. Are you ready for the test?
Put away your books. Take out a piece of paper.

Aram: Chan, can I borrow a pencil?

Chan: Sure, Aram.

4 PRACTICE

A **GROUPS OF 3.** Practice the conversation. Then make new conversations. Use the pictures.

A: Are you ready for the test?

Put away your _____. Take out a _____.

B: Can I borrow _____?

C: Sure.

> Remember:
> *a piece of paper*
> *an eraser*

B **ROLE PLAY. GROUPS OF 3.** Make your own conversations.
Student A, you are the teacher. Students B and C, you are the students.

Give and follow classroom instructions

Grammar

Imperatives		
Affirmative		
Take out **Use**	your notebooks. a pencil.	

Negative		
Don't	**look at** **open**	your books. your dictionaries.

> **Grammar Watch**
>
> Use *please* to be polite: ***Please*** *turn off your cell phones.*

1 PRACTICE

Match the sentences and the pictures.

_d_ 1. Turn off the computer.

____ 2. Don't open your dictionary.

____ 3. Write in your book.

____ 4. Don't take out your notebook.

____ 5. Don't turn off the computer.

____ 6. Open your dictionary.

____ 7. Take out your notebook.

____ 8. Don't write in your book.

a.

b.

c.

d.

e.

f.

g.

h.

2 LIFE SKILLS WRITING

Complete a school registration form. See page 255.

3 PRACTICE

A **Read the test directions. Underline the correct words.**

1.

Use / **Don't use** a Number 2 pencil.

2.

Use / **Don't use** a pen.

3.
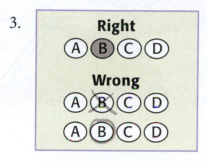

Make / Don't make dark marks in the circles.

4.

Look / **Don't look** at your classmate's test.

B **Complete the sentences about classroom rules. Use the words in the box. Use capital letters and add _don't_ when necessary.**

answer	~~bring~~	~~eat~~	interrupt	listen	try to

1. ____**Bring**____ a notebook and pencil.

2. ____**Don't eat**____ in class.

3. _____ the class when you are late.

4. _____ to your classmates.

5. _____ your cell phone in class.

6. _____ come on time.

Show what you know! Give and follow classroom instructions

GROUPS OF 3. Make a list of *Dos* and *Don'ts* for your class in your notebook. Use the sentences in Exercise B as a model.

Can you... give and follow classroom instructions? ☐

Read about good study habits

Reading

1 BEFORE YOU READ

A **CLASS.** What are your *study habits*? For example, when do you usually study? At lunch? At night? Where do you usually study? At home? At school?

B **PAIRS.** Match the sentences about study habits with the pictures. Write one sentence from the box under each picture.

> Set study goals.
> Study for a short time.
> Throw out papers you don't need.
> ~~Turn off your cell phone.~~

1. _Turn off your cell phone._

2. _____

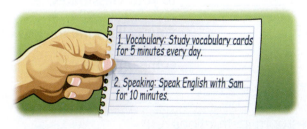

3. _____

4. _____

CD1 T54

Ally Einstein is not a good student. Her study habits are terrible. Listen. Read Professor Studywell's letter of advice to Ms. Einstein.

Ask the Professor

Dear Ms. Einstein,

Don't worry! You can be a good student. Good study habits help. Here are some ideas.

1) **Set study goals each week.** Write your goals in your notebook. Be sure your goals are small. For example, "Listening: Watch TV in English for ten minutes."

2) **Look at your list of goals every day.** Check off each goal when you finish.

3) **Study in a quiet place.** Sit at a table. Turn off your TV, radio, and cell phone.

4) **Be organized.** Keep important papers. Throw out other papers. Put your important papers in one binder.

5) **Plan your study time.** Try to study for fifteen minutes. Then review for five minutes.

3 CHECK YOUR UNDERSTANDING

A Read the sentences. There is one mistake in each sentence. Correct the mistake.

1. Set study goals each ~~year~~ *week*.

2. Be sure your goals are big.

3. Turn off your computer.

4. Throw out important papers.

5. Put your papers in a notebook.

6. Review for fifteen minutes.

B Read the letter again. What is the main idea? Complete the sentence.

Good _____ can help you be a good student.

Show what you know!

STEP 1. Choose one language skill you want to practice (for example, listening, speaking, or vocabulary). In your notebook, write one goal for that skill.

STEP 2. NETWORK. Who wants to practice the same skill as you? Find those classmates. Form a group. Ask the people in your group, *What is your study goal?*

Listening and Speaking

1 **BEFORE YOU LISTEN**

PAIRS. Look at the picture. Write the words from the box on the lines.

keyboard
~~CD~~
mouse
monitor
DVD

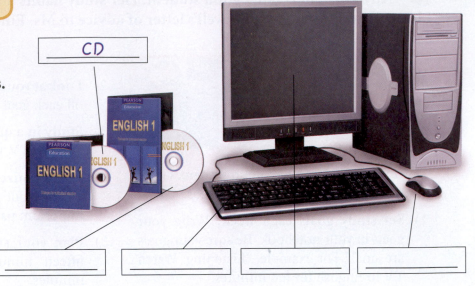

CD

2 **LISTEN**

A Look at the picture. Carlos and Kamaria are learning new words in English.

Guess: What is Carlos's question? What is Kamaria's answer?

CD1 T55

B Listen to the conversation. Was your guess in Exercise A correct?

Listen again. What is Carlos asking about? Check (✓) all the correct answers.

☐ a mouse   ☐ a keyboard

☐ DVDs   ☐ CDs

CD1 T56

C Listen to the whole conversation. Complete the sentence.

Carlos says, "This is a _____ of a _____, and that's a _____ of _____."

3 CONVERSATION

A CD1 T57 🔘 **Listen. Then listen and repeat.**

This	**This** is a computer.
These	**These** are CDs.
That's	**That's** a mouse.

Pronunciation Watch

To say the *th* sound in *this*, *these*, and *that's*, put your tongue between your teeth.

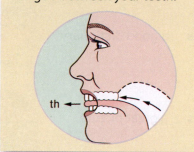

th ←

B CD1 T58 🔘 **Listen and read the conversation. Then listen and repeat.**

Carlos: What's this called in English?

Kamaria: It's a mouse.

Carlos: And these? What are these called?

Kamaria: They're CDs.

4 PRACTICE

A **PAIRS.** Practice the conversation. Then make new conversations. Use the pictures.

A: What's this called in English?

B: It's _____ .

A: And these? What are these called?

B: They're _____ .

B **MAKE IT PERSONAL. PAIRS.** Make your own conversations. Ask about things in your classroom.

Talk about things in the classroom

Grammar

This, that, these, those: Statements

	Singular			Plural	
This is	a good dictionary.		**These are**	good dictionaries.	
That's	a great picture.		**Those are**	great pictures.	

Grammar Watch

- Use **this** and **these** for people or things near you.
- Use **that** or **those** for people or things <u>not</u> near you.

Contractions
that is = **that's**

1 PRACTICE

A Underline the correct words.

1. <u>This is</u> / These are a good book.
2. That's / Those are my classmates.
3. This is / These are my markers.
4. That's / Those are my folders.
5. That's / Those are called a monitor.

B Look at the pictures. Complete the sentences with *This is*, *That's*, *These are*, and *Those are*.

1. <u>These are</u> our books.
2. _____ our teacher.
3. _____ good binders.
4. _____ my backpack.

C WRITE. Write two sentences in your notebook about things in your classroom. Use *this*, *that*, *these*, or *those*.

> This is my book.

This, that, these, those: Questions and answers

Is	this that	your book?	Yes, **it** is.

Are	these those	your books?	Yes, **they** are.

What is	this? that?	**It**'s a pen.

What are	these? those?	**They**'re pens.

2 PRACTICE

PAIRS. Look at the picture. Complete the conversations.

Pairs
Practice this, that, these, those

What is ___this___ called in English? **1.**

_____ **2.**

What _____? **3.**

_____ **4.**

_____ a good book? **5.**

___, ___ **6.**

_____ markers? **7.**

___, ___. **8.**

Show what you know! Talk about things in the classroom

PAIRS. Student A, you have ten seconds. Draw a picture of one or two things in your classroom. Student B, guess the object or objects.

A: *What are these?*
B: *Are they folders?*
A: *No. They're notebooks.*

Can you... talk about things in the classroom? ☐

Talk about places at school

Life Skills

1 USE NUMBERS 10–100

CD1 T59

A 🔘 **Look at the numbers. Listen and point. Then listen and repeat.**

10	11	12	13	14
ten	eleven	twelve	thirteen	fourteen

15	16	17	18	19
fifteen	sixteen	seventeen	eighteen	nineteen

B **PAIRS.** Student A, say a number from Exercise A. Student B, write the number. Take turns. Don't repeat a number.

_____ _____ _____ _____ _____

CD1 T60

C 🔘 **Listen and point. Then listen and repeat.**

20	21	22	23	30	40
twenty	twenty-one	twenty-two	twenty-three	thirty	forty

50	60	70	80	90	100
fifty	sixty	seventy	eighty	ninety	one hundred

2 PRACTICE

A **Read the words. Write the numbers.**

1. twenty-four ___24___   3. fifty-three ____   5. forty-seven ____

2. sixty-one ____   4. ninety-nine ____   6. eighty-six ____

CD1 T61

B 🔘 **Listen to the conversations. Circle the number you hear.**

1. 9 (19)   3. 35 45   5. 14 40   7. 17 70

2. 12 20   4. 59 69   6. 13 30   8. 82 92

Can you...use numbers 10–100? ☐

3   TALK ABOUT PLACES AT SCHOOL

A   **PAIRS.**   Look at the floor plan. How many places around school do you know? Write the words from the box on the lines.

> cafeteria   computer lab   elevator   hall
> library   office   ~~restroom~~   stairs

1. _restroom_
2. _____
3. _____
4. _____
5. _____
6. _____
7. _____
8. _____

CD1 T62

B   Listen and check your answers. Then listen and repeat.

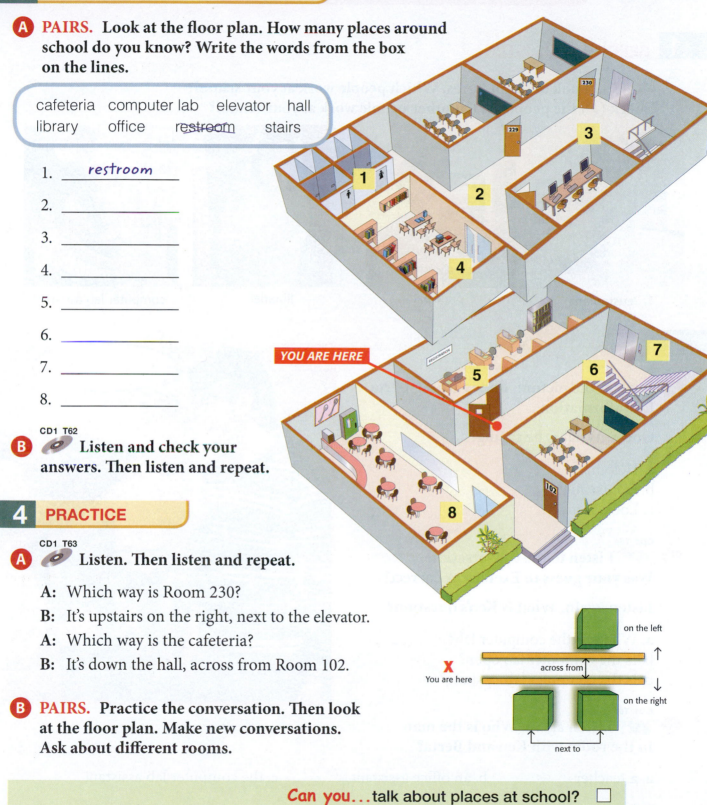

4   PRACTICE

CD1 T63

A   Listen. Then listen and repeat.

A: Which way is Room 230?
B: It's upstairs on the right, next to the elevator.
A: Which way is the cafeteria?
B: It's down the hall, across from Room 102.

B   **PAIRS.**   Practice the conversation. Then look at the floor plan. Make new conversations. Ask about different rooms.

Can you… talk about places at school? ☐

Listening and Speaking

1 BEFORE YOU LISTEN

CLASS. Look at the pictures. Which people work at your school?
Check (✓) the people. What other people work at your school?

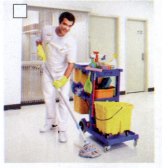
custodian

principal

librarian

computer lab assistant

2 LISTEN

A Look at the picture. Ken is asking Berta
for information.

Guess: What is he saying?

a. Help me.
b. Excuse me.
c. Look at me.

CD1 T64

B Listen to the conversation.
Was your guess in Exercise A correct?

Listen again. What is Ken's question?

a. Where is the computer lab?
b. Is the computer lab open?
c. Is the computer lab upstairs?

CD1 T65

C Listen again. Who is the man
in the room with Ken and Berta?

a. a teacher   b. an office assistant   c. the computer lab assistant

3 CONVERSATION

CD1 T66

A Listen. Then listen and repeat.

•	•	•	•	•
office	ex**cuse**	**li**brary	li**brar**ian	cafe**te**ria

Pronunciation Watch

A syllable is part of a word. One syllable in each word is stressed.

CD1 T67

B Listen to the words. Mark (•) the stressed syllable.

1. o pen   2. com pu ter   3. as sist ant   4. prin ci pal   5. cus to di an

CD1 T68

C Listen and read the conversation. Then listen and repeat.

Ken: Excuse me. Is the computer lab open?

Berta: Sorry. I don't know. Ask him.

Ken: Oh, OK. But . . . Who is he?

Berta: He's the computer lab assistant!

4 PRACTICE

A PAIRS. Practice the conversation. Then make new conversations.
Use the words in the boxes.

A: Excuse me. Is the _____ open?

B: Sorry. I don't know. Ask _____ .

A: Oh, OK. But . . . Who is _____ ?

B: _____ 's the _____ .

Ask *him*.   Ask *her*.

cafeteria	him	he	custodian
office	her	she	office assistant
library	him	he	librarian
principal's office	her	she	principal

B ROLE PLAY. PAIRS. Make your own conversations.
Talk about places at your school.

Grammar

Object pronouns

Subject pronouns			Object pronouns	
I	am			**me.**
He	is			**him.**
She	is	new here.	Please help	**her.**
We	are			**us.**
They	are			**them.**

Subject Pronoun	Object Pronoun	
you	**you**	Are you the librarian? Can I ask **you** a question?
it	**it**	It's interesting. Read **it**.

PRACTICE

A   **Underline the correct word.**

1. **A:** Where's the cafeteria?
   B: Sorry. I don't know. Ask **he** / <u>**him**</u>.

2. **A:** Are these the answers?
   B: Yes, but don't look at **they** / **them**.

3. **A:** Please show **we** / **us** your new pictures.
   B: Sure. Here they are.

4. **A:** What's the word for this in English?
   B: Sorry. I don't know. Ask **she** / **her**.

Where's the cafeteria?

Ask him.

B   **Read Ms. Reed's instructions to her class. Replace the underlined words. Use *him, her, it, us,* or *them.***

1. Take out your book. Open <u>the book</u> to page 10.
   it

2. Please close <u>your notebooks</u>. Thanks.

3. Please don't use your cell phone in class. Use <u>your cell phone</u> in the cafeteria.

4. Ask <u>Ms. Thomas</u> about the computer lab hours. She's the computer lab assistant.

5. Mr. and Mrs. Lin are new here. Please show <u>Mr. and Mrs. Lin</u> the library.

6. Mr. Tran doesn't understand. Please help <u>Mr. Tran</u>.

7. Ask <u>Mr. Benson and me</u> your English questions. We're both level 1 teachers.

1 GRAMMAR

Complete Ms. Reed's instructions to her class. Write the correct words.

OK, class. ____Open____ your books to page 10. _____ is a picture story.
1. (Open / Close)   2. (This / These)

Now, work with a partner. _____ at the picture. Ask questions. For example,
                          3. (Look / Don't look)

"Is _____ a DVD? Are _____ CDs?" Now look at the picture on page 11.
   4. (that / those)   5. (that / those)

_____ about _____ with your partner. Tell _____ or
6. (Talk / Don't talk)   7. (it / them)   8. (he / him)

_____ about the picture. _____ four sentences about it.
9. (she / her)   10. (Write / Don't write)

Show _____ to your partner.
     11. (they / them)

2 WRITING

STEP 1. Complete the sentences. Use words from the box. Choose affirmative or negative. There may be more than one correct answer.

Tips for Learning English

1. ___Speak___ English in class as much as possible!

2. _____ your language in class.

3. _____ English books at home.

4. _____ TV in English.

5. _____ new words in a notebook.

ask
listen
practice
read
speak
use
study
watch
write

STEP 2. Write four more tips for learning English. Use words from the box in Step 1.

_____

_____

_____

_____

3 ACT IT OUT   What do you say?

STEP 1. CD1 T69 **Listen to the conversation.**

STEP 2. PAIRS. You are in the office at school. Student A, you are a new student. Student B, you are an office assistant.

> **Student A:** Ask the office assistant for the location of different places around school.

> **Student B:** The new student needs information about your school. Answer the student's questions.

4 READ AND REACT   Problem-solving

STEP 1. Read about Ali's problem.

Ali is a student at the Greenville Adult School. He is in a level 1 class. Ali has good study habits. He practices English every day.

Today Ali's teacher is giving a test. The teacher says, "Please don't talk. Don't look at your classmates' test papers." Ali is not happy. A classmate is looking at his test paper.

STEP 2. PAIRS. Talk about it. What is Ali's problem? What can Ali do? Here are some ideas.

- He can say, "Please don't look at my paper."
- He can move his paper.
- He can talk to his teacher.
- He can _____.

5 CONNECT   For your Study Skills Activity, go to page 247.
For your Team Project, go to page 267.

Which goals can you check off? Go back to page 45.

Family Ties

Preview

Look at the picture. Who are the people? Where are they?

UNIT GOALS

- [ ] Talk about family
- [ ] Describe people
- [ ] Talk about months and dates
- [ ] Write dates in numbers and words
- [ ] Give your birthday and date of birth
- [ ] Give a child's age and grade in school
- [ ] Complete an emergency contact form

1   WHAT DO YOU KNOW?

A   **CLASS.** Look at the pictures of Susan's family. What words for family members do you know?

Susan

> Number 6 is her husband.

CD2 T2

B   Listen and point to the people. Then listen and repeat.

2   PRACTICE

A   **PAIRS.** Student A, point to a person and ask, "Who's this?" Student B, answer.

A: *Who's this?*
B: *Susan's mother. Who's this?*
A: *Susan's . . .*

B   **WORD PLAY. PAIRS.** Student A, look at the list of family members on page 67. Say a family member. Student B, say the matching male or female word.

A: *Brother.*
B: *Sister.*

C   **GROUPS OF 3.** Look at Susan's family tree. Talk about the people.

A: *David is Susan's husband.*
B: *Right. And Carol is Susan's mother.*

Tai-Ling   Bi-Yun

Carol   Thomas

Michael   Karen   Susan   David

Emma   Tommy

Family Members

1. sister
2. brother
3. mother
4. father
5. parents
6. husband
7. wife
8. daughter
9. son
10. children
11. grandmother
12. grandfather

Learning Strategy

Write personal sentences

Write three sentences in your notebook about your family.

Pedro and Carlos are my brothers.

Show what you know!

STEP 1. Draw your family tree in your notebook. Don't use pictures. Use names.

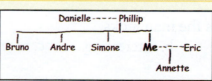

STEP 2. PAIRS. Show your partner your family tree. Ask and answer questions about your family.

A: *Who's Bruno?*
B: *He's my brother.*

Listening and Speaking

1 **BEFORE YOU LISTEN**

A **READ.** Read the sentences.

This is Justin Timberlake.
He is a singer.

This is my brother.
He **looks like** Justin Timberlake.

B **CLASS.** Who do people in your family look like?

> My sister looks like me.

2 **LISTEN**

A Look at the picture. Dora is showing a photo to Sen.

Guess: Who is the man in the photo?

a. Dora's brother   b. Dora's husband   c. Dora's father

CD2 T3

B Listen to the conversation. Was your guess in Exercise A correct?

Listen again. Complete the sentences.

1. Sen says the photo is _____.
   a. great   b. interesting   c. nice

2. Sen says the man looks _____.
   a. great   b. interesting   c. nice

CD2 T4

C Listen to the whole conversation.
Read the sentences. Circle *True* or *False*.

1. Sen thinks Dora looks like   **True   False**
   the woman in the photo.

2. The woman is Dora's sister.   **True   False**

3 CONVERSATION

CD2 T5

Listen and read the conversation. Then listen and repeat.

Sen: That's a great photo. Who's that?
Dora: My father.
Sen: Oh, he looks nice.
Dora: Thanks.

4 PRACTICE

A **PAIRS.** Practice the conversation. Then make new conversations. Use the family tree.

A: That's a great photo. Who's that?

B: My _____.
      (family member)

A: Oh, _____ looks nice.
         (he / she)

B: Thanks.

Notice three new words:
uncle, aunt, cousin

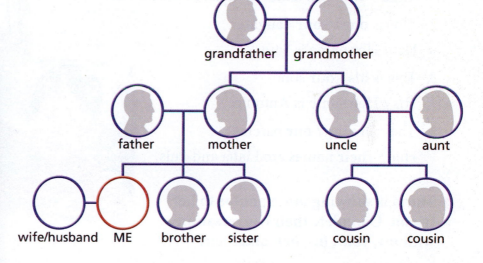

B **MAKE IT PERSONAL. PAIRS.** Make your own conversations. Bring a family photo to class or draw a picture of a person in your family. Talk about that person.

UNIT 4 **69**

Grammar

Possessive adjectives

Subject pronouns			Possessive adjectives	
I	am		**My**	
You	are		**Your**	
He	is	in the U.S.	**His**	family is in Peru.
She	is		**Her**	
We	are		**Our**	
They	are		**Their**	

1 PRACTICE

A Maria is showing family photos to a friend. Complete the sentences. Underline the correct word.

1. This is **his** / <u>**my**</u> husband and me.

   Their / **Our** two children aren't in the picture.

2. This is **our** / **your** daughter.

   His / **Her** name is Sara.

3. This is **his** / **our** son.

   His / **Her** name is Antonio.

4. These are **my** / **our** parents.

   Her / **Their** names are Liana and Luis.

B Maria is showing more photos to her friend. Complete their conversation with *my*, *your*, *his*, *her*, and *their*.

Maria: This is _m_y_ daughter with _ _ _ friend from school.

This is _ _ son with _ _ _ cousin.

And here are the children with _ _ _ _ _ classmates.

Friend: Nice. _ _ _ _ _ son looks like you.

Maria: I know. And _ _ daughter looks like my husband.

C CD2 T6 Listen and check your answers.

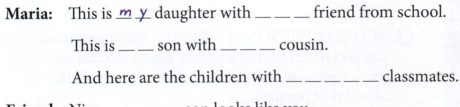

Possessive nouns

Grammar Watch

Dora Luis	is in the U.S.	Dora's Luis's Dora and Luis's	family is in Peru.

Add **'s** to names to show possession.

2 PRACTICE

A Look at the family tree. Complete the sentences.

1. Ryan is _____Eva's_____ husband.

2. Megan is _____ wife.

3. Eva is Ross and _____ daughter.

4. Tess is _____ grandmother.

5. Ed is _____ husband.

6. Diana is Mary and _____ granddaughter.

CD2 T7

B 🔘 Listen and check your answers. Then listen and repeat.

Ross Mary
Ryan Eva Tess Ed
Diana Mike Megan
Jake

Pronunciation Watch

The **'s** adds an extra syllable after the sounds *s, z, sh,* and *ch* (*Luis's, Alex's, Liz's, Josh's,* and *Mitch's*).

Show what you know! Talk about family

GROUPS OF 3. Talk about the people in the picture. Who are they? Guess.

A: *Who's Ramiro?*
B: *I think he's Rosa's husband.*
C: *Oh. I think he's Rosa's brother. He looks like her.*

Omar, Rosa, Pancho, Ramiro, Lila, Adriana, Miranda

Can you… talk about family? ☐

Read about blended families

Reading

1 BEFORE YOU READ

A **CLASS.** Read the information. Then answer the questions.

In the United States, 48% of married couples get divorced. And 75% of divorced people get married again.

Do many people in your country get divorced? Do they get married again?

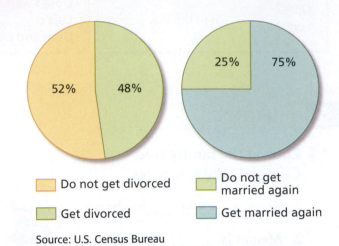

52%   48%

25%   75%

☐ Do not get divorced   ☐ Do not get married again

☐ Get divorced   ☐ Get married again

Source: U.S. Census Bureau

B Look at the pictures and dates. Complete the information. Use the words in the box.

| divorced | ~~married~~ | parents | son | step-mother | step-sister |

1 1997

Ann and Bob Peterson get _married_

2 1998

Ann and Bob with their _____, Jimmy

3 2005

Jimmy with his _____

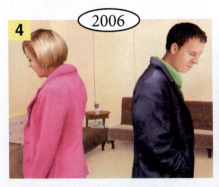

4 2006

Ann and Bob get _____

5 2008

Jimmy with his mother, step-father, and _____

6 2008

Jimmy with his father, _____, and step-brothers

CD2 T8

🔘 **Listen. Read the article.**

The American Family Today

In 2005, Jimmy had a small family. He had a mother and a father. He had no brothers or sisters. Then, in 2006, his parents got divorced.

In 2008, Jimmy's parents both got married again. Jimmy now lives with two "blended families." From Monday to Friday, Jimmy lives with his mother, his step-father, and his step-sister. On Saturdays and Sundays, he lives with his father, his step-mother and his two step-brothers. Jimmy says, "It's a little crazy. But I like my big family."

Jimmy's life isn't simple, but his story is common. Today, one out of three people in the United States is part of a blended family.

10-year-old Jimmy with his new family

3 CHECK YOUR UNDERSTANDING

A **PAIRS.** Read the article again. Look at the days of the week.
Underline the days Jimmy lives with his mother, his step-father, and his step-sister.
Circle the days Jimmy lives with his father, his step-mother, and his two step-brothers.

Sunday   Monday   Tuesday   Wednesday   Thursday   Friday   Saturday

B What is the main idea of the article? Complete the sentence.

_____ are common in the U.S. today.

Show what you know!

PAIRS. Talk about it. Do you know someone in a blended family? Who?
How many brothers and sisters does that person have?

Listening and Speaking

1   BEFORE YOU LISTEN

CD2 T9

READ. Look at the picture of Zofia's parents and brother. Listen and read the description. Answer the questions.

Zofia's father is *average height* and *heavy*. He has *a mustache*. Her mother is *short* and *average weight*. She has *long hair*. Her brother is *tall* and *thin*. He has *a beard*.

1. Who has a mustache? _____

2. Who has a beard? _____

3. Who is average weight? _____

2   LISTEN

A CD2 T10

Look at the picture. Ernesto is showing Zofia a photo. Listen to their conversation. Who are they talking about?

a. Ernesto's father   b. Ernesto's mother   c. Ernesto's brother

B CD2 T10

Listen again. Check (✓) all the things that are true.

Ernesto's brother is _____.

☐ a painter   ☐ a carpenter
☐ great   ☐ interesting   ☐ fun   ☐ smart
☐ short   ☐ tall   ☐ heavy   ☐ thin

C CD2 T11

Listen to the whole conversation. Answer the questions.

1. Which picture shows Ernesto's brother?

a.   b.   c.

2. Is Ernesto's brother married?
   a. yes   b. no

74   UNIT 4

3 CONVERSATION

CD2 T12

🔘 **Listen and read the conversation. Then listen and repeat.**

Zofia: Is your family here in this country?

Ernesto: My brother is here. He's a carpenter.

Zofia: Oh. What's he like?

Ernesto: He's great. He's a lot of fun.

Zofia: Does he look like you?

Ernesto: No. He's tall and thin and he has long hair.

4 PRACTICE

A **PAIRS.** Practice the conversation. Then make new conversations. Look at the picture. Imagine these are your uncle, cousin, and aunt.

A: Is your family here in this country?

B: My _____ is here.
      (family member)

A: Oh. What's _____ like?
         (he / she)

B: _____'s great.
  (He / She)

     _____'s a lot of fun.
    (He / She)

A: Does _____ look like you?
       (he / she)

B: Yes/No. _____'s
        (He / She)

  _____ and _____
 (height)   **(weight)**

  and has _____.
         (hair)

B **MAKE IT PERSONAL. PAIRS.** Make your own conversations. Student A, ask about your partner's family. Student B, talk about one person. Use true or made-up information.

Grammar

Descriptions with *have*

I You We They	**have**	long hair.

He She Ernesto	**has**	short hair.

1 PRACTICE

A Look at the picture. Underline the correct word.

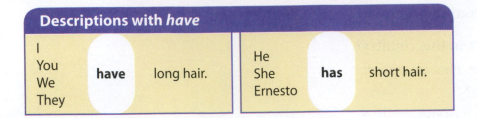

1. My name is Paul. I **have** / **has** short hair.

2. My parents both **have** / **has** short hair, too.

3. My brother and I both **have** / **has** mustaches.
   But I also **have** / **has** a beard.

4. Our sister looks like our mother. But she
   have / **has** long hair.

B PAIRS. Look at the picture again. Circle Paul.

C PAIRS. Look at the pictures. Describe the people. Use *have* or *has*. Use periods.

1. Elias *has a mustache.*

2. Ayantu _____

3. Sue and Edna _____

4. Feng _____

5. Jim and Bob _____

6. Rafael _____

Descriptions with *be* and *have*

	Be	
I	**am**	short.
She	**is**	tall.
We	**are**	average height.
They	**are**	heavy.

	Have	
I	**have**	a mustache.
She	**has**	long hair.
We	**have**	short hair.
They	**have**	beards.

2 PRACTICE

A Read about Donna's family. Underline the correct words.

Donna's mother **is** / **has** average height and weight, but her sister **is** / **are** short and heavy. Her sister and her mother both **has** / **have** short hair. Donna's father **is** / **has** a beard, and her brother **is** / **has** a mustache. Her father and her brother both **are** / **have** short hair. Her father **is** / **has** thin, but her brother **is** / **has** heavy.

B PAIRS. Look at the pictures of Donna and her husband. Talk about the differences.

A: *In Picture A, Donna is average weight. In Picture B, she's heavy.*
B: *In Picture A, she has . . .*

May 2001

April 2007

Show what you know!   Describe people

GROUPS OF 3. Look at your classmates. Complete the chart. Write the number of students.

Beard	Mustache	Long hair	Short hair	Tall	Short

A: *Who has a beard?*
B: *Carlos and Chen have beards.*
A: *Viktor has a beard, too.*
B: *OK. So, three men have beards. What about mustaches?*

Can you... describe people? ☐

Life Skills

1 TALK ABOUT MONTHS AND DATES

A **CLASS.** What are some important dates in your family?

CD2 T13
B Look at the calendar pages. Listen and point. Then listen and repeat.

2 PRACTICE

A **GROUPS OF 3.** Student A, say a month.
Student B, repeat the month and say the next month.
Student C, keep going. Then Student B, say a new month.

A: *March.*
B: *March, April.*
C: *March, April, May.*
B: *August.*
C: *August, . . .*

Sunday	Monday	Tuesday	Wednesday	Thursday	Friday	Saturday
	1	2	3	4	5	6	7
8	9	10	11	12	13	14
15	16	17	18	19	20	21
22	23	24	25	26	27	28
29	30	31				

January
February
March
April
May
June
July
August
September
October
November
December

CD2 T14
B Look at the numbers. Listen and point. Then listen and repeat.

1st first	2nd second	3rd third	4th fourth	5th fifth	6th sixth
7th seventh	8th eighth	9th ninth	10th tenth	11th eleventh	12th twelfth
13th thirteenth	14th fourteenth	15th fifteenth	16th sixteenth	17th seventeenth	18th eighteenth
19th nineteenth	20th twentieth	30th thirtieth	31st thirty-first		

> For dates we say *first, second, third,* but we write 1, 2, 3.
> For example, we say *January fifteenth,* but we write *January 15.*

CD2 T15
C Look at the calendar above for January. Listen and point to the dates.

Can you. . .talk about months and dates? ☐

D Look at the calendars. Write the dates. Use this year.

February						
SUN	MON	TUES	WED	THUR	FRI	SAT
1	2	3	4	5	6	7
8	9	10	11	12	13	14
15	16	17	18	19	20	21
22	23	24	25	26	27	28

May						
SUN	MON	TUES	WED	THUR	FRI	SAT
1	2	3	4	5	6	7
8	9	10	11	12	13	14
15	16	17	18	19	20	21
22	23	24	25	26	27	28
29	30	31				

July						
SUN	MON	TUES	WED	THUR	FRI	SAT
1	2	3	4	5	6	7
8	9	10	11	12	13	14
15	16	17	18	19	20	21
22	23	24	25	26	27	28
29	30	31				

November						
SUN	MON	TUES	WED	THUR	FRI	SAT
1	2	3	4	5	6	7
8	9	10	11	12	13	14
15	16	17	18	19	20	21
22	23	24	25	26	27	28
29	30					

February 24, 20__ __ _____ _____ _____

E Look at the calendars again. Write the dates in numbers.

1. ___2-24-10___   2. _____   3. _____   4. _____

CD2 T16

F Listen to the conversations. Which date do you hear?

1. a. 3–4–77   (b.) 3–14–77   4. a. 8–30–95   b. 8–31–95

2. a. 10–2–01   b. 2–10–01   5. a. 12–17–59   b. 12–7–59

3. a. 6–28–88   b. 5–28–88   6. a. 9–2–62   b. 9–22–52

3   GIVE YOUR BIRTHDAY

CD2 T17

Listen and read the conversation. Then listen and repeat.

A: Yu-Ping, when is your birthday?

B: My birthday is July 29. When is your birthday?

4   PRACTICE

A Walk around the room. Practice the conversation above. Use your own names and birthdays.

B NETWORK. Find classmates with the same birthday month as you. Form a group. Then create a calendar page for your birthday month. Write your names on the dates of your birthdays.

Can you...give your birthday and date of birth?   ☐

Listening and Speaking

1 BEFORE YOU LISTEN

A Look at picture 1. Label the people in the picture. Use the words in the box.

> boys   girls   children (kids)

B **CLASS.** Look at picture 2. Read the conversation. Then read the information.

In the U.S., it's OK to ask children their age. We usually do not ask adults their age. What about in your country?

How old are you?

I'm ten. I'm in the fourth grade.

2 LISTEN

A Look at the picture. Zofia is babysitting for her friend's children.

Guess: How old are the children?

CD2 T18

B Listen to Zofia's phone conversation with Assefa. Was your guess in Exercise A correct?

Listen again. Complete the sentences.

1. The boy is in the _____ grade.
   a. fourth   b. fifth   c. sixth

2. The girl is in the _____ grade.
   a. first   b. third   c. fourth

CD2 T19

C Listen to the whole conversation. Answer the questions.

1. Who says Terry is friendly?
   a. Zofia   b. Zofia's friend   c. Kevin

2. Who calls Terry "Terry the Terrible"?
   a. Zofia   b. Zofia's friend   c. Kevin

3 CONVERSATION

A 🔘 Listen. Then listen and repeat.

Her son is eleven.

He's in the fifth grade.

Where are you?

CD2 T21

B 🔘 Listen and read the conversation. Then listen and repeat.

Assefa: Hi, Zofia. Where are you?
Zofia: I'm at my friend's house. I'm babysitting for her kids.
Assefa: Oh. How old are they?
Zofia: Well, her son is eleven. He's in the fifth grade.
And her daughter is six. She's in the first grade.

4 PRACTICE

A **PAIRS.** Practice the conversation. Then make new conversations. Use the information in the boxes.

A: Hi! Where are you?

B: I'm at my friend's house. I'm babysitting for her kids.

A: Oh. How old are they?

B: Well, her son is _____. He's in the _____.
And her daughter is _____. She's in the _____.

B **MAKE IT PERSONAL. PAIRS.** Make your own conversations. Talk about children you know. Use true or made-up information.

A: *My sister has two children.*
B: *Oh, really? How old are they?*

12 (years old)
6th grade

8 (years old)
3rd grade

16 (years old)
11th grade

15 (years old)
10th grade

7 (years old)
2nd grade

10 (years old)
4th grade

5 LIFE SKILLS WRITING

Complete an emergency contact form. See page 256.

Grammar

Questions with *How old*

How old	are	you? they? your friend's children?

How old	is	he? she? Terry?

PRACTICE

A Complete the conversations. Ask about age. Use capital letters when necessary.

 Date of birth:
Jan. 4, 1975

 Date of birth:
May 6, 2003

 Date of birth:
Oct. 4, 1987

1. **A:** How old _____*is*_____
   Ya-Wen's son?

   B: He's _____.

2. **A:** How old _____
   Eric's cousins?

   B: They're _____.

3. **A:** _____
   Diego's sisters?

   B: _____.

 Date of birth:
Aug. 11, 1926

 Date of birth:
June 2, 2000

Date of birth:
Sept. 30, 2003

 Date of birth:

You

4. **A:** _____
   Soo-Jin's grandmother?

   B: _____.

5. **A:** _____ Eva's kids?

   B: Her son _____ and
   her daughter _____.

6. **A:** How old _____ you?

   B: I'd rather not say!

B PAIRS. Look at these photos of famous people. Guess. How old are they?

 Zhang Ziyi

 George Clooney

 Diego Maradona

 Oprah Winfrey

A: *How old is Zhang Ziyi?*
B: *I don't know. I think she's (around) twenty-five.*
A: *Oh, no. I think she's (around) thirty-five.*

1   GRAMMAR

Look at the picture. Who is Tina? Complete the paragraph about her. Choose the correct words.

Back: Mike, Tina, Morris, Anna, Cindy, and Ben
Front: Laurel, Chris, Jennie, and Amanda

_____My_____ name is Tina. _____
1. (Our / My)   **2. (My / Her)**

husband's name is Mike. We _____
       3. (are / have)

both 53 years old, and we're both tall and thin.

_____ have two children. _____
4. (Our / We)   **5. (Your / Our)**

son's name is Chris, and our daughter's name is

Laurel. Chris is married. _____ wife's name is Jennie. Chris and Jennie have a
       6. (His / Her)

daughter. _____ name is Amanda. She _____ ten years old. Amanda is
       7. (Their / Her)   **8. (has / is)**

_____ first granddaughter! She _____ tall, and she _____ long
9. (our / their)   **10. (is / has)**   **11. (is / has)**

hair. Amanda looks just like _____ Aunt Laurel!
       12. (my / her)

2   WRITING

STEP 1. Look at the picture again. Who is Morris? Complete the sentences about him. Use _my_, _their_, or the correct form of _be_ or _have_. Use capital letters when necessary.

_____My_____ name is Morris. I _____ 75 years old. I _____ tall

and I _____ a beard. _____ wife's name is Anna. She _____

tall, too, and she _____ short hair. We _____ two daughters.

_____ names _____ Tina and Cindy.

STEP 2. Look at the picture and read the paragraph about Tina. Imagine you are Mike. Write about yourself and your family. Use the paragraph about Morris as an example.

My name is Mike. I . . .

_____

_____

_____

_____

3 ACT IT OUT   What do you say?

STEP 1. CD2 T22 Listen to the conversation.

STEP 2. PAIRS. You are co-workers.

Student A: Ask about your friend's family.
- Ask who is in your friend's family.
- Choose a family member. Ask, "What is he/she like?"
- Are there children in your friend's family? Ask about their ages and grades in school.
- Ask about the children's birthdays.

Student B: Answer your friend's questions about your family. Use your own information, or choose a picture to talk about.

4 READ AND REACT   Problem-solving

STEP 1. Read about Hae-Jin's problem.

Hae-Jin lives in Los Angeles with her family. Her grandfather lives in a different part of L.A. He lives alone.

Hae-Jin works at a bank. Her grandfather calls her at work every day. He just wants to talk. But Hae-Jin can't talk on the phone at work.

STEP 2. PAIRS. Talk about it. What is Hae-Jin's problem? What can Hae-Jin do? Here are some ideas.

- She can turn her phone off.
- She can say, "Please don't call me at work."
- She can talk to her manager.
- She can _____.

5 CONNECT   For your Goal-setting Activity, go to page 247.
For your Team Project, go to page 267.

Which goals can you check off? Go back to page 65.

Shop, Shop, Shop

5

Preview

Look at the picture. What do you see?

UNIT GOALS

- ☐ Talk about colors
- ☐ Talk about clothes
- ☐ Talk about things you need, want, or have
- ☐ Use U.S. money
- ☐ Talk about prices
- ☐ Read price tags
- ☐ Read a receipt
- ☐ Write a personal check
- ☐ Ask about sizes and colors
- ☐ Return something to a store

1   WHAT DO YOU KNOW?

A   **CLASS.** Look at the pictures. Which clothes do you know? Which colors do you know?

> Number 1 is a dress.
> Number 5 is orange.

CD2 T23

B   Listen and point to the pictures. Then listen and repeat.

2   PRACTICE

A   **WORD PLAY.** Look at the pictures and the list of clothes on page 87. Which clothes come in pairs? Write the words.

___*pants*___

_____

_____

_____

_____

> These clothes are plural.
> Example: *The pants are black.*

B   **PAIRS.** Ask and answer questions about the pictures.

A: *What's number 12?*
B: *Shoes.*
A: *What color are they?*
B: *Brown. What's number 3?*
A: *A skirt.*
B: *What color is it?*
A: *Red.*

C   **NETWORK.** What is your favorite color? Find classmates with the same favorite color as you. Form a group. Ask the people in your group, *What clothes do you have in that color?*

1   2

5   6

9   10

11   12

3

4

7

8

Colors and Clothes

1. **a** yellow dress
2. **a** green shirt
3. **a** red skirt
4. white sneakers
5. **an** orange blouse
6. **a** pink sweater
7. black jeans
8. **a** blue jacket
9. gray socks
10. **a** purple T-shirt
11. beige pants
12. brown shoes

Learning Strategy

Make word groups

Look at the list of clothes. Which clothes do men wear? Which clothes do women wear? Which clothes do both men and women wear? Make three lists in your notebook.

Show what you know!

STEP 1. PAIRS. Describe your clothes.

A: *I'm wearing a green T-shirt, blue jeans, and black sneakers.*
B: *And I'm wearing . . .*

STEP 2. NEW PAIRS. What are your classmates wearing? Look around the room.

Student A, ask: "Who's wearing _____?"
Student B, name the student.

A: *Who's wearing gray pants and a red sweater?*
B: *Roberto.*
A: *Right!*
B: *Who's wearing . . . ?*

Listening and Speaking

1 BEFORE YOU LISTEN

CD2 T24

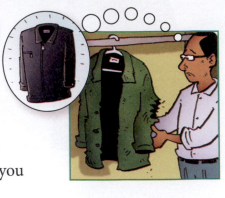

READ. Look at the picture. Listen and read about Mr. Monro's birthday. Then complete the sentences. Underline the correct word.

It's Mr. Monro's birthday next week. His wife always gives him a gift for his birthday. This year, she asks him, "What do you want for your birthday?"

"How about a jacket?" Mr. Monro says.

"Well," his wife says, "I know you *need* a jacket. Your green jacket is old. But what do you *want*?"

"Oh," Mr. Monro says. "I need a jacket *and* I want a jacket. I want a black jacket!"

1. Mr. Monro needs a **gift / jacket**.

2. Mr. Monro wants a **black / green** jacket.

2 LISTEN

CD2 T25

A Look at the picture. Zofia and Carlos are friends. Listen to their conversation. Who is Robert?

a. Zofia's brother   b. Zofia's friend   c. Zofia's father

CD2 T25

B Listen again. Read the sentences. Circle *True* or *False*.

1. Zofia's birthday is next week.   True   False

2. Robert needs clothes.   True   False

3. Robert wants clothes.   True   False

CD2 T26

C Listen to the whole conversation. Complete the sentence.

Carlos wants a _____.

a.    b.   c.

3 CONVERSATION

CD2 T27

 Listen and read the conversation. Then listen and repeat.

Zofia: I need a gift for my brother, Robert. It's his birthday next week.
Carlos: How about clothes?
Zofia: Well, he needs clothes, but he wants a backpack!

4 PRACTICE

A PAIRS. Practice the conversation. Then make new conversations. Use the information in the boxes.

A: I need a gift for my _____. It's _____ birthday next week.
(his / her)

B: How about clothes?

A: Well, _____ needs clothes, but _____ wants _____ !
(he / she)   (he / she)

friend

mother

father

a wallet

a handbag

a watch

B ROLE PLAY. PAIRS. Make your own conversations. Use different people and gifts.

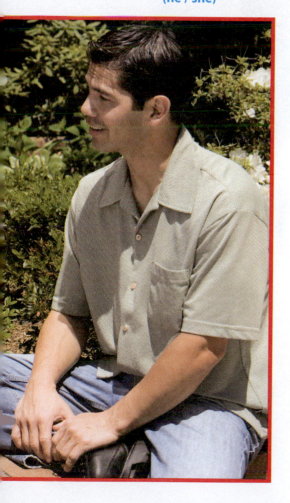

Talk about things you need, want, or have

Grammar

Simple present affirmative

I You We They	**need** **want** **have**	new clothes.

He She Robert	**needs** **wants** **has**	new clothes.

1 **PRACTICE**

A **Underline the correct word.**

1. Mr. Garcia **have / <u>has</u>** a blue shirt.
2. He **want / wants** a green shirt.
3. Amy and Jeff **have / has** black sneakers.
4. I **want / wants** black sneakers, too.
5. Our teacher **need / needs** a new jacket.
6. He **need / needs** new pants, too.

B **Complete the sentences.**
Use the verbs in parentheses.

1. My sister _____*needs*_____ a skirt.
   (need)
2. She _____ a red skirt.
   (want)
3. My brothers _____ new shoes.
   (have)
4. Now they _____ new socks.
   (need)
5. Allen _____ brown jeans.
   (have)
6. We _____ brown jeans, too.
   (want)
7. You _____ a nice new wallet.
   (have)
8. I _____ a new wallet, too.
   (want)

A **PAIRS.** Look at the picture of Joe and Ellen. What do they need? What do they want? Decide together. There is more than one correct answer.

A: *What does Joe need?*
B: *He needs new shoes.*
A: *Right. He also needs . . .*

B Complete the sentences.

Joe needs _____new shoes_____.

He wants _____.

Ellen needs _____.

She wants _____.

C **WRITE.** Look at the picture again. What do Joe and Ellen both need? What do they both want? Write sentences. Use capital letters and periods.

Joe and Ellen need _____

_____

Show what you know! Talk about things you need, want, or have

STEP 1. Complete the sentence with true information.

I want _____a red dress_____.

I want _____.

STEP 2. GROUPS OF 5. Play the Memory Game. Talk about clothes you want.

Agnes: *I want a red dress.*
Pedro: *Agnes wants a red dress. I want new jeans.*
Maury: *Agnes wants a red dress. Pedro wants new jeans. I want a green shirt.*

Can you...talk about things you need, want, or have? ☐

Use U.S. money

Life Skills

1 USE U.S. MONEY

A CLASS. Where do you shop for clothes? Do you pay with cash?

CD2 T28

B Look at the U.S. money. Listen and point. Then listen and repeat.

1. one dollar ($1.00)

2. five dollars ($5.00)

3. ten dollars ($10.00)

4. twenty dollars ($20.00)

CD2 T29

C Look at the coins. Listen and point. Then listen and repeat.

1. a penny (1¢)   2. a nickel (5¢)   3. a dime (10¢)   4. a quarter (25¢)

2 PRACTICE

A Count the money. Write the amount.

1. ___65¢___

2. _____

3. _____

4. _____

CD2 T30

B Listen and check your answers. Then listen and repeat.

3 TALK ABOUT PRICES

CD2 T31

Listen. A customer in a clothing store is asking about prices. Listen and repeat the conversation. Then practice with a partner.

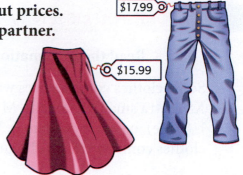

Customer: Excuse me. How much is this **skirt**?
Assistant: It's **$15.99**.
Customer: And how much are these **jeans**?
Assistant: They're **$17.99**.

4 PRACTICE

CD2 T32

A Listen. Fill in the price tags.

1.

2.

3

4.

B **PAIRS.** Practice the conversation above. Use the pictures in Exercise A.

C Look at the receipt. Answer the questions.

1. What is the date on the receipt?

   Write it in words. _____

2. How much are the jeans? _____

3. How much is the tax? _____

4. How much are the clothes before tax? _____

5. How much are the clothes after tax? _____

6. How much is the change? _____

```
            IMAGINE
      Los Angeles, CA 90027
         (213) 555-6111

   08-06-10
                        2:25 P.M.

   WOMEN'S JEANS
   WOMEN'S SWEATERS           11.99
   WOMEN'S T-SHIRTS            8.99
                              5.99
   SUBTOTAL
   TAX 8% ON 26.97           26.97
                             2.16
   TOTAL
                            29.13
   CASH AMOUNT PAID
   CHANGE DUE                30.00
                             .87
   Please keep receipt for returns.
     Thank you for shopping at
            IMAGINE.
```

5 LIFE SKILLS WRITING

Write a personal check. See page 257.

Can you... talk about prices and read price tags and receipts? ☐

Listening and Speaking

1   BEFORE YOU LISTEN

CLASS. Read the information. Answer the question.

Some clothes come in sizes with letters:
XS (extra small), S (small), M (medium),
L (large), or XL (extra large). What
clothes come in sizes with numbers?

2   LISTEN

A   Look at the picture. Assefa is shopping.

Guess: What is he asking the sales assistant about?

a. the price   b. the color   c. the size

CD2 T33

B   Listen to the conversation.
Was your guess in Exercise A correct?

Listen again. Complete the sentences.

1. Assefa wants a _____ for his sister.

a.    b.    c.

2. Assefa's sister needs a _____.

a.   b.   c.

CD2 T34

C   Listen to the whole conversation. Which sweater does the store have?

a.    b.   c.

3 CONVERSATION

A 🔵 CD2 T35 Listen. Then listen and repeat.

Do you **have** this **sweater** in a **large**?

It's **for** my **sister**.

Does she **like blue**?

Pronunciation Watch

Important words in a sentence are stressed. Other words are often unstressed. Unstressed words sound short and weak.

B 🔵 CD2 T36 Listen. Underline the stressed words.

1. Do you <u>like</u> <u>green</u>?

2. Do you need a small?

3. He wants a watch.

C 🔵 CD2 T37 Listen and read the conversation. Then listen and repeat.

Assefa: Do you have this sweater in a large?
Assistant: No, I'm sorry. We don't.
Assefa: Too bad. It's for my sister and she needs a large.

a large
an extra small

4 PRACTICE

A PAIRS. Practice the conversation. Then make new conversations. Use the pictures.

A: Do you have this _____ in _____?

B: No, I'm sorry. We don't.

A: Too bad. It's for my sister and she needs _____.

B ROLE PLAY. PAIRS. Make your own conversations. Use different clothes and sizes.

Grammar

Simple present: *Yes/no* questions and short answers

Do	I / we / you / they	**need** new shoes?	Yes,	you / we / I / they	**do.**	No,	you / we / I / they	**don't.**
Does	he / she			he / she	**does.**		he / she	**doesn't.**

1 PRACTICE

A Match the questions with the short answers.

1. Do you have these shoes in a size 9? __d__   a. Yes, he does.

2. Does your son like his new sneakers? _____   b. No, she doesn't.

3. Does Ms. Cho have a backpack? _____   c. Yes, they do.

4. Do your sisters want new clothes? _____   d. Yes, we do.

B Complete the conversations. Use *do, does, don't,* or *doesn't*. Use capital letters when necessary.

1. **A:** _____Do_____ you have this jacket in black?

   B: Yes, we _____do_____. Here you go.

2. **A:** _____ Cindy want a new watch?

   B: No, she _____. She likes her old watch.

3. **A:** _____ you need these jeans in a size 14?

   B: No, I _____. I need a size 12.

4. **A:** _____ you have this shirt in an extra small?

   B: No, we _____. But we have it in a small.

5. **A:** _____ Mr. Miller like this green sweater?

   B: No, he _____. He likes the blue sweater.

C PAIRS. Practice the conversations in Exercise B.

2 PRACTICE

Complete the questions. Use *do* or *does* and the verbs in parentheses. Use capital letters when necessary. Then look at the pictures. Answer the questions.

1. **A:** _____Does_____ Ben _____have_____ an extra-large white T-shirt?
     (have)
   B: Yes, he does.

2. **A:** _____ Ben and Tina _____ blue shirts?
     (have)
   B: _____

3. **A:** _____ Tina _____ a large red jacket?
     (need)
   B: _____

4. **A:** _____ Ben and Tina _____ red sweaters?
     (need)
   B: _____

5. **A:** _____ Tina _____ a small green sweater?
     (have)
   B: _____

BEN'S CLOTHES

TINA'S CLOTHES

Show what you know! Ask about sizes and colors

STEP 1. Write *yes/no* questions. Use *you*.

1. like / red ties   Do you like red ties?

2. have / a favorite color _____

3. need / new clothes   _____

4. want / new jeans   _____

STEP 2. PAIRS. Ask and answer the questions in Step 1.

Paula: *Do you like red ties?*
Ed: *Yes, I do.*

STEP 3. NEW PAIRS. Ask your new partner about his or her old partner.

Dan: *Does Ed like red ties?*
Paula: *Yes, he does.*

Can you… ask about sizes and colors? ☐

Read about U.S. dollar coins

Reading

1 BEFORE YOU READ

A CLASS. Look at the $5 bill. Who is the man in the picture?

B Look at other bills you have. Who are the people on the bills?

C Look at the U.S. presidents on the coins. Which presidents do you know?

 1    2    3    4

D GROUPS OF 3. Look at the coins again. Answer the questions in the chart.

	Which president is on the coin?	When was he president?	Which president was he?
1	George Washington	1789–1797	first
2			
3			
4			

CD2 T38

Listen. Read the article.

The New One-Dollar Coin

Many Americans don't know the names of the U.S. presidents. But now people can learn their names. How? With money! The U.S. government is making four new $1 coins every year. Each coin shows a different U.S. president.

The new George Washington $1 coin

The front of each coin has a lot of information about the president. It has the president's picture, his name, the dates he was president, and which president he was. For example, the George Washington coin says that he was the president from 1789 to 1797. It also says he was the first president.

The back of the coin shows the Statue of Liberty. The date of the coin is on the edge.

Some people like the new coins. But other people don't like them. In the past, the U.S. government made other $1 coins. Those coins were not popular. Will the U.S. president $1 coins be popular? We'll have to wait and see.

---

3 CHECK YOUR UNDERSTANDING

A Read the article again. What is the main idea? Complete the sentence.

The U.S. government is making new _____.

B Read the sentences. Circle *True* or *False*.

1. Most Americans know all the U.S. presidents.   True   (False)
2. The new $1 coins show different U.S. presidents.   True   False
3. On the front of the coin, you see the Statue of Liberty.   True   False
4. The old $1 coins were not popular   True   False

Show what you know!

PAIRS. Talk about it. Do you have any $1 coins? What is on them? Do you use them? Do you like them?

Return something to a store

Listening and Speaking

1 BEFORE YOU LISTEN

CLASS. Read the information. Answer the question.

Sometimes people return clothes to stores. You usually need your receipt to get your money back. Do you ever return clothes?

2 LISTEN

A Look at the pictures. Why do people return clothes? Read the reasons.

ON THE AIR

Four Reasons People Return Clothes

◯ They don't fit. They're too big.

① It doesn't look good. I don't like it.

◯ They don't match. The colors don't look good together.

◯ The zipper doesn't work. It's broken.

CD1 T39

B Matt Spencer is interviewing people on a radio show. He's at the customer service desk in a clothing store. Listen. Who is Matt interviewing?

a. cashiers   b. customer service assistants   c. customers

CD2 T39

C Listen again. Number the reasons in Exercise A in the order you hear them.

3 CONVERSATION

A Look at the picture on the right. A customer is returning a shirt. Guess: What is she looking for?

a. her money   b. her receipt   c. her credit card

B CD2 T40 Listen to the conversation. Was your guess in Exercise A correct?

C CD2 T41 Listen and read the conversation. Then listen and repeat.

Assistant: Hello. May I help you?

Customer: Yes. Hi. I need to return **this shirt**.

Assistant: What's the problem?

Customer: **It doesn't fit**.

Assistant: Do you have your receipt?

Customer: Yes, I do. It's here somewhere!

4 PRACTICE

A PAIRS. Practice the conversation. Then make new conversations. Use different clothes and reasons from page 100.

B CLASS. What are other reasons people return things?

C ROLE PLAY. PAIRS. Make your own conversations. Use different clothes and problems.

Grammar

Simple present negative

I		need		
You		want		
We	**don't**	**have**	this color.	
		like		
They		**fit**.		

He		need		
She		want		
The customer	**doesn't**	**have**	this color.	
		like		
It		**fit**.		

Grammar Watch

Use the base form of the verb after *don't* or *doesn't*.

PRACTICE

A Underline the correct word.

1. The zipper on my jacket **don't** / <u>**doesn't**</u> work.

2. Your new jeans **don't** / **doesn't** fit.

3. I **don't** / **doesn't** have my receipt.

4. They **don't** / **doesn't** like their new shoes.

5. Ms. Wong **don't** / **doesn't** like her new skirt.

6. My husband **don't** / **doesn't** need a tie.

B **PAIRS.** Look at the picture. Find the problems with the clothes. Tell your partner. There is more than one correct answer.

A: *What's the problem in A?*
B: *The jeans don't fit.*
A: *Right.*
B: *What's the problem . . . ?*

C **WRITE.** Write three problems from Exercise B.

1. _____

2. _____

3. _____

1 GRAMMAR

Complete the sentences. Use the verbs in parentheses.

A: Hi. I _____*need*_____ a gift for my friend.
            (need)

_____ you _____ this shirt in white?
                        (have)

B: No, we _____. But we _____ it in yellow.
                              (have)

A: Hmm. My friend _____ yellow.
                        (not like)

B: _____ your friend _____ blue?
                                  (like)

A: Yes, he _____. He _____ a large.
                                (need)

B: OK. Here you go.

2 WRITING

STEP 1. Complete the questions. Use words from the box or your own ideas. Add *a* or *an* when necessary.

Do you have __*red shoes*_____ ?

1. Do you have _____ ?

2. Do you want _____ ?

3. Do you need _____ ?

4. Do you like _____ ?

red	white	sweater	jacket
yellow	pink	jeans	shoes
blue	orange	pants	shirt
beige	purple		
black			

STEP 2. PAIRS. Take turns. Student A, ask a question from Step 1. Student B, give true answers. Then add information.

Eric: *Do you have red shoes?*
Mai: *No, I don't. But I have pink shoes. Do you have . . . ?*

STEP 3. Write sentences about your partner.

__*Mai has pink shoes.*_____

1. _____

2. _____

3. _____

3 ACT IT OUT What do you say?

CD2 T42
STEP 1. Listen to the conversation.

STEP 2. You are in a clothing store.
Student A, you are a customer. Student B,
you are an assistant.

> **Student A:** You need a gift. You
> want a red sweater.
> • Don't look at the picture.
> • Ask the assistant for a sweater.
> • Ask for the size you need.
> • Ask the price.
> • Thank the assistant.

> **Student B:** The customer wants a
> sweater.
> • Look at the sweaters.
> • Answer the customer's
>   questions.

STEP 3. Review the conversation on
page 101 (CD 2 Track 40).

STEP 4. It's the next day.

> **Student A:** You want to return the
> sweater.
> • The zipper doesn't work.
> • You have the receipt.

> **Student B:** The customer wants to
> return the sweater.
> • Ask why.
> • Ask for the receipt.

ON SALE!
$19.99

XS S M L XL

4 READ AND REACT Problem-solving

STEP 1. Read about Luis's problem.

Luis's birthday is today! His friends give him some gifts. His friend Paula gives
him a CD. His friend Solomon gives him a T-shirt. His friend Ayantu gives him a tie.
The tie is nice, but Luis doesn't need a tie. He wants a new wallet. He doesn't have
the receipt, but the box has the name of the store on it.

**STEP 2. PAIRS. Talk about it. What is Luis's problem? What can Luis do?
Here are some ideas.**

- He can return the tie and buy a wallet.
- He can give the tie to another friend.
- He can keep the tie.
- He can _____.

5 CONNECT

For your Community-building Activity, go to page 248.
For your Team Project, go to page 268.

Which goals can you check off? Go back to page 85.

Home, Sweet Home

Preview

Look at the picture.
Where are the people?
Why are they there?

UNIT GOALS

☐ Describe a house

☐ Ask about an apartment for rent

☐ Ask about things in a house

☐ Read addresses

☐ Give your address

☐ Address an envelope

☐ Read apartment ads

☐ Give directions

1 WHAT DO YOU KNOW?

A CLASS. Look at the pictures. Which rooms do you know? Which things in the rooms do you know?

> D is a bedroom.
> Number 13 is a bathtub.

B CD2 T43 Listen and point to the pictures. Then listen and repeat.

2 PRACTICE

A PAIRS. Student A, look at the pictures. Name the things in a room. Student B, guess the room.

A: *A table and chairs.*
B: *Is it the living room?*
A: *No.*
B: *The dining room?*
A: *Right.*

B WORD PLAY. GROUPS OF 3. Student A, look at the list of things in a house on page 107. Draw a picture of one thing. Students B and C, guess the thing.

B: *A dresser.*
A: *No.*
C: *A refrigerator.*
A: *Right.*

B

D

Rooms and Things in a House

A. kitchen	D. bedroom
1. sink	9. dresser
2. stove	10. bed
3. microwave	11. closet
4. refrigerator	
	E. bathroom
B. dining room	12. shower
5. table	13. bathtub
6. chair	14. toilet
C. living room	
7. lamp	
8. sofa	

Show what you know!

STEP 1. Think about your dream house. Which rooms are in the house? Make a list in your notebook.

STEP 2. PAIRS. Talk about your dream house.

A: *My dream house has nine rooms. It has a living room, a dining room, a kitchen, three bedrooms, two bathrooms, and a laundry room.*

B: *My dream house . . .*

> living room
> dining room
> kitchen
> 3 bedrooms
> 2 bathrooms
> laundry room

Talk about a house for rent

Listening and Speaking

1 BEFORE YOU LISTEN

PAIRS. Label the pictures. Use the words in the box.

cheap   dark   expensive   large   old   ~~new~~   small   sunny

a __new__ kitchen   an _____ kitchen   a _____ bathroom   a _____ bathroom

a _____ bedroom   a _____ bedroom   an _____ place   a _____ place

House for Rent! $2,000/month

House for Rent! $200/month

2 LISTEN

A Dan and Emily Reed are looking for a house. Look at the computer monitor. What can you say about the house?

CD2 T44

B Listen to the conversation. Check (✓) the correct answer.

1. Dan says the house looks _____.
   ☐ cheap   ☐ great   ☐ large

2. The house has _____. (Check (✓) two answers.)
   ☐ two bedrooms   ☐ three bedrooms
   ☐ a large kitchen   ☐ a dining room

CD2 T45

C Listen to the whole conversation. What's wrong with the house?

a. It's old.   b. It's very expensive.   c. It's not in the United States.

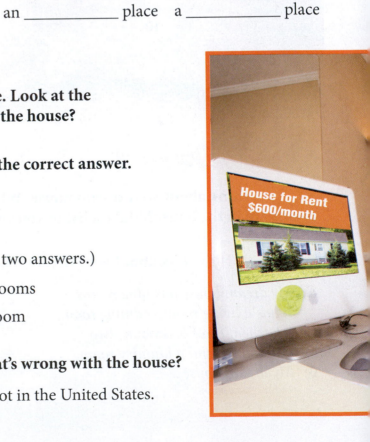

House for Rent $600/month

3 CONVERSATION

CD2 T46

Listen and read the conversation. Then listen and repeat.

Dan: Oh, wow! This house looks great!
Emily: Really?
Dan: Yes. There are two bedrooms and a large kitchen.
Emily: What about a dining room?
Dan: Well, no. There's no dining room.

4 PRACTICE

A **PAIRS. Practice the conversation. Then make new conversations. Use the information in the boxes.**

A: Oh, wow! This house looks great!

B: Really?

A: Yes. There are two bedrooms and a ⬚⬚⬚⬚ .

B: What about a ⬚⬚⬚⬚ ?

A: Well, no. There's no ⬚⬚⬚⬚ .

new bathroom — garage

sunny kitchen — laundry room

nice living room — yard

B **ROLE PLAY. PAIRS. Make your own conversations. Use different rooms.**

Grammar

There is/There are		
There is There's	a one	living room. bathroom.
There are	two	bedrooms.

There is There's	no	dining room. bathtub.
There are		closets.

Grammar Watch

Contractions
There's = There is

1 PRACTICE

A Look at the apartment ad. Read the sentences. Check (✓) *True* or *False*. Correct the false sentences.

	True	False
There's one bedroom. 1. ~~There are two bedrooms.~~	☐	✔
2. There's one bathroom.	☐	☐
3. There's no dining room.	☐	☐
4. There's a new kitchen.	☐	☐
5. There's one closet.	☐	☐
6. There's no garage.	☐	☐

FOR RENT

Large one-bedroom apartment with dining room, new bathroom, and new kitchen. Five closets! Garage. $700/month.

Call 213-555-4892

B Look at the picture on page 111. Complete the conversation. Use the words in the box. You will use some words more than once. Use capital letters when necessary.

> there's a   there are two   there's no

A: So, tell me about your new house!

B: Well, ___*there are two*___ sunny bedrooms.

A: Nice! What about bathrooms?

B: _____ bathrooms.

A: Great. And a dining room?

B: _____ dining room, but _____ table and chairs in the kitchen. _____ large yard, too. We love it!

WRITE. Look at the picture of the house. What's in each room? What's *not* in each room? Write sentences about the upstairs bathroom, the downstairs bathroom, the parents' bedroom, the children's bedroom, the living room, and the kitchen. Use *there is*, *there are*, *there's no*, and *there are no*.

In the parents' bedroom, there's a lamp. In the children's bedroom, there's no lamp.

_____

_____

_____

_____

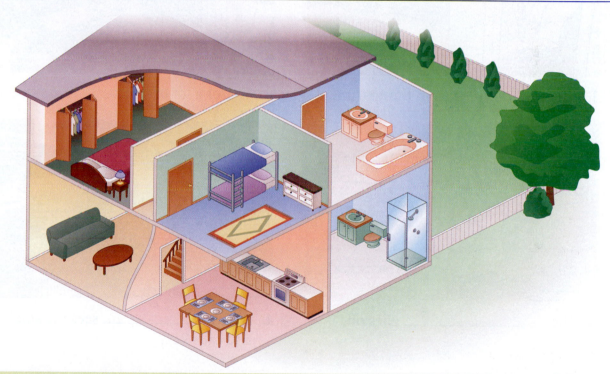

Show what you know!   Describe a house

GROUPS OF 3. Talk about things in the rooms of your house.

A: *In my bedroom, there's a bed and a dresser.*
B: *What about closets?*
A: *No, there are no closets.*
C: *In my bathroom . . .*

Can you. . . describe a house? ☐

Reading

1 BEFORE YOU READ

A Look at the pictures. Complete the sentences. Use the words in the box.

~~fire~~   neighbor   smoke   smoke alarm

1. There's a ___fire___ in the apartment.

2. There's a lot of _____.

3. The _____ goes off.

4. A _____ sees the smoke and calls 911.

B CLASS. Talk about it. What do smoke alarms do?

C Look at the pie chart. How many people get hurt every year from fires at home? How many people get killed every year?

D Do you have smoke alarms in your home? Where are they? For example, are they near the kitchen? The living room? The bedroom?

Number of people hurt or killed every year because of fires at home

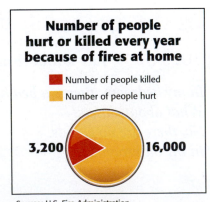

■ Number of people killed
■ Number of people hurt

3,200   16,000

Source: U.S. Fire Administration

CD2 T47

Listen. Read the article.

SMOKE ALARMS – A Life-Saver!

Every year in the U.S., about 16,000 people get hurt because of fires in their homes. And about 3,200 people get killed. Smoke alarms can keep you safe.

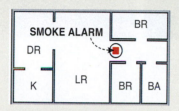

Where should you put your smoke alarms?

Put one smoke alarm near the bedroom area. You can also put smoke alarms in the living room or other rooms. But don't put an alarm in your kitchen. It will go off when you cook!

When should you check the smoke alarms?

Does your smoke alarm work? How do you know? Check the alarm every month. To check an alarm, push the test button and listen for the alarm sound.

When should you change the batteries?

Change the batteries every year. But if your alarm makes a "chirp" sound, put in a new battery right away. Your smoke alarms can't help you if they don't work!

3 **CHECK YOUR UNDERSTANDING**

A Read the article again. What is the main idea? Complete the sentence.

_____ can keep you safe from fires.

B Read the sentences. Underline the correct words.

1. In the U.S., about 16,000 people **get hurt / get killed** every year from fires in their homes.

2. You should put a smoke alarm near your **kitchen / bedroom**.

3. Check your smoke alarms every **month / year**.

4. Change the batteries every **month / year**.

Show what you know!

Draw a floor plan of your home. Put smoke alarms in the correct places.

Ask about an apartment for rent

Listening and Speaking

1 BEFORE YOU LISTEN

Studio apartments for rent!

A READ. Read about Amy and Lei Sun.

Amy and Lei Sun are looking for an apartment. They want a furnished apartment because they don't have furniture. They also want an apartment with appliances, like a refrigerator.

B CLASS. Look at the pictures. Which apartment is furnished? Which apartment is unfurnished?

2 LISTEN

A Look at the picture. Amy and Lei are talking to a building manager.

Guess: What is Amy asking about?

1 BEDROOM

B CD2 T48
🔘 Listen to the conversation. **Was your guess in Exercise A correct?**

Listen again. Underline the correct words.

1. The apartment is on the **second / seventh** floor.

2. The apartment has **beds / a dresser**.

3. The apartment has a **stove / refrigerator**.

C CD2 T49
🔘 Listen to the whole conversation. Answer the questions.

1. The building manager asks Amy and Lei: "Are you interested?"

   Who says "Yes"? _____   Who says "No"? _____

2. Do you think Amy and Lei want the apartment? Why?

   _____

Pronunciation Watch

In two-word nouns, the first word is stressed.

A  CD2 T50

 Listen. Then listen and repeat.

•
floor lamp   There's a floor lamp.

•
dining room   It's in the dining room.

B CD2 T51

 Listen to the sentences. Mark (•) the stress on the underlined words.

1. There's a <u>coffee table</u>.

2. There are two <u>desk lamps</u>.

C CD2 T52

 Listen and read the conversation. Then listen and repeat.

Amy: Excuse me. Is there an apartment for rent in this building?

Manager: Yes, there is. There's a one-bedroom apartment on the second floor.

Amy: Oh, great. Is it furnished?

Manager: Well, yes and no. There's a dresser, but no beds.

Lei: Oh. Well, are there appliances?

Manager: Uh, yes and no. There's a stove, but no refrigerator.

4 **PRACTICE**

A **PAIRS.** Practice the conversation. Then make new conversations. Use the words in the boxes.

A: Excuse me. Is there an apartment for rent in this building?

B: Yes, there is. There's a _____ apartment on the second floor.

A: Oh, great. Is it furnished?

B: Well, yes and no. There's a _____, but no _____.

B **ROLE PLAY. PAIRS.** Make your own conversations. Student A, you are looking for an apartment. Student B, you are the building manager.

> studio
> two-bedroom
> three-bedroom

> sofa
> desk
> table

> coffee table
> lamp
> chairs

Grammar

Is there/Are there

Is there	a table?
Are there	lamps?

Yes,	there is.
	there are.

No,	there isn't.
	there aren't.

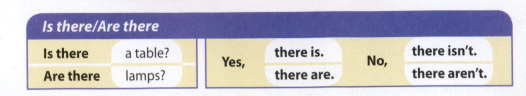

1 PRACTICE

A Complete the conversations. Underline the correct words.

1. **A: Is there** / **Are there** a bathtub in the bathroom?

   B: No, **there is** / **there isn't**. There's a shower.

2. **A: Is there** / **Are there** closets in the bedrooms?

   B: Yes, **there is** / **there are**. There's a closet in each bedroom.

3. **A: Is there** / **Are there** table lamps in the living room?

   B: No, **there are** / **there aren't**. There are floor lamps.

4. **A: Is there** / **Are there** a coffee table in the living room?

   B: Yes, **there is** / **there isn't**. There's a small coffee table and a sofa.

5. **A: Is there** / **Are there** a dining room in the apartment?

   B: No, **there isn't** / **there aren't**.

6. **A: Is there** / **Are there** a sunny kitchen?

   B: Yes, **there is** / **there are**. The kitchen is very sunny.

7. **A: Is there** / **Are there** a table in the kitchen?

   B: Yes, **there is** / **there are**. There's a table and four chairs.

CD2 T53

B Listen and check your answers.

C PAIRS. Practice the conversations in Exercise A.

WRITE. Write questions. Use the words in parentheses. Then look at the picture and write short answers.

Remember:
• Start sentences with a capital letter.
• End questions with a question mark.
• End short answers with a period.

1. (there / two / are / tables)

   A: *Are there two tables?*

   B: *Yes, there are.*

2. (lamps / are / on the tables / there)

   A: _____

   B: _____

3. (a sofa / in the room / there / is)

   A: _____

   B: _____

4. (book / on the sofa / is / there / a)

   A: _____

   B: _____

5. (pictures / there / are / in the room)

   A: _____

   B: _____

Show what you know!   Ask about things in a house

STEP 1. Complete this picture of a kitchen.

STEP 2. PAIRS. Don't look at your partner's picture! Ask questions about your partner's picture. Draw the picture on a piece of paper.

A: *Is there a refrigerator?*
B: *Yes, there is. It's across from the stove.*

STEP 3. SAME PAIRS. Look at your partner's picture. Is the picture on your paper the same?

Can you... ask about things in a house?   ☐

Life Skills

1 READ ADDRESSES

CD2 T54

A Listen and read the addresses. Then listen and repeat.

6103 Lake Drive, Apartment 27

98 East High Street

45720 Foothill Road

3095 Sunset Boulevard

1463 2nd Avenue, Apartment 10

852 Mission Street, Apartment 903

B PAIRS. Listen to your teacher. Repeat the conversation. Then practice with a partner.

A: *What's the address, please?*
B: *It's 6103 Lake Drive, Apartment 27.*

2 PRACTICE

A PAIRS. Make new conversations. Use the addresses above.

B Look at the addresses again. Write the words for each abbreviation.

1. St. _____Street_____   3. Dr. _____   5. Blvd. _____

2. Ave. _____   4. Rd. _____   6. Apt. _____

Writing Watch

Use periods in abbreviations in addresses. Example: *St.*

C Write your street address. Use abbreviations. _____

D CLASS. Walk around the room. Ask three classmates for their addresses. Use true or made-up information. Write the addresses in your notebook.

A: *What's your address?*
B: *1451 Pine Street, Apartment 3.*

E NETWORK. Who lives in your neighborhood (area)? Find those classmates. Form a group. Ask the people in your group, *What street do you live on?*

3 LIFE SKILLS WRITING   Address an envelope. See page 258.

Can you...read addresses and give your address? ☐

4 READ APARTMENT ADS

PAIRS. Look at the words. Find their abbreviations in the apartment ads below. Write the abbreviations.

1. air conditioning _A/C_
2. bathroom _____
3. bedroom _____
4. building _____

5. dining room _____
6. included _____
7. kitchen _____
8. large _____

9. laundry _____
10. living room _____
11. parking _____
12. utilities _____

A BR/1BA Apt. in New Bldg.
$975 Utils. incl.
259 Water St.
Citywide Rentals (213) 555-4488

B 2 BR/1BA Apt. $1,300
New Kit, A/C
4177 Los Feliz Blvd.
(323) 555-3276

utilities = gas, electricity, water

C 2 BR/2BA House $1,850
Lndry, Pkg
561 Franklin Ave.
(818) 555-0200

D 3 BR/ 2 BA House $2,100
Lg DR & LR
2319 Greenleaf Ave.
(562) 555-9264

5 PRACTICE

A Look at the ads again. Answer the questions. Write the letter of the ad.

Which apartment or house . . .

1. __D__ has three bedrooms?
2. _____ has a large dining room?
3. _____ has air conditioning?
4. _____ is $1,850 a month?

5. _____ has laundry and parking?
6. _____ has a new kitchen?
7. _____ has utilities included in the rent?
8. _____ is new?

B **PAIRS.** Talk about it. Which apartment or house do you like?

A: *Which apartment or house do you like?*
B: *I like B.*
A: *Why?*
B: *Because I need two bedrooms, and it has a new kitchen.*

Can you... read apartment ads? ☐

Listening and Speaking

1 BEFORE YOU LISTEN

CLASS. Look at these words: *north, south, east, west*. Where can you see these words?

2 LISTEN

A Look at the picture. Lei and Amy need a new sofa. Lei is calling Joe's Furniture Store.

Guess: Why is he calling?

a. for directions

b. for the store hours

c. for prices

CD2 T55

B Listen to the phone call. Was your guess in Exercise A correct?

Listen again. Answer the questions.

1. Which number do you press for store hours? _____

2. Which number do you press for directions to the store? _____

3. Which number do you press for directions from the north? _____

4. Which number do you press for directions from the south? _____

CD2 T56

C Listen to the whole phone call. Complete the directions to Joe's Furniture Store. Listen again and draw the route.

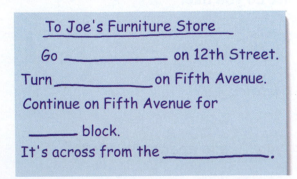

To Joe's Furniture Store

Go _____ on 12th Street.

Turn _____ on Fifth Avenue.

Continue on Fifth Avenue for

_____ block.

It's across from the _____.

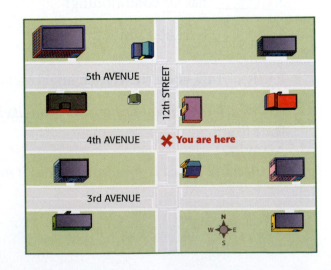

3 CONVERSATION

CD2 T57

🔘 **Two friends are talking. Listen and read the conversation. Then listen and repeat.**

A: How do you get to Joe's Furniture Store?

B: Joe's Furniture Store? Let's see . . . First, go north on 12th Street.

A: North?

B: Uh-huh. Then turn left on Fifth Avenue. Continue for one block. It's on the left across from the hospital. You can't miss it.

A: Thanks.

4 PRACTICE

A **PAIRS.** **Practice the conversation. Then make new conversations. Use the words in the boxes.**

A: How do you get to _____ ?

B: _____ ? Let's see . . . First, go _____ on 12th Street.

A: _____ ?

B: Uh-huh. Then turn left on Fifth Avenue.

Continue for one block. It's on the left across from

the _____ . You can't miss it.

A: Thanks.

| Sam's Appliances |
| Ali's Air Conditioners |
| Kitty's Kitchen |

| south |
| east |
| west |

| computer store |
| bookstore |
| hotel |

B **MAKE IT PERSONAL. PAIRS.** **Make your own conversations. Ask for directions from your school to a store your partner likes.**

A: *What's your favorite department store?*
B: *I like Kale's.*
A: *How do you get there from here?*
B: *Go north on . . .*

Give directions

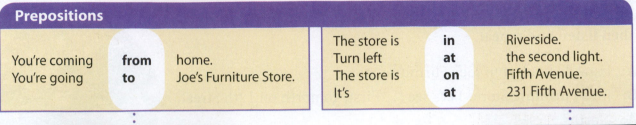

Grammar

Prepositions

You're coming	**from**	home.
You're going	**to**	Joe's Furniture Store.

The store is	**in**	Riverside.
Turn left	**at**	the second light.
The store is	**on**	Fifth Avenue.
It's	**at**	231 Fifth Avenue.

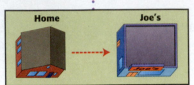

PRACTICE

A Complete the directions. Underline the correct words.

Directions to Our New Apartment

• Our apartment is **on** / **in** Tenth Avenue **in** / **at** Greenville.

• If you're coming **from** / **to** the school, go **from** / **to** the first light.

• Turn right **at** / **on** the light. You're now **on** / **in** Tenth Avenue.

• Our apartment is **on** / **to** the corner of Tenth Avenue and Elm Street. It's **in** / **at** 3245 Tenth Avenue.

B Complete the conversation. Use the words in the box.

at~~~~   at   from   in   on   to

A: Where is Eric's office?

B: It's _____*at*_____ 649 Second Avenue _____ Riverside.

A: OK. How do I get there _____ here?

B: It's easy. Go _____ First Street and turn right _____ the light. Continue for three blocks. Eric's office is on the right.

A: Is there a coffee shop near his office?

B: Yes. There's a nice coffee shop _____ Second Avenue.

1 GRAMMAR

Complete the conversation between Ana and a building manager. Use *is there*, *there's*, *there's no*, and *there are no*. Use capital letters when necessary.

Ana: This apartment is very nice. ___*Is there*___ a laundry room in the building?

Manager: Yes, _____ a laundry room on the second floor.

Ana: Good. _____ a garage?

Manager: Yes, _____ a garage, too.

Ana: OK. One more thing. What about furniture? There's a table in the living room, but _____ sofa, and _____ chairs in the dining room.

Manager: Well, _____ a furniture store in Smithfield. Their furniture is good, and it's not expensive. And _____ a good sale on now.

2 WRITING

STEP 1. Look at the map. Complete the directions from Ana's apartment to the furniture store.

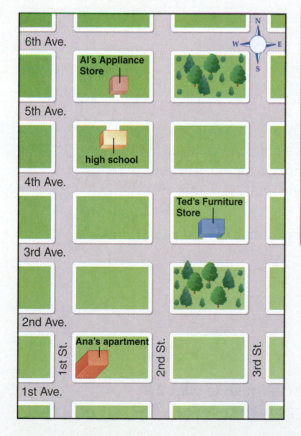

Directions ___*from*___ Ana's apartment _____ Ted's Furniture Store:

Go _____ on 1st Avenue _____ 2nd Street. Turn _____ on 2nd Street.

Go _____ 3rd Avenue. Turn _____ on 3rd Avenue. The store is _____ 3rd Avenue between 2nd and 3rd Streets across from a small park.

STEP 2. Now write directions from Ted's Furniture Store to Al's Appliance Store.

_____

_____

_____

_____

3 ACT IT OUT   What do you say?

STEP 1. CD2 T58 **Listen to the conversation.**

STEP 2. PAIRS. Student A, you want to rent an apartment. Student B, you are an apartment manager.

> **Student A:** You are calling about an apartment.
> - Ask the manager about the rooms in the apartment.
> - Ask about the furniture and the appliances.
> - Ask for directions to the apartment.

> **Student B:** Someone calls you to ask about an apartment you manage.
> - Answer the questions about the apartment.
> - Give directions to the apartment.

APARTMENT FOR RENT

2 Bedrooms
Call 310-555-8927

4 READ AND REACT   Problem-solving

STEP 1. Read about Silvia's problem.

Silvia lives in a two-bedroom apartment. She lives with her mother, her husband, and their daughter. The apartment is small, but it's nice. The living room is sunny. The kitchen is new. The appliances are good. The rent is $800. But now the building manager wants to raise the rent. He wants $900.

STEP 2. PAIRS. Talk about it. What is Silvia's problem? What can Silvia do? Here are some ideas.

- She can get a second job.
- She can find another apartment.
- She can talk to the building manager.
- She can _____.

5 CONNECT

For your Goal-setting Activity, go to page 248.
For your Team Project, go to page 269.

Which goals can you check off? Go back to page 105.

Day After Day

Preview

**Look at the picture.
What do you see?**

UNIT GOALS

- ☐ Talk about daily activities
- ☐ Talk about times of day
- ☐ Talk about work schedules
- ☐ Read and complete a time sheet
- ☐ Write a note asking for time off
- ☐ Talk about weekend activities
- ☐ Talk about how often you do something

1 WHAT DO YOU KNOW?

A **CLASS.** Look at the pictures. Which activities do you know?

> Number 4 is "eat breakfast."

B CD3 T2  Listen and point to the pictures. Then listen and repeat.

2 PRACTICE

A **WORD PLAY. PAIRS.** Student A, look at the list of daily activities on page 127. Act out an activity. Student B, guess the activity.

B: *Wash the dishes?*
A: *No.*
B: *Cook dinner?*
A: *Right!*

B CD3 T3  Look at the time in each picture. Listen and point. Then listen and repeat.

C **PAIRS.** Look at the pictures. Student A, ask about an activity. Student B, say the time.

A: *What time does he go to work?*
B: *At nine.*
A: A.M. *or* P.M.*?*
B: A.M.
A: *Right!*
B: *What time does he . . . ?*

> A.M. = **in the morning**
> P.M. = **in the afternoon,**
> **in the evening, or**
> **at night**

1

2

7

8

8

11

12

3 8:30 A.M.

4 8:45 A.M.

5 9:00 A.M.

6 7:15 P.M.

9 9:15 P.M.

10 9:30 P.M.

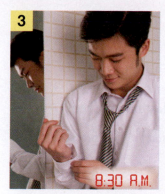

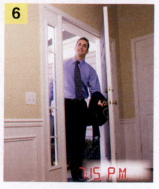

Daily Activities

1. get up
2. take a shower
3. get dressed
4. eat breakfast
5. go to work
6. get home

7. exercise
8. cook dinner
9. eat dinner
10. wash the dishes
11. watch TV
12. go to sleep

Learning Strategy

Write personal sentences

Look at the list of daily activities. Make cards for three or four activities. On one side, write a sentence with a blank about your daily schedule. On the other side, write the activity you do at that time.

Show what you know!

STEP 1. What do you do every day? Complete the sentences. Write activities and times.

I ___go to work___ at ___7:00 A.M.___. I _____ at _____.

I _____ at _____. I _____ at _____.

STEP 2. GROUPS OF 3. Ask about your classmates' daily activities.

A: *What's your schedule like?*
B: *I go to work at seven. I eat lunch at. . . .*

STEP 3. Report to the class.

Carolina goes to work at seven.

go → goes
wash → washes
watch → watches

Listening and Speaking

1   BEFORE YOU LISTEN

A **CLASS.** Look at Gloria's schedule. Which days is she busy? Which day is she free?

Sunday	Monday	Tuesday	Wednesday	Thursday	Friday	Saturday
Work	Class	Work	Class	Work		Work

B **PAIRS.** When are you free? What do you do in your free time? Check (✓) the activities. What other activities do you do?

☐ see a movie

☐ go to the mall

☐ play soccer

☐ go to the park

2   LISTEN

A Look at the picture. Gloria and Sen are classmates.

Guess: What are they talking about?

a. homework   b. plans for Saturday   c. directions to the mall

B CD3 T4   Listen to the conversation. Was your guess in Exercise A correct?

Listen again. Complete the sentences.

1. On Saturdays Sen _____.
   a. works   b. goes to school   c. babysits for her cousin

2. Sen gets home at _____ on Saturdays.
   a. 6:00   b. 7:00   c. 8:00

C CD3 T5   Listen to the whole conversation. What does Gloria want to do on Saturday?

a.

b.

3 CONVERSATION

A CD3 T6 **Listen. Then listen and repeat.**

When do you get home?
What do you mean?

Pronunciation Watch

In informal conversation, *do you* often sounds like "d'ya."

B CD3 T7 **Listen. Complete the sentences.**

1. ___*What do you*___ do in your free time?

2. _____ have English class?

3. _____ go to work?

C CD3 T8 **Listen and read the conversation. Then listen and repeat.**

Gloria: Are you free tomorrow? How about a movie?
Sen: Sorry, I'm busy. I work on Saturdays.
Gloria: Oh. Well, when do you get home?
Sen: At 8:00.

4 PRACTICE

A PAIRS. **Practice the conversation. Then make new conversations. Use the information in the boxes.**

A: Are you free tomorrow?
How about a movie?

B: Sorry, I'm busy. I ▭▭▭
on ▭▭▭ .

A: Oh. Well, when do you get home?

B: At ▭▭▭ .

B MAKE IT PERSONAL. PAIRS.
Make your own conversations. Use different activities, days, and times.

take a computer class

babysit

visit my grandparents

Fridays

Thursdays

Sundays

Grammar

Simple present: Questions with *When* and *What time*				Prepositions of time
When	**does**	Sen	**work?**	**On** Saturdays.
		she	**get home?**	**At** 8:00.
	do	you	**have class?**	**From** Monday **to** Friday.
What time	**does**	the movie / it	**start?**	**At** 6:00.
	do	they	**have dinner?**	**From** 7:00 **to** 8:00.

1 PRACTICE

A **Complete the sentences about Alicia's schedule. Use *on*, *at*, *from*, or *to*.**

1. Alicia starts work ___at___ 8:00 ___on___ Mondays.

2. She works _____ Monday _____ Friday.

3. _____ Fridays she has dinner with her father.

   They eat _____ 7:00.

4. Alicia has English class _____ 10:00 _____ 12:00

   _____ Saturdays.

5. She meets her friends at the mall _____ 3:00.

6. _____ Sundays she plays soccer _____ 11:00.

7. She watches TV _____ 9:00 _____ 11:00. She goes to sleep _____ 11:30.

> **Grammar Watch**
> - Use *from . . . to . . .* with days and times. This shows when an activity starts and ends.
> - *on Mondays* = every Monday
> - For more prepositions of time, see page 273.

B **Complete the conversation. Read the answers. Then complete the questions.**

1. **A:** When _____do_____ Paul and Elise _____go_____ to work?
   B: They go to work at 9:00. They work from Monday to Friday.

2. **A:** What time _____ they _____?
   B: Paul gets home at six. Elise gets home at 6:30.

3. **A:** And when _____ Paul _____?
   B: He cooks dinner at 7:00. They eat together from 7:30 to 8:30.

Friday	Saturday	Sunday
work—8:00	soccer game—9:00	exercise—2:00
	study with Maria—1:00	dinner with Mom—6:00

2 PRACTICE

A Look at Claude's schedule. Write questions about his activities. Use the words in parentheses.

1. <u>What time does Claude start work on Fridays?</u>
   (What time / Claude / start work on Fridays)

2. _____
   (What time / Claude / play soccer on Saturdays)

3. _____
   (What time / Claude and Maria / study on Saturdays)

4. _____
   (When / Claude / exercise)

5. _____
   (When / Claude and his mother / have dinner)

B PAIRS. Ask and answer the questions in Exercise A.

Show what you know! Talk about daily activities

STEP 1. When do you do each activity? Fill in the "You" columns.

	You		Partner	
	Friday	Saturday	Friday	Saturday
get up				
eat dinner				
watch TV				

STEP 2. PAIRS. When does your partner do each activity? Ask questions. Complete the chart.

You: *Ana, when do you get up on Fridays?*
Ana: *I get up at 7:00.*

STEP 3. WRITE. In your notebook, write about activities you and your partner do at the same time.

Ana and I both watch TV from 6:00 to 7:00 on Fridays.

Can you… talk about daily activities? ☐

Talk about work schedules and time sheets

Life Skills

1 TALK ABOUT WORK SCHEDULES

CLASS. Look at the calendar. Say the days of the week.

DECEMBER						
Sun.	Mon.	Tues.	Wed.	Thurs.	Fri.	Sat.

> **Writing Watch**
>
> Start days of the week with capital letters.
> Example: *Sunday*
> End abbreviations for days of the week with a period.
> Example: *Sun.*

2 PRACTICE

PAIRS. Student A, look at the work schedule on the left. Student B, look at the schedule on the right. Don't look at your partner's schedule. Ask and answer questions. Complete the information.

A: *When does Ming work?*
B: *She works Tuesday to Saturday, from 11:00 to 5:00.*

> • For *Mon.–Fri.,* we say *Monday to Friday* or *from Monday to Friday.*
> • For *Mon., Wed., Fri.,* we say *Monday, Wednesday, and Friday.*
> • For *11:00–5:00,* we say *eleven to five* or *from eleven to five.*

Student A

The Computer Store

Work Schedule: December 9–15

Ming Chu	Tues.–Sat., 11:00 A.M.–5:00 P.M.
Pedro Molina	Mon.–Fri., 2:30 P.M.–8:30 P.M.
Maya Kabir	_____
Danny Wu	Wed., Thurs., Fri., 6:30 A.M.–10:30 A.M.
Bruno Duval	_____

Student B

The Computer Store

Work Schedule: December 9–15

Ming Chu	Tues.–Sat., 11:00 A.M.–5:00 P.M.
Pedro Molina	_____
Maya Kabir	Tues., Thurs., Sat., 7:00 A.M.–4:00 P.M.
Danny Wu	_____
Bruno Duval	Wed.–Sun., 3:00 P.M.–10:00 P.M.

Can you...talk about work schedules? ☐

3 READ A TIME SHEET

Look at Mariam's time sheet. Complete the sentences.

① employee = worker

③ Time In = the time you start work

TIME SHEET

① EMPLOYEE NAME
Last   First
Said,   Mariam

② EMPLOYEE I.D. # 987-65-4321

Week ending 7/15

DAY	**③** TIME IN	**④** TIME OUT	HOURS
Mon.	8:30 A.M.	1:00 P.M.	4.5
Tues.	9:00 A.M.	5:00 P.M.	8
Wed.	8:30 A.M.	3:30 P.M.	7
Thurs.	off		
Fri.	off		
Sat.	12:00 P.M.	5:00 P.M.	5
Sun.	off		

Employee Signature *Mariam Said*   TOTAL HOURS
24.5

② I.D. # = Identification Number
Some companies use Social Security numbers (SSNs) for employee I.D. numbers.

④ Time Out = the time you finish work

1. Mariam worked on <u>Monday, Tuesday, Wednesday, and Saturday</u>.

2. On Tuesday she started work at _____.

3. On _____ she finished work at 3:30.

4. She was off on _____.

5. She worked _____ hours on Monday.

4 PRACTICE

Read the information. Complete your time sheet for the week.

You work from 7:00 A.M. to 3:00 P.M. at City Center Hospital. You are off on Tuesdays and Thursdays. Your employee I.D. number is 00312. Today is Saturday, March 11.

5 LIFE SKILLS WRITING

Write a note to your manager. Ask for time off. See page 259.

TIME SHEET

EMPLOYEE NAME _____   EMPLOYEE I.D. #

First   Last

Week ending _____

	TIME IN	TIME OUT	HOURS
Sun.			
Mon.			
Tues.			
Wed.			
Thurs.			
Fri.			
Sat.			
Employee Signature		TOTAL HOURS	

Can you...read and complete a time sheet? ☐

Talk about weekend activities

Listening and Speaking

1 BEFORE YOU LISTEN

A **READ.** Read the information.

In the U.S. and Canada, many people work from Monday to Friday.
They are free on the weekend (Saturday and Sunday).

B **CLASS.** Are you free on the weekend? What do you do? Check (✓) the activities. What other activities do you do?

☐ clean

☐ spend time with my family

☐ shop for food

2 LISTEN

A Look at the picture. Mei-Yu and Ernesto are leaving work.

Guess: What day is it?

B CD3 T9 Listen to the conversation. Was your guess in Exercise A correct?
Listen again. Complete the schedules.

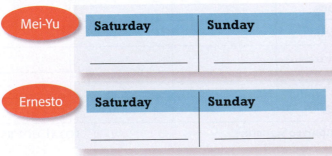

Mei-Yu	Saturday	Sunday
	_____	_____

Ernesto	Saturday	Sunday
	_____	_____

C CD3 T10 Listen to the whole conversation. In Ernesto's house, what do they call Sunday?

a. "work day"   b. "play day"   c. "fun day"

3 CONVERSATION

Listen and read the conversation. Then listen and repeat.

Mei-Yu: Gee, I'm so glad it's Friday!

Ernesto: Me, too. What do you usually do on the weekend?

Mei-Yu: Well, I always clean the house on Saturdays, and I always spend time with my family on Sundays. What about you?

Ernesto: I usually shop for food on Saturdays, and I sometimes go to the park on Sundays.

4 PRACTICE

A PAIRS. Practice the conversation. Then make new conversations. Use the pictures.

A: Gee, I'm so glad it's Friday!

B: Me, too. What do you usually do on the weekend?

A: Well, I always _____ on Saturdays, and I always _____ on Sundays. What about you?

B: I usually _____ on Saturdays, and I sometimes _____ on Sundays.

 cook

 ride my bike

 do my homework

 play basketball

 read the paper

 go dancing

 do the laundry

 go to the beach

 work on my car

 play cards

 play video games

 go swimming

B MAKE IT PERSONAL. PAIRS. Make your own conversations. Talk about your weekend activities.

Talk about weekend activities

Grammar

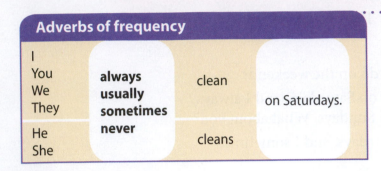

Adverbs of frequency

| I You We They | **always usually sometimes never** | clean | on Saturdays. |
| He She | | cleans | |

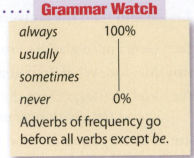

Grammar Watch

always	100%
usually	
sometimes	
never	0%

Adverbs of frequency go before all verbs except *be*.

PRACTICE

A Marcos is a student at Greenville Adult School. Look at his schedule. Complete the e-mail with *always, usually, sometimes,* or *never* and the correct form of the verb.

	Mon.	**Tue.**	**Wed.**	**Th.**	**Fri.**	**Sat.**	**Sun.**
7:00	exercise	exercise	exercise	exercise	exercise		
8:00–12:00	class	work	class	work	class		
12:30	lunch	lunch	lunch	lunch	lunch	lunch	lunch
1:00–5:00	work		work		work	work	soccer?

Hi Cristina,

How are you? I'm fine. My new job is great. I ___*usually*___ ___*work*___ in the
                  1. (work)

afternoon, but I _____ _____ in the morning. In my free time, I do a lot of
             2. (work)

things. I _____ _____ at 7:00 A.M. Then, on Mondays, Wednesdays, and
     3. (exercise)

Fridays, I _____ _____ class. I _____ _____ lunch at
     4. (have)   **5. (have)**

12:30. I _____ _____ on Sundays. It's my only day off! I _____
     6. (work)

_____ soccer in the afternoon with my brothers. I love Sundays!
   7. (play)

Write soon,

Marcos

B Look at Marcos and his family's Sunday activities. Imagine that you are Marcos. Write sentences about your activities. Use the words in parentheses.

1. <u>I always visit my family on Sundays.</u>
   (I / always / on Sundays)

2. _____
   (We / always / at 12:30)

3. _____
   (My brothers and I / sometimes / in the park)

4. _____
   (My father and sister / usually)

5. _____
   (My mother / usually / after lunch)

6. _____
   (My mother / never / on Sundays)

Show what you know! Talk about weekend activities

STEP 1. Complete the sentences with true or false information.

1. I usually _____ at night.

2. I always _____ on Sundays.

3. I never _____.

4. I _____.

STEP 2. PAIRS. Student A, read a sentence. Student B, guess *True* or *False*.

A: *I usually watch TV at night.*
B: *True.*
A: *No. I never watch TV at night. I work nights!*

Can you...talk about weekend activities? ☐

Reading

1 BEFORE YOU READ

PAIRS. Talk about it. How much free time do you have a day?
What do you do in your free time?

2 READ

CD3 T12

Listen. Read the article.

How much free time do Americans have? American men
have about 5 hours and 37 minutes of free time a day.
American women have about 5 hours.

What do Americans do with their free time? These are three common activities.

They watch TV. Men watch 2 hours and 48 minutes of TV a day. Women watch less TV. They watch 2 hours and 22 minutes.

They exercise. Men exercise or play sports for about 23 minutes a day. Women exercise only 12 minutes a day.

They spend time with family and friends. Men talk on the phone or spend time with family and friends for about 50 minutes a day. Women talk on the phone or spend time with family and friends for about an hour a day.

What's one reason American men have more free time than American women? Men cook and clean for only 30 minutes a day. Women cook and clean for 1 hour and 43 minutes a day!

Source: American Time Use Survey. U.S. Department of Labor, Bureau of Labor Statistics, 2005

3 CHECK YOUR UNDERSTANDING

A Read the article again. Circle *True* or *False*.

1. Women have more free time than men.	True	(False)
2. Men watch more TV than women.	True	False
3. Women play more sports than men.	True	False
4. Men spend more time with family and friends than women do.	True	False
5. Women cook and clean more than men.	True	False

B **PAIRS.** Talk about it. Are the sentences in Exercise A true or false in your country?

C Look at the bar graphs. How do Americans spend their free time? Complete the sentences.

a.

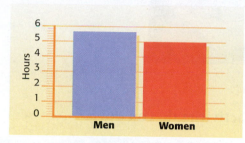

Hours of free time a day

Men have about _____ hours and 37 minutes of free time every day.

Women have about _____ hours of free time every day.

c.

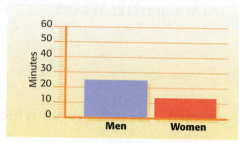

Minutes of exercise a day

Men exercise for about _____ minutes every day.

Women exercise about _____ minutes every day.

b.

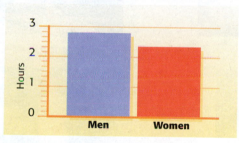

Hours of TV a day

Men watch about _____ hours and 48 minutes of TV every day.

Women watch about _____ hours and 22 minutes of TV every day.

d.

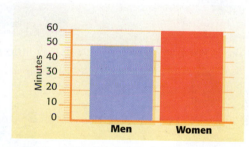

Minutes with family and friends a day

Men spend about _____ minutes every day with family and friends.

Women spend about _____ minutes every day with family and friends.

Show what you know!

CLASS. How much free time do you have? Take a survey. Make a bar graph for your class. Use the bar graphs above as a model.

Talk about how often you do something

Listening and Speaking

1 BEFORE YOU LISTEN

CLASS. Do you relax? When?

2 LISTEN

A Look at some ways people relax. Which of these activities do you do?

ON THE AIR Ways to Relax

☐ take a hot bath   ☐ do puzzles   ☐ go running

☐ knit   ☐ listen to music   ☐ take a long walk

CD3 T13

B 🔘 Listen to the radio show. The host, Sue Miller, talks about relaxing. Look at the pictures in Exercise A. Check (✓) the four activities Sue Miller talks about.

CD3 T13

C 🔘 Listen again. Complete the sentence. Check (✓) all the correct answers.

Sue Miller says, "You need to relax every day. It helps you _____."

☐ study better   ☐ work better   ☐ be a better friend   ☐ be a better parent

3 CONVERSATION

CD3 T14

A Listen. Then listen and repeat.

Pronunciation Watch

The **-es** ending on verbs adds an extra syllable after some sounds, for example, *'s'*, *'z'*, *'sh'*, and *'ch'*.

wash	I **wash** the dishes after dinner.
washes	He **washes** the dishes in the morning.
relax	We **relax** at night.
relaxes	She **relaxes** on Sundays.

B Look at the pictures. Listen to your teacher. Repeat the words.

happy	relaxed	excited	bored	sad	stressed

CD3 T15

C Cover the conversation in Exercise D. Listen. How does the woman feel?

CD3 T15

D Listen again. Read the conversation. Was your answer in Exercise C correct?

Alan: You look stressed.

Brenda: I know. I *am* stressed. I really need to relax.

Alan: Well, I **play soccer** to relax.

Brenda: That's a good idea. How often do you **play soccer**?

Alan: Every **weekend**!

CD3 T16

E Listen and repeat the conversation.

4 PRACTICE

A PAIRS. Practice the conversation. Then make new conversations. Use the activities from page 140.

B ROLE PLAY. PAIRS. Make your own conversations. Use different ways of relaxing and different times.

Talk about how often you do something

Grammar

Simple present: Questions with *How often*		
How often	do	I you we they
		play soccer?
	does	he she

Expressions of frequency

Every day.
Once a week.
Twice a week.
Three times a week.

Grammar Watch

every day = Monday – Sunday
once = one time
twice = two times

PRACTICE

A   WRITE. Artur is a student at Greenville Adult School. Look at his schedule.

Write questions. Use *How often* and the activities in the schedule.

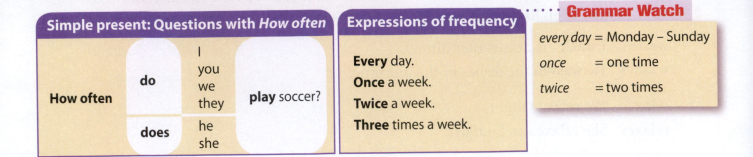

Sun.	Mon.	Tues.	Wed.	Thurs.	Fri.	Sat.
ride my bike	have class	ride my bike	have class	ride my bike	have class	ride my bike
play soccer	ride my bike	see friends	ride my bike	see friends	ride my bike	play soccer
		go food shopping		do laundry		

1. _How often does Artur ride his bike?_____
2. _How often does he . . .?_____
3. _____
4. _____
5. _____
6. _____

B   PAIRS. Ask and answer the questions in Exercise A. Give two answers
for every question.

A: *How often does Artur play soccer?*
B: *Twice a week. Every Saturday and Sunday.*
A: *Right.*
B: *How often does Artur . . . ?*

1 GRAMMAR

CD3 T17

A 🔊 **DICTATION.** **Listen. Complete the conversation.**

A: Hey, Brenda. You look great.

B: Thanks, Alan. I feel great! I think it's my bike rides in the park.

A: Oh? _____How_____ often _____ you ride your bike?

B: Three _____ a week.

A: Really? _____?

B: I _____ ride my bike before work, _____ 6:00 to 7:00,

and I _____ ride on Saturdays from 9:00 to 10:00.

A: Good for you!

B **PAIRS.** **Practice the conversation.**

2 WRITING

STEP 1. PAIRS. **Talk about a free-time activity.**

A: *What do you do in your free time?*
B: *I play soccer.*
A: *Oh. How often do you play?*
B: *Once a week. I play on Thursdays from five to seven.*

STEP 2. **Write three sentences about your partner's free-time activity.**

David plays soccer once a week. He plays on Thursdays. He plays from 5:00 to 7:00.

_____

_____

_____

_____

STEP 3. NETWORK. **Find classmates with the same free-time activity as you.
Form a group. Ask the people in your group,** *How often do you_____?*

3   ACT IT OUT   What do you say?

STEP 1. Review the Lesson 2 conversation between Gloria and Sen (CD 3 Track 4).

STEP 2. Imagine you are making plans to do something together this week. Use your weekly schedule. Decide on an activity, a day, and a time.

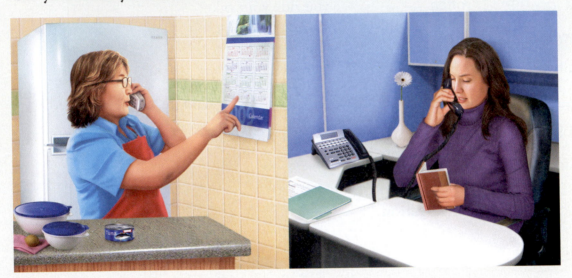

4   READ AND REACT   Problem-solving

STEP 1. Read about Diran's problem.

Diran has a busy life. He is a construction worker, and he works from Monday to Saturday. He also takes English classes at night from Monday to Thursday. On Sundays, he spends time with his family. He also goes food shopping, and he pays the bills. Life at home is not relaxing. Diran is always tired and stressed. He needs to relax, but he doesn't have time.

STEP 2. PAIRS. Talk about it. What is Diran's problem? What can Diran do? Here are some ideas.

- He can listen to music on the way to work.
- He can read on his lunch break.
- He can go out with friends on Friday nights.
- He can _____.

5   CONNECT   For your Study Skills Activity, go to page 249.
For your Team Project, go to page 269.

Which goals can you check off? Go back to page 125.

From Soup to Nuts

Preview

Look at the picture.
Where are the people?
What are they doing?

UNIT GOALS

- ☐ Talk about common foods
- ☐ Write a note about things you need at the store
- ☐ Read a menu
- ☐ Order a meal in a restaurant
- ☐ Use food measurements
- ☐ Compare food prices
- ☐ Read food labels
- ☐ Talk about the nutritional value of foods
- ☐ Plan a healthy meal

1 WHAT DO YOU KNOW?

A CLASS. Look at the pictures. Which foods do you know?

> Number 19 is eggs.

CD3 T18

B Listen and point to the pictures. Then listen and repeat.

2 PRACTICE

A PAIRS. Student A, name a food group. Student B, name two foods in the group.

A: *Vegetables.*
B: *Cabbage and lettuce.*

B WORD PLAY. GROUPS OF 4. Student A, look at the list of foods on page 147. Choose a food, but don't say it. Students B, C, and D, ask *yes/no* questions and guess the food.

B: *Do you eat it for breakfast?*
A: *Sometimes.*
C: *Is it in the "fruit" group?*
A: *Yes.*
D: *Is it red?*
A: *No.*
B: *Bananas?*
A: *Yes!*

C PAIRS. Look at the food pyramid. The colors show the amount of food you need from each food group. Match the colors in the pyramid to the food groups.

Source: www.MyPyramid.gov

Common Foods

1. bread	**6.** cabbage	**11.** vegetable oil	**16.** chicken
2. cereal	**7.** lettuce	**12.** butter	**17.** fish
3. rice	**8.** apples	**13.** milk	**18.** beef
4. potatoes	**9.** oranges	**14.** cheese	**19.** eggs
5. onions	**10.** bananas	**15.** yogurt	**20.** beans

Learning Strategy

Make word groups

Look at the list of foods. Make a chart of foods you eat.
At the top of the chart, write *breakfast*, *lunch*, and *dinner*.
In each column, write one or two foods.

Fruit

8

9

10

Oils

11

12

Show what you know!

STEP 1. Which foods do you eat? Fill in the "You" columns in the chart. Write one food from each food group. Write how often you eat each food.

Food Groups	You		Your Partner	
	What?	**How often?**	**What?**	**How often?**
Vegetables	potatoes	twice a week		
Fruit				
Meat and beans				

STEP 2. PAIRS. Talk about the foods you eat. Talk about how often. Complete the chart with your partner's information.

Marcus: *What vegetables do you eat?*
Agnes: *Potatoes.*
Marcus: *How often do you eat potatoes?*
Agnes: *Twice a week. What kind of vegetables…?*

STEP 3. Report to the class.

Agnes eats potatoes twice a week.

Listening and Speaking

1 BEFORE YOU LISTEN

CD3 T19

READ. Look at the pictures. Listen and read about Jason's lunch. Answer the questions.

It's 12:00. It's time for lunch. Jason is hungry. He is at the mall. Jason likes hamburgers, so he eats a hamburger. But he is still hungry, so he eats a piece of pizza. But he is *still* hungry, so he eats a taco. It's now 12:30. It's time for dessert!

1. Where is Jason? _____

2. How does he feel? _____

3. What does he eat for lunch? _____

2 LISTEN

A Look at the picture. Marius and Gabriela are friends.

Guess: What are they talking about?

CD3 T20

B Listen to the conversation. Was your guess in Exercise A correct?

Listen again. Answer the questions.

1. Who is hungry?
   a. Marius   b. Gabriela   c. Marius and Gabriela

2. What does Marius want for lunch?
   a. pizza   b. tacos   c. a hamburger

3. What does Gabriela want for lunch?
   a. pizza   b. tacos   c. a hamburger

CD3 T21

C Listen to the whole conversation. Complete the sentence.

Gabriela says, "Let's have pizza and tacos for _____."
a. breakfast   b. lunch   c. dinner

3 CONVERSATION

CD3 T22

Listen and read the conversation. Then listen and repeat.

Marius: Wow, I'm hungry!

Gabriela: Yeah, me too. What do you want for lunch?

Marius: Pizza. I love pizza! What about you?

Gabriela: I don't really like pizza, but I love tacos!

4 PRACTICE

A **PAIRS.** Practice the conversation. Then make new conversations. Use the information in the boxes.

A: What do you want for _____?

B: _____. I love _____! What about you?

A: I don't really like _____, but I love _____!

breakfast — scrambled eggs — pancakes

dinner — steak — pasta

dessert — cake — cookies

B **MAKE IT PERSONAL. PAIRS.** Make your own conversations. Use different meals and foods.

Talk about common foods

Grammar

Count nouns		Non-count nouns	
Gabriela wants	**a taco**.	I want	**pasta**.
She loves	**tacos**.	I love	**pasta**.

Grammar Watch

- You can count some nouns. They are called **count nouns:** *one taco, two tacos*
- You can't count some nouns. They are called **non-count nouns:** ~~*one pasta, two pastas*~~
- For a list of more non-count nouns, see page 274.
- For spelling rules for plural count nouns, see page 274.

1   PRACTICE

Complete the shopping list.

TO BUY

4 oranges _____

6 _____

black _____

apple _____

2 large _____

banana _____

3 _____

5 green _____

2   LIFE SKILLS WRITING

Write a note about things you need at the store.
See page 260.

Look at the pictures. Complete the conversations. Write the correct form of the word.

1.

A: ___Apples___ are good for you.

B: I know. I eat an _____ every day.

2.

A: I love _____.

B: Me too! I often have two _____ for breakfast.

3.

A: Do you have any _____?

B: Of course! I always have _____ in the house. It's in the refrigerator.

4.

A: I eat _____ every day.

B: Me too. I love _____!

Show what you know!   Talk about common foods

STEP 1. WRITE.   You have five minutes. Write foods for each color.

yellow: _bananas,_____

white: _____

red: _____

green: _____

Writing Watch

Use commas (,) between things in a list. Example: *bananas, cheese, . . .*

STEP 2. GROUPS OF 3.   Compare answers.

A: *What foods are yellow?*
B: *Bananas.*
C: *Cheese.*

Can you...talk about common foods? ☐

Reading

A Look at the pictures. Where do you keep each food? Write each food in the box for the place you keep it.

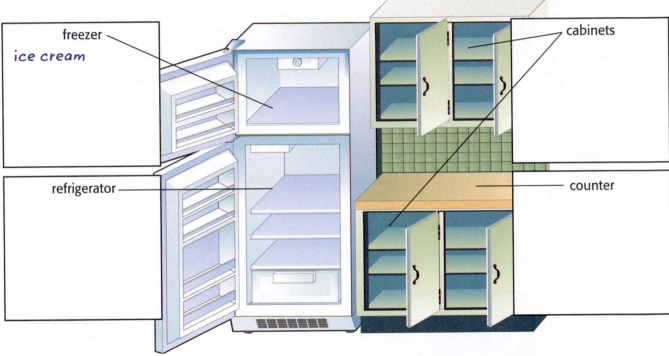

freezer

ice cream

cabinets

refrigerator

counter

B Sometimes there's a date on food. Why? Read the information and the label.

C CLASS. Look at the label again. Can a store sell this milk on October 15? Can you drink this milk on October 15?

Stores cannot sell food after a sell-by date. If you have food at home with an old sell-by date, it's usually OK to eat it a short time after the date.

2 READ

CD3 T23

🖸 **Listen. Read the article.**

Eat Fresh!

This careful shopper always checks the date on food.

Do you buy fresh food? Are you sure? Be careful! Stores sometimes sell old food. Check the dates.

How long can you keep your food at home? Here are some tips.

Milk is good for two to ten days after its sell-by date.

Eggs are good for three to five weeks after their sell-by dates. Just keep them in the refrigerator!

Chicken is different. The sell-by date on chicken is information for the store. The refrigerators in stores are very cold. But your home refrigerator isn't as cold. Cook or freeze chicken a day or two after you buy it. You can keep chicken in the freezer for twelve months.

Some food, like **canned food**, doesn't have a sell-by date. But it isn't good forever. Try to use your canned food in twelve months.

3 CHECK YOUR UNDERSTANDING

A **Read the article again. What is the main idea?**

a. Make sure your food is fresh. Check the dates.

b. Put your food in the right place. Keep milk in the refrigerator.

B **Read the sentences. Circle *True* or *False*.**

1. Stores sometimes sell old food.	(True)	False
2. It's OK to use milk two days after its sell-by date.	True	False
3. It's OK to keep eggs on the counter for three weeks.	True	False
4. It's OK to keep chicken in the refrigerator for a week.	True	False
5. Canned food is good for one year.	True	False

Show what you know!

PAIRS. Talk about it. How can you use the information from the article at home?
What other foods have expiration dates?

> I want to check the dates on the chicken in my refrigerator.

Listening and Speaking

1 BEFORE YOU LISTEN

CLASS. Look at the pictures. Which foods do you eat or drink?

tomato soup   coffee   turkey sandwich   fries   soda   baked potato

hamburger   iced tea   green salad   fruit cup   apple pie   ice cream

2 LISTEN

A Look at the picture. Greg and his wife are ordering lunch. Greg says, "I'd like a hamburger." What does this mean?

a. He likes hamburgers.

b. He wants a hamburger.

CD3 T24

B Listen to the conversation. Was your answer in Exercise A correct?

Listen again. What does Greg order? Check (✓) the pictures in Before You Listen.

CD3 T25

C Listen to the whole conversation. Answer the questions.

1. What does Greg's wife think? _____

2. What does Greg order for dessert? _____

3 CONVERSATION

CD3 T26

A 🔘 Listen. Notice the pronunciation of *I like* and *I'd like*. Then listen and repeat.

I like coffee.   **I'd like** coffee.   **I like** yogurt.   **I'd like** yogurt.

CD3 T27

B 🔘 Listen and read the conversation. Then listen and repeat.

Waitress: Can I help you?
Greg: Yes. I'd like a hamburger and a soda.
Waitress: Is that a large soda or a small soda?
Greg: Large, please.
Waitress: OK, a large soda. . . . Anything else?
Greg: Yes. A small order of fries.

4 PRACTICE

A **PAIRS.** Practice the conversation. Then make new conversations. Use the menu.

A: Can I help you?

B: Yes. I'd like _____
    (food)
    and _____.
        (drink)

A: Is that a large _____
            (drink)
    or a small _____?
            (drink)

B: Large, please.

A: OK, a large _____. . . .
            (drink)
    Anything else?

B: Yes. _____.
        (food)

B **ROLE PLAY. PAIRS.** Make your own conversations. Use the menu.

Starters		
tomato soup..cup $1.00		
bowl $1.25		
green salad $1.00		

Sides
baked potato $1.85
fries ..... small $1.25
large $1.75

Desserts
apple pie $1.75
ice cream $2.25
fruit cup $2.00

Sandwiches
hamburger............................. $3.25
chicken sandwich...................... $3.75

Drinks
soda ...... small $1.00
large $1.25
iced tea .... small $1.00
large $1.25
coffee ..... small $1.00
large $1.25

Grammar

Choice questions with *or*			
Would you like **coffee**	**or**	**tea**?	**Tea**, please.
Do you want **a large soda**		**a small soda**?	I want **a large soda**.

Grammar Watch

Some questions with *or* are choice questions.
Answer with your choice.
Do not say *yes* or *no*.

PRACTICE

A Complete the questions. Use the words in parentheses.

1. Do you want _____?
   (chicken soup / salad)

2. Would you like _____?
   (a fish sandwich / a hamburger)

3. Do you want _____?
   (fries / a baked potato)

4. Do you want _____?
   (soda / juice)

5. Would you like _____?
   (ice cream / apple pie)

CD3 T28

B Listen and check your answers.
Then listen and repeat.

In *choice questions with or*, the voice goes up ↗ on the first choice and down ↘ on the last choice.

Do you want soup or salad?

Show what you know!   Order a meal in a restaurant

STEP 1. PAIRS. Student A, you are a waiter. Student B, you are a customer. Student A, ask Student B the questions in Exercise A. Write Student B's answers on the order pad.

STEP 2. Report to the class.

> Maria wants chicken soup, a …

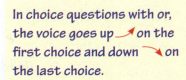

Can you… order a meal in a restaurant? ☐

Life Skills

69¢/lb. = sixty-nine cents a pound
or
sixty-nine cents per pound

1 COMPARE FOOD PRICES

CD3 T29

A Look at the ad for Farmer Tom's. Listen and repeat the prices and amounts.

CD3 T30

B Look at the ad for Country Market. Listen and fill in the prices.

2 PRACTICE

A Look at the prices in the ads again. Where is each food cheaper? Circle the cheaper price.

CD3 T31

B Two friends are comparing prices at the two stores. Listen to the conversation. Then listen and repeat.

A: Where are **onions** cheaper, Farmer Tom's or Country Market?

B: Farmer Tom's. They're **79 cents a pound**.

A: Where is **bread** cheaper, Farmer Tom's or Country Market?

B: Country Market. It's **$2.59**.

C PAIRS. Practice the conversations. Then make new conversations. Use different foods from the ads.

D NETWORK. Talk to your classmates. Ask, *Where do you shop for food?* Then ask, *Is that a good place to shop? Why?*

Can you...use measurements and compare food prices? ☐

3 TALK ABOUT NUTRITION

How do you stay healthy? Here are some tips.

Tips to Stay Healthy

• Don't eat a lot of fat.

• Don't eat a lot of sodium.

• Don't eat a lot of sugar.

12 calories   300 calories

Eat the right number of calories. How many calories can you eat? Every person is different. Talk to a doctor or nurse.

4 PRACTICE

A Look at the pictures. Check (✓) the foods that are healthy.

B PAIRS. Talk about your answers in Exercise A.

A: Green beans are good for you.
B: Why?
A: Because they don't have fat.

A: Ice cream isn't good for you.
B: Why not?
A: Because it has a lot of fat and sugar.

C GROUPS OF 3. Which healthy foods do you usually eat?

A: *I eat a lot of beans.*
B: *Really? Well, I eat rice every day. What about you, Li?*
C: *I eat . . .*

D Food labels give you important information about the food. Look at this label for bread. Then answer the questions.

g = gram
or grams
mg = milligram
or milligrams

Nutrition Facts

Serving Size: 1 slice

Servings per Container: 18

Calories 90
Total Fat................... 1 g
Sodium .... 180 mg
Sugars..................... 3 g
Net Wt. = ...1 lb. 8 oz.

Serving Size = the amount you eat at one time

Net Wt. = Net Weight = how much food is in the container

1. How much is one serving? _1 slice_

2. How many servings are in the package? _____

3. How many calories are in one serving? _____

4. How much fat is in one serving? _____

5. How much sodium is in one serving? _____

6. How much sugar is in one serving? _____

E WRITE. Look at the labels. Which drink is better for your health? Why?

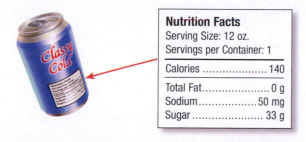

Nutrition Facts
Serving Size: 12 oz.
Servings per Container: 1

Calories 140

Total Fat.................... 0 g
Sodium.................50 mg
Sugar .... 33 g

Nutrition Facts
Serving Size: 12 oz.
Servings per Container: 1

Calories 75

Total Fat.................... 0 g
Sodium.................. 0 mg
Sugar .... 16 g

_____ is better for your health because _____

_____.

Can you...talk about the nutritional value of foods? ☐

Listening and Speaking

1 BEFORE YOU LISTEN

CLASS. Look at the pictures.
Which other foods are steamed,
grilled, or fried?

steamed vegetables   grilled chicken   fried fish

2 LISTEN

CD3 T32

A **CLASS.** Listen to the radio talk show. Answer the questions.

1. What is the talk show about?
2. What information does the caller want?
3. Does he get the information?

CD3 T32

B Listen again. Answer the questions in the chart about each food.

ON THE AIR How Healthy Is It?	How many calories?	How much fat? (in grams)
Fried chicken		12
Grilled chicken		3
French fries (small)	290	
Baked potato	130	

C **GROUPS OF 3.** Look at the pictures. Plan a healthy dinner for Greg.
Choose from the pictures.

A: *How about salad, a baked potato, and fruit?*
B: *No, he needs meat. How about . . . ?*

3 CONVERSATION

A **CLASS.** Look at the pictures. Which of these foods do you like?

CD3 T33

B Greg and Liz are planning dinner. Listen and read their conversation. Then listen and repeat.

Liz: Let's have **chicken** for dinner.

Greg: OK. How much **chicken** do we need?

Liz: Two pounds.

Greg: OK. And let's have salad with it.

Liz: Good idea. We have lettuce, but we need **onions**.

Greg: How many **onions** do we need?

Liz: Just one.

shrimp   turkey

salmon   roast beef

tomatoes   red peppers

cucumbers   avocados

4 PRACTICE

A **PAIRS.** Practice the conversation. Then make new conversations. Use the pictures.

B **MAKE IT PERSONAL. PAIRS.** Plan an interesting salad.

Maria: *Let's put nuts in the salad.*

Roberto: *OK. And how about avocados?*

Maria: *Oh, I don't like avocados. Let's put a mango in it.*

C **CLASS.** Tell your classmates about the salad.

Roberto: *Our salad has nuts, mango, . . .*

Grammar

Simple present: Questions with *How many* and *How much*					
How many	**eggs**	do we have? are there?	**A lot.**		**Not many.**
How much	**milk**	do we have? is there?	**A lot.**		**Not much.**

Grammar Watch
- Use *how many* with plural count nouns.
- Use *how much* with non-count nouns.

PRACTICE

A Look at the picture. Read the answers. Complete the questions with *How many* or *How much* and a noun.

1. **A:** _How many oranges_ are there?

   B: Not many. We only have three.

2. **A:** _____ do we have?

   B: Not much. Let's get more milk!

3. **A:** _____ are there?

   B: Twelve. We don't need more.

4. **A:** _____ is there?

   B: There is no cheese! Put it on the shopping list.

5. **A:** _____ are there?

   B: Six. And they're big!

   A: Great. Let's have baked potatoes tonight.

B PAIRS. Look at the picture again. Continue the conversation in Exercise A. Ask about other food in the refrigerator.

A: *How much orange juice is there?*
B: *There's a lot. We don't need orange juice.*
A: *How many apples…?*

1 GRAMMAR

CD3 T34

DICTATION. Two friends are talking about a recipe for a cheese omelet. **Listen and complete the conversation.**

A: This omelet is really good. What's in it?

B: ___Eggs___ and cheese. Oh, and there's _____, but not much.

A: Eggs? How _____ eggs?

B: Three.

A: And how _____ cheese?

B: Just one slice.

A: What do you cook it in? Do you use butter _____ oil?

B: I use _____, but it's good with _____, too.

2 WRITING

STEP 1. **You are planning a meal. Which foods do you want? Circle one thing in each pair.**

1. soup or salad
2. meat or fish
3. rice or potatoes
4. carrots or green beans
5. coffee or tea
6. ice cream or cake

STEP 2. GROUPS OF 5. **Ask your classmates about their choices. Count the students. Write the number next to each food.**

How many people want soup?

soup __2__ salad __3__

1. soup _____ salad _____
2. meat _____ fish _____
3. rice _____ potatoes _____
4. carrots _____ green beans _____
5. coffee _____ tea _____
6. ice cream _____ cake _____

STEP 3. **Write six sentences in your notebook about your group's choices.**

Two students want soup, and three students want salad.

STEP 4. **Tell the class about your group's meal.**

Our group wants salad, fish, ...

3 ACT IT OUT   What do you say?

STEP 1. Review the Lesson 5 conversation between Greg and the waitress (CD 3 Track 24).

STEP 2. PAIRS. You are at a small restaurant. Student A, you are a waiter or waitress. Student B, you are a customer.

> **Student A:** Take the customer's order. Ask about the size of the drink.

> **Student B:** Order something to eat and drink.

Kitty's Kitchen — MENU

Sandwiches ... $5.95 *chicken, fish, turkey*	Soda: cola, orange *Small* .... $1.00 *Large* $1.50
Hamburger $4.50	
Tacos (2) $4.95	Juice: orange, apple, tomato *Small* .... $1.95 *Large* $2.75
Pizza .... $7.25 *Today's special:* *Vegetable* $8.25	
	Coffee *Small* .... $1.00 *Large* $1.60
Salads: *Green* .... $3.95 *Fruit* $4.75	
	Tea *Small* .... $.85 *Large* $1.50
French fries ... $2.95	

4 READ AND REACT   Problem-solving

STEP 1. Read about Eduardo's problem.

Eduardo is 45 years old. He is heavy. Eduardo's doctor tells him, "Be careful. You need to eat healthy foods. Don't eat foods with a lot of calories and fat." Eduardo usually has lunch at a fast-food restaurant. He has a big cheeseburger, fries, and a large soda every day. He eats dinner at home with his family. His wife is a great cook, and the children love her food. But she cooks a lot of fried food.

STEP 2. PAIRS. Talk about it. What is Eduardo's problem? What can Eduardo do? Here are some ideas.

- He can bring a sandwich from home for lunch.
- He can eat small servings.
- He can ask his wife to cook different food for him.
- He can _____.

5 CONNECT   For your Community-building Activity, go to page 249. For your Team Project, go to page 270.

Which goals can you check off? Go back to page 145.

Rain or Shine

Preview

Look at the picture. What do you see? Does it often rain where you live? What do you do when it rains?

UNIT GOALS

- [ ] Talk about the weather and seasons
- [ ] Talk about what you are doing now
- [ ] Write a postcard
- [ ] Talk about weather conditions
- [ ] Plan for an emergency
- [ ] Ask what someone is doing now
- [ ] Understand a weather report

1 WHAT DO YOU KNOW?

A CLASS. Look at the pictures. Which seasons do you know? Which words about weather do you know?

> C is spring. Number 8 is sunny.

CD3 T35

B Listen and point to the pictures. Then listen and repeat.

2 PRACTICE

A PAIRS. Student A, point to a picture and ask about the weather. Student B, answer.

A: *What's the weather like?*
B: *It's hot and sunny.*

B WORD PLAY. PAIRS. Look at the list of weather words on page 167. Talk about the weather in your home country.

A: *I'm from Colombia. It's usually cool and sunny there.*
B: *Oh, really? In Korea, the winter is . . . .*

B

3

4

C

5

6

Weather and Seasons

A. fall	B. winter	C. spring	D. summer
1. cool	3. cold	5. warm	7. hot
2. cloudy	4. snowy	6. rainy	8. sunny

Show what you know!

STEP 1. CLASS. Walk around the room. Ask four classmates about their favorite seasons. Complete the chart.

Sylvia: *What's your favorite season?*
Paul: *I like spring.*
Sylvia: *Why?*
Paul: *Because I like the weather. It's warm, but not hot.*

Name	Favorite Season	Reason
Paul	spring	warm, not hot

STEP 2. Report to the class. How many people like each season?

Listening and Speaking

1   BEFORE YOU LISTEN

READ. **Look at the map. Read about Laura and her family. Then complete the sentences. Underline the correct words in each sentence.**

Laura lives in Green Bay, Wisconsin. In Green Bay, winter is usually cold and snowy. Laura often visits her family in winter. Her family lives in Tampa, Florida. Winter there is usually nice. It's warm and sunny.

1. Laura usually visits her family in **Green Bay / Tampa** in the winter.
2. Winter in Tampa is usually **cold and snowy / warm and sunny**.

2   LISTEN

A   **Look at the picture. Laura is in Tampa. She is calling her friend David in Green Bay. Guess: How does Laura feel?**

   a. happy   b. excited   c. bored

CD3 T36

B   **Listen to the conversation. What do you think? Was your guess in Exercise A correct?**

CD3 T36

C   **Listen again. Answer the questions.**

1. Who is Laura visiting?
   a. friends   b. family   c. classmates

2. Where is Laura's family now?
   a. at home   b. at work   c. at school

3. How is the weather in Tampa?
   a. hot and rainy   b. warm and rainy   c. cold and rainy

CD3 T37

D   **Listen to the whole conversation. What does David say about the weather in Green Bay? Complete the sentence.**

"It's not _____, but it's _____."

3 CONVERSATION

A Listen. Notice the pronunciation of *-ing*. Then listen and repeat.

It rains in Tampa.   It's rain**ing** in Tampa.
It snows in Green Bay.   It's snow**ing** in Green Bay.

CD3 T39

B Listen and read the conversation. Then listen and repeat.

David: Hello?
Laura: Hi! It's me. How are you?
David: Fine, thanks. Where are you?
Laura: I'm in Tampa. I'm visiting family, but they're at work now.
David: Tampa! That's great! How's the weather there?
Laura: Well, it's cold and rainy.

4 PRACTICE

A **PAIRS.** Practice the conversation.
Then make new conversations.
Use the information in the boxes.

A: Hello?

B: Hi! It's me. How are you?

A: Fine, thanks. Where are you?

B: I'm in _____. I'm visiting
_____, but they're at work now.

A: _____! That's great! How's
the weather there?

B: Well, it's _____ and
_____.

Dallas		
San Francisco	hot	humid
Boston		
friends	cool	foggy
my aunt and uncle		
my cousins	warm	windy

B **ROLE PLAY. PAIRS.** Make your own conversations.
Use different cities, people, and weather.

Grammar

Present continuous: Statements

Affirmative				
I	am			
You We They	are	visiting	family.	
He She Laura	is			
It	is	raining.		

Negative				
I	am			
You We They	are		not	working.
He She David	is			
It	is			snowing.

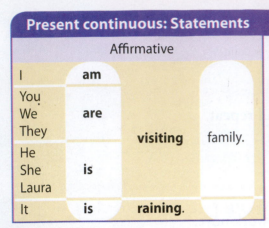

1 PRACTICE

Amy is calling her cousin Ben in Seattle. Complete the conversation.

Ben: What are you doing?

Amy: I _I'm watching_ TV. What are *you* doing?
              1. (watch)

Ben: I _____ to you!
          2. (talk)

Amy: Very funny. How's the weather there?

Ben: Well, it _____, but it's cold. How's the weather in Chicago?
          3. (not rain)

Amy: It _____ here.
        4. (snow)

Ben: Oh. Is it cold?

Amy: Yes. I _____ two sweaters.
        5. (wear)

Ben: Is Jason home?

Amy: Yes. He _____ today.
        6. (not work)

Ben: What about the kids? What are they doing?

Amy: They're outside. They _____ a snowman!
        7. (make)

Grammar Watch

- Use the present continuous for things that are happening now.
- Remember: We usually use contractions with *be* in conversations.
- *make → making* For spelling rules for the present continuous, see page 274.

2 LIFE SKILLS WRITING
Write a postcard. See page 261.

PAIRS. Look at the pictures. Find at least 10 differences. Talk about them.

A: *In Picture 1, a woman is eating an apple.*
B: *Right. And in Picture 2, she isn't eating an apple. She's eating a banana.*

Show what you know! Talk about what you are doing now

STEP 1. WRITE. Imagine that you're visiting friends in another city. It's a beautiful day. What are you doing? Complete the sentence.

I _____.

STEP 2. GROUPS OF 5. Play the Memory Game. Talk about what you are doing.

Ana: *I'm taking a walk in the park with my family.*
Boris: *Ana is taking a walk. I'm eating lunch outside with my family.*
Lucy: *Ana is taking a walk. Boris is . . . .*

Can you... talk about what you are doing now? ☐

Life Skills

1 TALK ABOUT WEATHER CONDITIONS

A **PAIRS.** Which words for bad weather and emergencies do you know? Write the correct words from the box under each picture.

an earthquake	a snowstorm
a flood	a thunderstorm
~~a heat wave~~	a tornado
a hurricane	a wild fire

1. _a heat wave_

2. _____

3. _____

4. _____

5. _____

6. _____

7. _____

8. _____

CD3 T40
B Listen and check your answers. Then listen and repeat.

2 PRACTICE

A What do you do in bad weather or an emergency? Check (✓) *Do* or *Don't.*

B **PAIRS.** Compare answers.

	DO	DON'T	DOs and DON'Ts in an Emergency
1.	☐	☐	go downstairs in a tornado
2.	☐	☐	go under a piece of furniture, like a desk, in an earthquake
3.	☐	☐	stay in your house in a flood
4.	☐	☐	cover your windows before a hurricane
5.	☐	☐	go swimming in a thunderstorm
6.	☐	☐	drink a lot of water in a heat wave
7.	☐	☐	go outside for a long time in a snowstorm
8.	☐	☐	leave your house when a wild fire is near

3 PLAN FOR AN EMERGENCY

A CLASS. Look at the Garcia family's emergency plan. What information is important to include in an emergency plan?

B Make an emergency plan for your family. Write the emergency plan in your notebook.

Emergency Family Plan

Places to meet
1. Outside our apartment building
2. Main post office: 2209 7th Street

Emergency phone numbers
Carla
   Work (510) 555-8317
   Cell (510) 555-1194
Luis
   Work (510) 555-7835
   Cell (510) 555-7834
Maria
   School (510) 555-4965
Uncle Alex (312) 555-0552

In an emergency, you can't always call someone in your area code. Include a long distance number.

4 PRACTICE

A GROUPS OF 3. What do you need in an emergency? Match the words and pictures.

batteries   candles   a first aid kit   a flashlight

matches   medicine   a radio   ~~water~~

1. ___water___   2. _____   3. _____   4. _____

5. _____   6. _____   7. _____   8. _____

CD3 T41

B Listen and check your answers. Then listen and repeat.

C WRITE. Make a list in your notebook of things you have for an emergency.

Can you...plan for an emergency? ☐

Ask what someone is doing now

Listening and Speaking

Can you turn on the TV? I want to check the weather.

1 BEFORE YOU LISTEN

CLASS. Look at the picture and read.
Where are the people? What are they doing?

Do you watch the weather report on
TV? What channel do you watch?

2 LISTEN

A Look at the picture of Dan Reed.
Where is he? What is he buying?
Guess: Why is he buying these things?

CD3 T42

B 🔘 Listen to Dan's conversation with Emily.
Was your guess in Exercise A correct?
Listen again. Answer the questions.

1. What is Emily doing?
   a. She's shopping.
   b. She's watching TV.
   c. She's reading a magazine.

2. Why is Dan going home early?
   a. A storm is coming.
   b. The supermarket is closing.
   c. He wants to watch the news on TV.

CD3 T43

C 🔘 Listen to the whole conversation. Complete the sentences.
Check (✓) the correct answers.

1. Dan is buying _____. (Check more than one answer.)
   ☐ water   ☐ food   ☐ a flashlight   ☐ batteries   ☐ clothes

2. Emily says, "Get _____, too."
   ☐ candles   ☐ matches   ☐ a first aid kit

3. Emily says, "We need _____!"
   ☐ good friends   ☐ a good TV   ☐ good weather

CD3 T44

🔘 **Listen and read the conversation. Then listen and repeat.**

Dan: Are you watching the news?

Emily: No, I'm not. I'm reading a magazine.

Dan: Well, turn on the TV. A big storm is coming.

Emily: Really?

Dan: Yes. In fact, I'm coming home early. I'm at the supermarket now.

4 PRACTICE

🅐 **PAIRS. Practice the conversation. Then make new conversations. Use the information in the boxes.**

A: Are you watching the news?

B: No, I'm not. I'm ▯▯▯▯▯.

A: Well, turn on the TV. A ▯▯▯▯▯ is coming.

A: Really?

B: Yes. In fact, I'm coming home early. I'm at the ▯▯▯▯▯ now.

checking e-mail	making lunch	cleaning the apartment
hurricane	thunderstorm	snowstorm

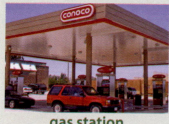

gas station

grocery store

drugstore

🅑 **ROLE PLAY. PAIRS. Make your own conversations. Use different activities and locations.**

Grammar

Present continuous: *Yes/no* questions and short answers

Are	you they you		
	he	**watching**	the news?
Is	she Emily		
	it	**raining**?	

Yes,	I **am**. they **are**. we **are**.	No,	I'm **not**. they'**re not** OR they **aren't**. we'**re not** OR we **aren't**.
	he **is**.		he'**s not** OR he **isn't**.
	she **is**.		she'**s not** OR she **isn't**.
	it **is**.		it'**s not** OR it **isn't**.

1 **PRACTICE**

Look at the picture. Daron and Lena are on vacation. Answer the questions. Use short answers.

Grammar Watch

shop → shopping
See page 274 for spelling rules.

1. **A:** Are Lena and Daron working?

   B: _No, they're not._

2. **A:** Is it raining?

   B: _____

3. **A:** Is Lena wearing a T-shirt?

   B: _____

4. **A:** Are they shopping for food?

   B: _____

5. **A:** Is Daron talking to a man?

   B: _____

6. **A:** Is Lena looking at Daron?

   B: _____

South Seas Jewelry

LENA

DARON

A **WRITE.** Write *yes/no* questions. Use the words in parentheses.
Use capital letters and question marks.

1. (Lena and Daron / shop) <u>*Are Lena and Daron shopping?*</u>

2. (they / eat) _____

3. (Lena / wear a skirt) _____

4. (Daron / wear a jacket) _____

5. (he / listen to music) _____

6. (they / buy / CDs) _____

B **PAIRS.** Look at the picture on page 176. Ask and
answer the questions in Exercise A.

A: *Are Lena and Daron shopping?*
B: *Yes, they are. Are they . . . ?*

C **NETWORK.** You have the day off from work and
school. Where do you go? Find classmates with the
same answer as you. Then ask, *What do you do there?*

Show what you know! Ask what someone is doing now

STEP 1. WRITE. It's raining. You're at home.
What are you doing? Write the activity.

> I'm studying.

_____

STEP 2. GROUPS OF 3. Student A, act out your activity from Step 1.
Students B and C, guess the activity.

B: *Are you reading a magazine?*
A: *No, I'm not.*
C: *Are you studying?*
A: *Yes, I am.*

Can you . . . ask what someone is doing now? ☐

Reading

1 | **BEFORE YOU READ**

CLASS. Talk about it. Look at the cartoons.
Answer the questions.

1. Where are the people in each cartoon?
   What are they doing?

2. The people in the cartoons are strangers. What are they talking about?

a.

b.

c.

d.

e.

CD3 T45

Listen. Read the article.

Small Talk Is Big!

We tell children, "Don't talk to strangers." But we do it all the time. We talk to strangers at the supermarket, at the bus stop, and at the coffee shop. We make small talk every day.

What do we talk about? Only a few topics are OK. The weather is a good topic. Everyone talks about the weather. We say, "What a nice day!" or "It's so hot!" Some other good topics for small talk are sports, food, transportation, and shopping.

Two strangers make small talk at a bus stop.

We don't talk about personal things. In the United States, we don't make small talk about money, love, or health problems.

Answer a person's small talk in a friendly way. Smile and say something more about the topic. For example, when someone says, "This is such great weather!" you can say, "I know. It's so beautiful out! I love the spring."

In the U.S., small talk is a big part of our culture. We think it's a way to be friendly!

3 CHECK YOUR UNDERSTANDING

A Read the article again. What is the main idea?

a. The weather is a good topic for small talk.

b. We make small talk with strangers, but only a few topics are OK.

B Read these sentences. Are they OK for small talk? Write *OK* or *Not OK* next to each one.

1. Look at all this rain!   __OK__

2. The food looks so good!   _____

3. What's your address?   _____

4. Are you married?   _____

5. How much money do you make?   _____

6. Great game last night, right?   _____

7. Oh, no! The bus is late again!   _____

8. I have a problem with my foot.   _____

Show what you know!

PAIRS. Imagine you are at work. You see a co-worker. You don't know the person. Try to make small talk. Write a short conversation. Role play your conversation.

Listening and Speaking

1 **BEFORE YOU LISTEN**

PAIRS. Do you know these words? Label the pictures. Use the words in the box.

boots	ear muffs	gloves	a hat	~~light clothes~~	a raincoat
a scarf	shorts	sunblock	sunglasses	an umbrella	a bottle of water

ON THE AIR **Weather!** Do you have the right clothes, accessories, and supplies?

1. light clothes

2. _____

3. _____

4. _____

5. _____

6. _____

7. _____

8. _____

9. _____

10. _____

11. _____

12. _____

2 LISTEN

CD3 T46

A Listen to the weather report. What clothes, accessories, and supplies do you hear? Check (✓) the pictures on page 180.

CD3 T46

B Listen again. Write the temperature for each city on the map.

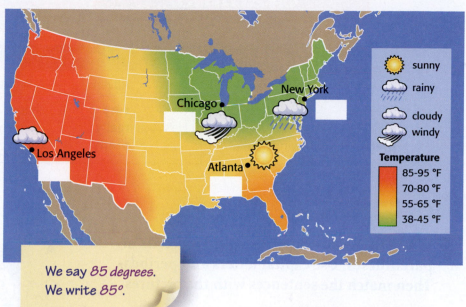

New York

Chicago

Los Angeles

Atlanta

sunny
rainy
cloudy
windy

Temperature
85-95 °F
70-80 °F
55-65 °F
38-45 °F

We say *85 degrees*.
We write *85°*.

3 CONVERSATION

A Look at the picture. Marta is ready to go outside.

Guess: How is the weather?

CD3 T47

B Listen to the conversation. Marta is talking to her husband, Joel.

Was your guess in Exercise A correct?

CD3 T48

C Listen and read the conversation. Then listen and repeat.

Joel: Are you going out?
Marta: Yes. Why?
Joel: Well, it's really **cold**, and it's pretty **windy**.
Marta: That's OK. I have a **scarf** and **gloves**!

4 PRACTICE

A PAIRS. Practice the conversation. Then make new conversations. Use different weather words and clothes, accessories, or supplies from page 180.

B ROLE PLAY. PAIRS. Make your own conversations. Talk about today's weather.

Talk about the weather

Grammar

Adverbs of degree: *Very, really, pretty*						
	Adverb	Adjective			Adverb	Adjective
It's	**very** **really** **pretty**	hot. cold. windy.		He's	**very** **really** **pretty**	happy. hungry. tired.

Grammar Watch

Use *very*, *really*, or *pretty* before an adjective to make it stronger.

PRACTICE

A WRITE. Write sentences with the words in parentheses. Use capital letters and periods. Then match the sentences with the pictures.

1. _____It's really cold._____   D
   (really / it's / cold)

2. _____   ____
   (out here / pretty / it's / hot)

3. _____   ____
   (very / it's / windy)

4. _____   ____
   (foggy / really / it's)

B PAIRS. Read the conversation. Find the three adjectives in blue. Add the word *very*, *really*, or *pretty* before each adjective. Use each word only once.

A: How's the weather?

B: It's **nice**.

A: Then let's take a walk!

B: OK. But I'm **hungry**. Let's eat first.

A: Well, there's a **good** restaurant on Main Street.

B: OK. Let's go there.

C SAME PAIRS. Perform your conversation for the class.

D WRITE. Write sentences in your notebook about today's weather.

1 GRAMMAR

CD3 T49

🔘 **DICTATION. Listen. Complete the sentences.**

A: Hi, Sandy. It's me, Gail. Are you at work?

B: _____, I _____ . I'm home. There's a _____ bad snowstorm here. Schools are closed again.

A: Wow! So, what _____ the kids _____?

B: Well, Tony and Dino are outside in the snow. They _____ pictures.

A: That's nice. What about Maria? _____ she _____ in the snow?

B: _____, she _____. She _____ computer games with my dad.

A: And you?

B: Well, I _____. And my mom and I _____ laundry. I'm not at work, but I'm _____ busy. And I'm _____ tired.

2 WRITING

STEP 1. PAIRS. Look at the picture. What are the people doing?

A: *In Apartment 1, the man is sleeping.*
B: *Right. And in Apartment 2 . . . .*

STEP 2. Choose six apartments. Write sentences about the people.

<u>In Apartment 1, the man is sleeping.</u>

_____

_____

_____

_____

_____

3 ACT IT OUT   What do you say?

STEP 1. Review the Lesson 2 conversation between Laura and David (CD 3 Track 36).

STEP 2. PAIRS. You are friends. You are talking on the phone.

Student A: You're on vacation. Choose a place.
- Call your friend at home.
- Talk about the weather.
- Talk about what you are doing.

Student B: You're at home. Your friend calls you.
- Ask "Where are you?"
- Ask about the weather.
- Ask "What are you doing?"
  Continue the conversation.

4 READ AND REACT   Problem-solving

STEP 1. Read about Danielle's problem.

Danielle is at home one morning with her mother and her baby. Her husband is out of the country. He is visiting his sick father. There is a big storm, and there is no electricity. The power is out in the whole neighborhood. Danielle is very worried. There are no candles in the house, and there are no batteries for the flashlight. She doesn't have any canned food.

STEP 2. PAIRS. Talk about it. What is Danielle's problem? What can Danielle do? Here are some ideas.

- She can call a neighbor to ask for supplies.
- She can go get supplies.
- She can wait for the power to come back on.
- She can _____.

5 CONNECT   For your Community-building Activity, go to page 250.
For your Team Project, go to page 270.

Go back to page 165. Which goals can you check off?

Around Town

Preview

**Look at the picture.
What do you see?**

UNIT GOALS

- ☐ Give locations of places in the community
- ☐ Talk about forms of transportation
- ☐ Read traffic signs
- ☐ Read bus signs and schedules
- ☐ Ask about bus routes and costs
- ☐ Write directions to your home
- ☐ Ask about places in the community
- ☐ Talk about future plans

1   WHAT DO YOU KNOW?

A   **CLASS.** Look at the pictures. Which places do you know?

> Number 3 is a post office.

B   CD4 T2   Listen and point to the pictures. Then listen and repeat.

2   PRACTICE

A   **PAIRS.** Look at the pictures. Student A, choose a place. Say something you do there. Student B, name the place.

A: *I buy stamps there.*
B: *The post office.*
A: *Right.*

B   **WORD PLAY.** Look at the list of places on page 187. Which places have the word *station*? Which places have the word *store*? Which place has the word *shop*? Make three lists.

Words with *station*   **Words with *store***

    fire station   _____

_____   _____

_____

Word with *shop*

_____

C   Do you know other words with *station*, *store*, or *shop*? Write other words you know.

_____   _____   _____

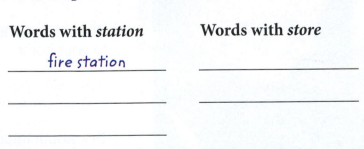

Places in the Community

1. **a** fire station
2. **a** police station
3. **a** post office
4. **a** bus stop
5. **a** park
6. **a** drugstore
7. **a** gas station
8. **a** supermarket
9. **a** bank
10. **an** ATM
11. **a** laundromat
12. **a** parking lot
13. **a** department store
14. **a** coffee shop
15. **a** hair salon

Show what you know!

STEP 1. GROUPS OF 3. Draw a map of the streets near your school. Talk about the places around your school. Put the places on the map.

A: *Is there a drugstore around here?*
B: *Yes. It's across the street.*
C: *Right. And there's a bank on Fifth Street, next to the supermarket.*

STEP 2. Show your map to another group. Are your maps the same?

Give locations of places in the community

Listening and Speaking

1   BEFORE YOU LISTEN

A   **READ.**   Look at the flyer. Read the information.
Foodsmart, a new supermarket, is opening
on Saturday, October 8.

The supermarket is **near** the library.
It's **around the corner from** the bank.
It's **down the block from** the post office.

B   **CLASS.**   What is near your school? What is
around the corner from your school?
What is down the block from your school?

2   LISTEN

A   Look at the picture. Berta is asking a
mail carrier for directions.

Where does she want to go?

B   CD4 T3   Listen to the conversation.
Was your answer in Exercise A correct?

Listen again. Where is the new supermarket?

a. 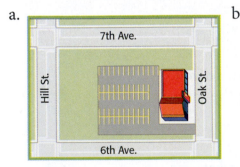   b. 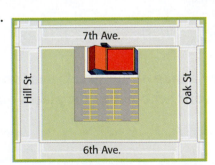   c.

C   CD4 T4   Listen to the whole conversation. Answer the questions.

1. Are there many people at the supermarket?   a. no   b. yes

2. When is the grand opening?   a. today   b. tomorrow

3 CONVERSATION

CD4 T5

A Listen. Then listen and repeat.

a **round**   **o** pen   to **day**   po **lice**   **sta** tion

Pronunciation Watch

In a two-syllable word, one syllable is stressed. The other syllable is unstressed. The vowel in the unstressed syllable often has a very short, quiet sound.

CD4 T6

B Listen and read the conversation. Then listen and repeat.

Berta: Excuse me. Can you help me? I'm looking for Foodsmart.

Mail Carrier: Sure. It's on Seventh between Hill and Oak.

Berta: Sorry?

Mail Carrier: It's on Seventh Avenue between Hill Street and Oak Street.

Berta: Thanks.

4 PRACTICE

A PAIRS. Practice the conversation. Then make new conversations. Use the pictures and map.

A: Excuse me. Can you help me?

I'm looking for _____.
            (place)

B: Sure. It's on _____ between
                (Avenue)

_____ and _____.
   (Street)   (Street)

A: Sorry?

B: It's on _____ between _____
            (Avenue)   (Street)

and _____.
      (Street)

A: Thanks.

B MAKE IT PERSONAL. PAIRS. Make your own conversations. Use places and streets near your school.

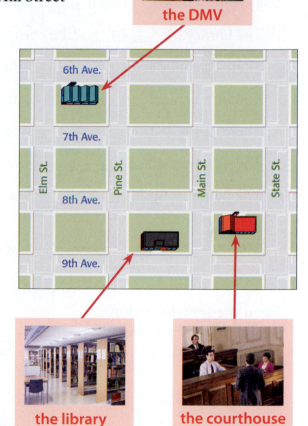

the DMV

the library

the courthouse

Give locations of places in the community

Grammar

Grammar Watch

For more prepositions of place, see page 274.

Prepositions of place

The supermarket is	around	the corner from the bank.
	down	the block / the street.
	between	Hill and Oak Streets.
	on	the corner of 10th Street and Pine Street.
	near	the library.

PRACTICE

**Complete the sentences about the location of some places in Riverside.
Use *around*, *down*, *between*, *on*, or *near*.**

1. The library is _____*on*_____ the corner of Oak and Elm Streets.

2. There's a coffee shop _____ the corner of 9th and Elm Streets.

3. There's a bank _____ the corner from the police station.

4. There's a fire station _____ the street from the police station.

5. There's a post office _____ the library.

6. The police station is _____ Park Street _____ 9th and 10th Streets.

Show what you know! Give locations of places in the community

Read the sentences above again. Write the names of the places on the map.

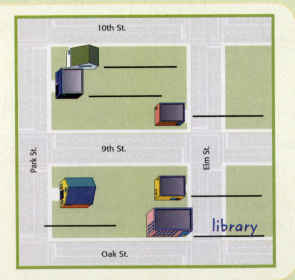

Can you...give locations of places in the community? ☐

Talk about transportation

Life Skills

1 TALK ABOUT FORMS OF TRANSPORTATION

CD4 T7

Look at the kinds of transportation. Listen and point. Then listen and repeat.

a bus

a subway

a train

a car

a bike

a taxi

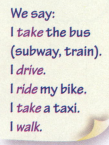
We say:
I *take* the bus
(subway, train).
I *drive.*
I *ride* my bike.
I *take* a taxi.
I *walk.*

2 PRACTICE

A **GROUPS OF 5.** Ask your classmates how they get to school. Write their names in the chart.

A: *How do you get to school?*
B: *I take the bus.*

Names	Take the bus	Take the train	Walk	Drive	Other
Susan	✓				

B **Report to the class.**

Susan takes the bus to school.

C **NETWORK.** Who gets to school the same way as you?
Find classmates who get to school the same way. Form a group.
Talk about problems with transportation.

Can you...talk about forms of transportation? ☐

3 READ TRAFFIC SIGNS

PAIRS. Look at the signs. Match the signs to their meanings. Write the meaning under each sign.

Don't turn left.	~~Stop.~~	Two-way traffic. Drive on the right.

☐ ☐ ☐

1. _Stop._   2. _____   3. _____

Drive slowly. Children often cross the street here.	Drive slowly. Wait for other cars.	Right lane ends ahead. Stay to the left.

☐ ☐ ☐

4. _____   5. _____   6. _____

Be ready to stop for trains.	Don't drive here.	Drive slowly. People often cross the street here.

☐ ☐ ☐

7. _____   8. _____   9. _____

4 PRACTICE

CD4 T8

Listen to the conversations. Which signs are the people talking about? Check (✓) the correct signs above.

Can you...read traffic signs? ☐

5 READ BUS SIGNS AND SCHEDULES

PAIRS. Student A, look at the buses on the left. Student B, look at the buses on the right. Don't look at your partner's buses. Ask and answer questions. Write the missing numbers on the buses.

A: *Which bus goes to Pine Street?*
B: *The Number 51. Which . . . ?*

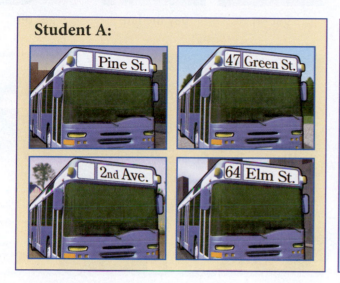

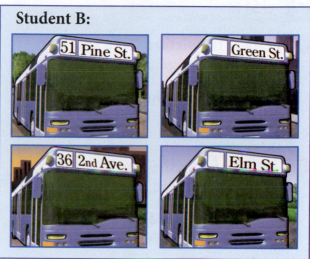

6 PRACTICE

CD4 T9

A Look at the bus schedules. Listen and fill in the missing times.

GREENVILLE BUS SCHEDULES

BUS 36		BUS 47		BUS 51	
39th Ave.	____	39th Ave.	8:14	King Dr.	8:15
River Rd.	8:16	Clay St.	8:23	State St.	8:22
16th Ave.	8:24	Park Ave.	____	Oak St.	8:31
2nd Ave.	8:35	Green St.	8:40	Pine St.	____

B **PAIRS.** Look at the schedules again. Answer the questions.

1. What time does Bus 36 leave 16th Avenue? ___*8:24*___

2. What time does Bus 47 leave 39th Avenue? _____

3. What time does Bus 51 leave State Street? _____

Can you . . . read bus signs and schedules? ☐

Listening and Speaking

1 BEFORE YOU LISTEN

CLASS. Look at the pictures. Listen to your teacher and repeat.

get on   pay the fare   get off

2 LISTEN

A Look at the picture. Tara and Matt are going to a concert.

Guess: Why are they talking to the police officer?

CD4 T10

B Listen to the conversation. Was your guess in Exercise A correct?

Listen again. Read the sentences. Circle *True* or *False*. Make the false sentences true.

1. They need the Number 5̶ bus.   **True**   (**False**)
    [4]

2. They get on at Second Street.   **True**   **False**

3. The fare is $2.00.   **True**   **False**

4. It is OK to give the driver a
    five-dollar bill.   **True**   **False**

CD4 T11

C Listen to the second part of the conversation.
Tara and Matt are getting off the bus. Answer the questions.

1. Matt asks the woman for _____.
    a. exact change   b. directions   c. a map

2. The woman _____ directions to Adams College.
    a. gives   b. doesn't give   c. gets

3. The woman says "_____"
    a. It's over there.   b. It's on Second Street.   c. Study, study, study!

3 CONVERSATION

A
CD4 T12
Listen. Then listen and repeat.

How **do you** get **to** Adams College?

Take **the** bus, **and** get off **at** Second Street.

Pronunciation Watch
Words like *do, the, to,* and *at* are usually unstressed.

B
CD4 T13
Listen and read the conversation. Then listen and repeat.

Tara: Excuse me. How do you get to Adams College?

Officer: Take the Number 4 bus, and get off at Second Street. It's not far from there.

Tara: Thanks. Oh, and how much does the bus cost?

Officer: Two dollars, but you need exact change.

4 PRACTICE

A
PAIRS. Practice the conversation. Then make new conversations. Use the pictures.

A: Excuse me. How do you get to ____?

B: Take the ____, and get off at Second Street. It's not far from there.

A: Thanks. Oh, and how much does the bus cost?

B: ____, but you need exact change.

Pine Hill Park

Green's

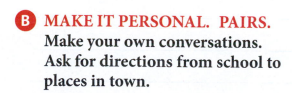
the main post office

B
MAKE IT PERSONAL. PAIRS. Make your own conversations. Ask for directions from school to places in town.

Ask about places in the community

Grammar

Simple present: Questions with *How*, *How much*, and *Where*		
How	do you get to Adams College?	Take the Number 4 bus.
How much	does it cost?	$2.00.
Where	do you get off?	Second Street.

> **Grammar Watch**
>
> Remember: For questions in the simple present, use ***does*** with *he, she* and *it*.

1 PRACTICE

A Maria is going shopping. Put the pictures in the correct order (1–4).

B Unscramble the words to ask questions about Maria. Use capital letters and question marks.

1. (Maria / does / shop for food / where) _Where does Maria shop for food?_____

2. (get there / how / she / does) _____

3. (does / cost / how much / the milk) _____

4. (she / does / get home / how) _____

5. (the bus / where / she / does / wait for) _____

C **PAIRS.** Ask and answer the questions in Exercise B.

   A: *Where does Maria shop for food?*
   B: *At Bob's supermarket. How . . . ?*

2 PRACTICE

A Pilar is new in town. She is asking a woman for directions. Complete the questions with *How*, *How much*, or *Where*. Use the words in parentheses and add *do* or *does*.

Pilar: Excuse me. ___How do you get to___ Pine Hill Park?
                            1. (you / get to)

Woman: Take the Number 4 train.

Pilar: OK. _____ the train?
               2. (you / get)

Woman: The train station is down the block. Do you see it?

Pilar: Oh, yes. And _____ a ticket?
                          3. (you / buy)

Woman: In the station.

Pilar: _____?
          4. (it / cost)

Woman: $2.00.

Pilar: OK. Sorry, one more question. _____ for the park?
                                         5. (you / get off)

Woman: Park Avenue. There's a big sign for the park. You can't miss it.

CD4 T14

B Listen and check your answers.

3 LIFE SKILLS WRITING   Write directions to your home. See page 262.

Show what you know!   Ask about places in the community

STEP 1. Look at the pictures. Where do you buy these things? Write the places.

milk— DVS Drugstore   _____

_____   _____

STEP 2. PAIRS. Talk about your answers in Step 1.

chocolate

tissues

A: *Where do you buy milk?*
B: *At DVS Drugstore.*
A: *Oh? How much does it cost there?*

milk   pens

Can you...ask about places in the community? ☐

Reading

1 **BEFORE YOU READ**

Match the sentences and pictures. Write one sentence from the box under each picture.

> ~~Mr. Park goes to the library with his children every Saturday.~~
> The librarian scans the books.
> They bring the books to the librarian at the front desk.
> They choose books to **borrow**.
> They **return** the books by the **due date**.
> They give the librarian their **library cards**.

1. *Mr. Park goes to the library with his children every Saturday.*

2. _____

3. _____

4. _____

5. _____

6. _____

CD4 T15

Listen. Read the article.

At the Library

Do you go to your public library? What can you do there? You can borrow books and magazines or read newspapers. What other things can you do at the library?

Story time at the Greenville Public Library

Most libraries have CDs and DVDs. Do you want to see a movie? Borrow it from the library. Do you like a song on the radio? Borrow the CD.

Most libraries also have computers. You can look up information on the Internet or check e-mail. You can also do your homework.

Many libraries have activities for children. Librarians read stories to young children. And there are often after-school programs or summer programs for older children.

The library can help you find a job. Libraries often have information about jobs in the area. And some libraries have classes to help you get a job or start a small business.

These are just some of the things you can do at the library. Go to your public library or check their website to find out more.

What's the best thing about the library? Everything there is free!

Read the article again. Answer the questions. Check (✓) all the correct answers.

1. What can you borrow from the library?

   ☐ books   ☐ CDs   ☐ computers

   ☐ DVDs   ☐ magazines ☐ radios

2. What can you do at the library?

   ☐ see a movie   ☐ look up information online

   ☐ listen to children's stories ☐ find job information

Show what you know!

Go to your public library. Get a library card. What activities do you want to do at your library? How can your library help you learn English?

Listening and Speaking

1 BEFORE YOU LISTEN

CLASS. Look at the pictures. Do you go to events like these in your community?

Where do you get information about events in your community? For example, do you look in the newspaper? Do you watch TV?

grand opening

concert

baseball game

yard sale

2 LISTEN

CD4 T16

A Look at the Greenville Weekend Community Schedule. Listen to the radio show and complete the information.

ON THE AIR

The Greenville Weekend Community Schedule

Grand Opening

Place: Foodsmart

Day: _____

Time: _____

Baseball Game

Place: Greenville _____

Day: _____

Time: 1:00 P.M.

Concert

Place: Greenville Community College

Day: _____

Time: _____

Yard Sale

Place: the Community Center across

from the _____ station

Day: _____

Time: 10:00 A.M. to _____

CD4 T16

B 🔘 **Listen again. Which events are free? Check (✓) all the correct answers.**

☐ the grand opening   ☐ the baseball game

☐ the concert   ☐ the yard sale

C **CLASS.** **Are there free events in your community? What are some examples?**

> There are free movies at the library.

3 CONVERSATION

A **Look at the picture. Sufia and Viet are classmates.**

Guess: What are they talking about?

CD4 T17

B 🔘 **Listen to the conversation. Was your guess in Exercise A correct?**

CD4 T18

C 🔘 **Listen and read the conversation. Then listen and repeat.**

Viet: What are you doing this weekend?
Sufia: I'm going to **a concert**.
Viet: Oh? Where's **the concert**?
Sufia: At **the community college**. Do you want to go?
Viet: Sounds great.

Pronunciation Watch

In informal conversation, *want to* often sounds like "wanna."

---

4 PRACTICE

A **PAIRS.** **Practice the conversation. Then make new conversations. Use the events in the Greenville Weekend Community Schedule on page 200.**

B **MAKE IT PERSONAL.** **PAIRS.** **Make your own conversations. Give true information.**

Talk about future plans

Grammar

Present continuous for future

What	**are** you **doing**	next weekend?	**I'm going**	to a concert.
How	**are** you **getting**	there?	**I'm taking**	the bus.
Who	**are** you **going**	with?	My sister. She's **meeting**	me there.

PRACTICE

A Ms. Reed's students are talking about their activities. Read each sentence. Is the person talking about the present or the future? Check (✓) the correct box.

	Present	Future
1. **Ernesto:** I'm working next weekend.	☐	✓
2. **Mei-Yu:** I'm doing my English homework now.	☐	☐
3. **Carlos:** Are you coming with us to the movie tomorrow?	☐	☐
4. **Assefa:** When are you visiting your grandparents?	☐	☐
5. **Dora:** I'm sorry, but I can't talk now. I'm cooking dinner.	☐	☐

B Complete the conversations. Use the present continuous form of the verbs in parentheses.

1. **A:** What ____are____ you ____doing____ tomorrow?
 (do)

 B: I _____ my friends at the mall.
 (meet)

 A: How _____ you _____ there?
 (get)

 B: I _____ the bus.
 (take)

2. **A:** Where _____ Sam _____ this weekend?
 (go)

 B: He _____ to Riverside for a concert.
 (go)

3. **A:** When _____ your children _____ you?
 (visit)

 B: They _____ for dinner next Sunday.
 (come)

1 GRAMMAR

Complete the conversation. Underline the correct words.

A: What **do you do** / <u>**are you doing**</u> tomorrow?

B: I **go** / **'m going** to the library in Greenville. I **go** / **'m going** every Friday.

A: Every Friday! **How** / **Where** do you get there?

B: Well, I always **take** / **am taking** the Number 2 bus. The library is on Oak **near** / **between** 7th and 8th Avenues. The bus stops **down** / **near** the block from the library.

A: Oh, really? **What** / **When** are you going?

B: At noon. Why?

A: I **go** / **'m going** to the DMV. It's right **around** / **between** the corner from the library. We can go together!

2 WRITING

STEP 1. Think about your weekend plans. Fill in the "You" rows. Write two activities.

	What?	When?	Who?
You	concert	Sat. afternoon	me, Amy, Joe
Your Partner			

STEP 2. PAIRS. Talk about your plans. Complete the chart.

Laura: *What are you doing this weekend?*
Antonio: *I'm going to a concert in the park.*
Laura: *Oh. When . . .*

STEP 3. Write two sentences about your plans and two sentences about your partner's plans.

I am going to a concert on Saturday afternoon. I am going with . . .

3 ACT IT OUT   What do you say?

STEP 1. Review the Lessons 2 and 5 conversations (CD 4 Tracks 3 and 10).

STEP 2. PAIRS. Student A, you are a visitor to Riverside. Student B, you live in Riverside.

Student A: You need directions to a place.
- Look at the pictures. Choose a place.
- Ask where the place is.
- Ask how to get to the place.

Student B: Help the visitor.
- Find the place on the map.
- Say where the place is.
- Give the visitor directions.

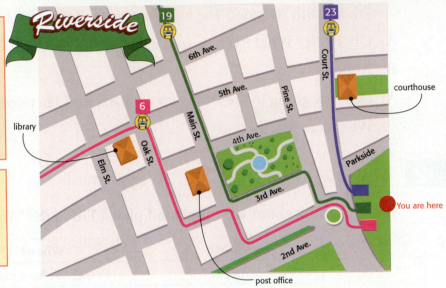

4 READ AND REACT   Problem-solving

STEP 1. Read about Minh's problem.

Minh takes the bus to work every day. He often reads the newspaper on the bus. Today, he gets off the bus at his usual stop. He gets to work and puts his coat away. But something is wrong. Where are his reading glasses? Are they still on the bus? He is worried. He can work without his glasses, but they are expensive. He doesn't want to lose them.

STEP 2. PAIRS. Talk about it. What is Minh's problem? What can Minh do? Here are some ideas.

- He can call the bus company's Lost and Found department.
- He can buy new glasses.
- He can ask the bus driver the next day.
- He can _____.

5 CONNECT

For your Goal-setting Activity, go to page 251.
For your Team Project, go to page 271.

Which goals can you check off? Go back to page 185.

Health Matters

11

Preview

Look at the picture.
What do you see?

UNIT GOALS

- ☐ Name parts of the body
- ☐ Call to explain an absence
- ☐ Talk about health problems
- ☐ Make a doctor's appointment
- ☐ Complete a medical history form
- ☐ Follow instructions during a medical exam
- ☐ Read medicine labels
- ☐ Talk about the past
- ☐ Give advice

1 WHAT DO YOU KNOW?

A CLASS. Look at the picture. Which parts of the body do you know?

> Number 3 is her leg.

CD4 T19

B Listen and point to the parts of the body. Then listen and repeat.

2 PRACTICE

A PAIRS. Look at the picture. Student A, say a part of the body. Student B, point to the part of the body.

> Ankle.

B WORD PLAY. PAIRS. Student A, look at the list of words on page 207. Say a part of the body. Student B, ask for the spelling. Then write the word on the picture.

A: *Stomach.*
B: *How do you spell that?*
A: *S-T-O-M-A-C-H.*
B: *Thanks.*

C Match the pictures and words. Write the correct letter.

a. shake   b. touch   c. nod   d. clap

1. __b__   2. ____   3. ____   4. ____

Parts of the Body

1. head
2. face
3. leg
4. ankle
5. shoulder
6. stomach
7. eye
8. nose
9. mouth
10. tooth/teeth
11. ear
12. chest
13. elbow
14. wrist
15. knee
16. neck
17. hand
18. back
19. arm
20. foot/feet

Learning Strategy

Make labels

Look at the list of parts of the body. Choose three or four words. Find a picture of a person in a magazine. Write each word in the correct place. For example, write the word *arm* on the person's arm.

Show what you know!

STEP 1. CD4 T20 Listen and follow the commands.

STEP 2. GROUPS OF 5. Student A, you are the leader. Give commands. Say *please* sometimes. Students B, C, D, and E, follow the command only when Student A says *please*. When you make a mistake, sit down.

A: *Clap your hands.*

B, C, D, E:

A: *Clap your hands, please.*

B, C, D, E:

This game is like "Simon Says."

Call to explain an absence

Listening and Speaking

1 BEFORE YOU LISTEN

CD4 T21

 READ. Look at the pictures. Listen and read about the children. Complete the sentences.

These children don't feel well. They feel sick. Barbara has a sore throat. Li has a stomachache. Asad has a toothache. And Rodolfo has a headache.

1. Barbara's ____*throat*____ hurts.

2. Li's _____ hurts.

3. Asad's _____ hurts.

4. Rodolfo's _____ hurts.

sore throat

stomachache

toothache

headache

2 LISTEN

A Look at the picture. Mrs. Lee is calling her son Alex's school.

Guess: What's the matter with Alex?

CD4 T22

B 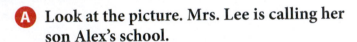 Listen to Mrs. Lee's conversation with the office assistant. Was your guess in Exercise A correct?

Listen again. Answer the questions.

1. Who is Ms. Wong?
   a. a teacher   b. an office assistant

2. Is Alex going to school today?
   a. yes   b. no

CD4 T23

C Listen to the whole conversation. Answer the questions. Circle *True* or *False*.

1. Mrs. Lee's other children feel well.   True   False

2. Mrs. Lee needs to call the school again later.   True   False

3 CONVERSATION

CD4 T24

Listen and read the conversation. Then listen and repeat.

Assistant: Good morning. Greenville Elementary.

Mrs. Lee: Hello. This is Terry Lee. I'm calling about my son Alex.

Assistant: Is that Alex Lee?

Mrs. Lee: Yes. He's sick today. He has a sore throat and a headache.

Assistant: I'm sorry to hear that. What class is he in?

Mrs. Lee: He's in Ms. Wong's class.

4 PRACTICE

A **PAIRS.** Practice the conversation. Then make new conversations. Use the information in the boxes. Change *he* to *she* when necessary.

A: Good morning. Greenville Elementary.

B: Hello. This is Terry Lee. I'm calling about my _____ Alex.

A: Is that Alex Lee?

B: Yes. **He**'s sick today. **He** has _____ and _____ .

A: I'm sorry to hear that. What class is **he** in?

B: **He**'s in Ms. Wong's class.

grandson	daughter	granddaughter
the flu	a cold	a cough
a fever	an earache	a stuffy nose

B **ROLE PLAY. PAIRS.** Student A, you're sick. Call work or school.

A: *Hi. This is _____. I can't come to work today. I have a . . . .*

B: *I'm sorry to hear that.*

Talk about health problems

Grammar

Review: Simple present

Information questions and answers		Yes/no questions and answers	
How do you **feel**? **How does** Alex **feel**?	My throat **hurts**. He **doesn't feel** well.	**Do** you **have** a fever? **Does** he **have** a fever?	**Yes**, I **do**. **No**, he **doesn't**.

PRACTICE

Maria and her mother are in Dr. Philip's office. Complete their conversation. Use the correct form of the verbs in parentheses. Give short answers.

Mom: Dr. Philip, I'm worried about Maria. I think she ___*has*___ the flu.
(have)

Doctor: How _____ you _____, Maria?
(feel)

Maria: Terrible. I _____ a cough and a stuffy nose.
(have)

Doctor: What about your throat? _____ it _____?
(hurt)

Maria: Yes, it _____. But just a little. _____ I _____ a fever?
(have)

Doctor: Let's see, . . . No, you _____.

Mom: _____ she _____ the flu, Dr. Philip?
(have)

Doctor: No. She _____ the flu. It's just a bad cold.
(not have)

Mom: That's good. I _____ a lot better now!
(feel)

Show what you know! Talk about health problems

PAIRS. You are friends. Student A, you are sick. Student B, ask questions. Find out your friend's symptoms. Use your imagination!

A: *I feel terrible.*
B: *What's wrong?*
A: *My _____ hurts.*
B: *Do you have . . . ?*

Can you. . . talk about health problems? ☐

See the doctor and get medicine

Life Skills

1 SEE THE DOCTOR

CD4 T25

Viktor Petrov is calling City Clinic to make an appointment. Listen and read his conversation with the office assistant. Then listen and repeat.

Assistant:	City Clinic. Can I help you?
Viktor:	This is Viktor Petrov. I'd like to make an appointment for a check-up.
Assistant:	Sure. For what day?
Viktor:	Can I come in tomorrow?
Assistant:	No, I'm sorry. There are no openings this week. How about next **Thursday afternoon** at **2:00**?
Viktor:	Okay. Next **Thursday** at **2:00** is good.
Assistant:	Okay, that's **Thursday**, **March third**, at **2:00** P.M. See you then.

2 PRACTICE

CD4 T26

A Listen to the conversation again. Circle the letter of the correct appointment card.

a.
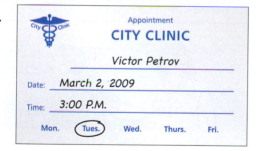

b.
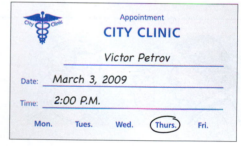

B PAIRS. Practice the conversation. Use your own name.

C PAIRS. Make a new conversation. Use different days, dates, and times. Complete the appointment card with your partner's information.

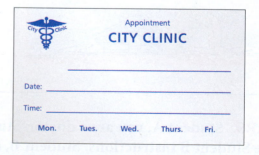

3 LIFE SKILLS WRITING

Complete a medical history form. See page 263.

A PAIRS. Viktor is at City Clinic for his check-up. Look at the pictures. Write an instruction under each picture. Use the instructions in the box.

> Lie down.   Open your mouth and say *Ahh*.
> Look straight ahead.   Roll up your sleeve.   ~~Step on the scale.~~
> Make a fist.   Sit on the table.   Take a deep breath.

1. _Step on the scale._

2. _____

3. _____

4. _____

5. _____

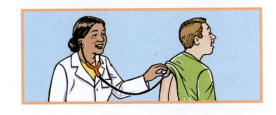

6. _____

7. _____

8. _____

B PAIRS. Student A, you are a doctor. Student B, you are a patient. Student A, give Student B instructions. Student B, act out the instructions.

Can you...see the doctor? ☐

5 READrMEDICINE LABELS

A Match the words and pictures. Write the correct words from the box under each picture.

> alcoholic beverage   ~~orally~~
> out of reach   tablet

1. ___*orally*___   2. _____   3. _____   4. _____

CD4 T27

B 🔘 Listen and check your answers.

6 PRACTICE

CD4 T28

A 🔘 Listen. Complete the medicine label.

Pain Away!
Pain Reliever / Fever Reducer

Directions:
Take _____ tablets orally every 6 _____.
Warnings:
• Do not take more than _____ tablets per day.
• Take with food or _____.
• Do not _____ alcoholic beverages.
• Do not give to children under _____.
• **Keep out of reach of _____.**

B Look at the medicine label. Answer the questions.

MAX-PROFEN
Pain Reliever / Fever Reducer

Directions: Take 1 tablet orally every 4–6 hours
Warnings:
• Do not take more than 6 tablets per day.
• Take with food or milk.
• Do not drink alcoholic beverages.
• Do not give to children under 12.
• **Keep out of reach of children.**

1. What is this medicine for? ___*pain or fever*_____

2. How much of the medicine do you take at one time? _____

3. How often do you take this medicine? _____

4. How much of this medicine can you take in one day? _____

5. What do you take this medicine with? _____

6. Where should you keep this medicine? _____

Can you...read medicine labels? ☐

Listening and Speaking

1 BEFORE YOU LISTEN

A Look at the calendar. Read the information.

January

MONDAY	TUESDAY	WEDNESDAY	THURSDAY	FRIDAY
2	3	4	5 Today!	6

Jan. 4 = *yesterday*
Jan. 4 at night = *last night*
Jan. 3 = *the day before yesterday*

B CLASS. Answer the questions.

Where were you yesterday?
Where were you last night?
Where were you the day before yesterday?

2 LISTEN

A Look at the picture. Tuan is talking to Luisa. Luisa wasn't at work yesterday.

What do you think? Why wasn't she at work?

B CD4 T29 Listen to the conversation. Was your guess in Exercise A correct? Listen again. Complete the sentences.

1. Luisa's daughter was home with _____.

a.

b.

c.

2. Her daughter is now _____.

a.

b.

c.

C CD4 T30 Listen to the whole conversation. Who is sick now? _____

3 CONVERSATION

CD4 T31

A 💿 Listen. Then listen and repeat.

- She was **sick**.
- It was the **flu**.
- They were **ab**sent.

- She **was**n't in **school**.
- It **was**n't a **cold**.
- They **were**n't **late**.

> **Pronunciation Watch**
>
> *Was* and *were* are often unstressed. *Wasn't* and *weren't* are stressed.

CD4 T32

B 💿 Listen to the sentences. Check (✓) the word you hear.

1. ☐ was ✓ wasn't
2. ☐ were ☐ weren't
3. ☐ was ☐ wasn't
4. ☐ were ☐ weren't

CD4 T33

C 💿 Listen and read the conversation. Then listen and repeat.

Tuan: You weren't here yesterday.

Luisa: I know. My daughter was home sick. She had a bad cold.

Tuan: Oh, too bad. How is she now?

Luisa: A lot better, thanks. She's back at school.

4 PRACTICE

A **PAIRS.** Practice the conversation. Then make new conversations. Use the words in the boxes. Change *she* to *he* when necessary.

A: You weren't here ⬚⬚⬚⬚.

B: I know. My ⬚⬚⬚⬚ was home sick.
   She had a bad ⬚⬚⬚⬚.

A: Oh, too bad. How is **she** now?

B: A lot better, thanks. **She's** back at school.

B **ROLE PLAY. PAIRS.** Make your own conversations. Use different times, people, and health problems.

> **Wednesday**
> **last night**
> **the day before yesterday**

> **son**
> **grandson**
> **granddaughter**

> **headache**
> **earache**
> **stomachache**

Grammar

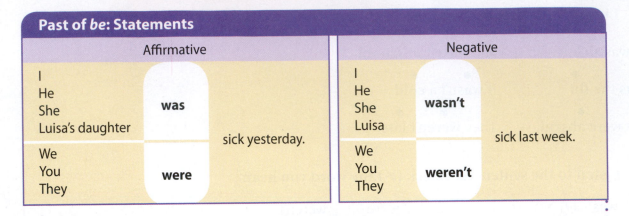

Past of *be*: Statements

Affirmative			Negative		
I He She Luisa's daughter	**was**		I He She Luisa	**wasn't**	
		sick yesterday.			sick last week.
We You They	**were**		We You They	**weren't**	

Grammar Watch

Contractions

wasn't = was not
weren't = were not

1 PRACTICE

A Some of Ms. Reed's students have the flu. Complete Ms. Reed's sentences. Underline the correct words.

1. Pierre and Miriam **are** / **were** here today, but they **are** / **were** absent yesterday.

2. Sen **is** / **was** OK now, but she **is** / **was** sick last night.

3. Ilya and Mei-Yu **are** / **were** in school yesterday, but they **aren't** / **weren't** here now.

4. Kamaria **is** / **was** at the doctor's office yesterday. Now she **is** / **was** at home in bed.

5. Assefa **isn't** / **wasn't** here now, but he **is** / **was** here yesterday.

6. I **am** / **was** OK last week, but now I **am** / **was** sick!

B Complete the paragraph about Sonia and her sister. Use *was* or *were*.

Sonia ____*was*____ home sick the day before yesterday.
1.

Her sister _____ sick, too. They _____
2.   3.

both in bed all day. Sonia's parents _____
4.

worried. Yesterday Sonia _____ a lot
5.

better. Her sister _____ better, too.
6.

Sonia's parents _____ very happy!
7.

A Look at yesterday's attendance sheet. Complete the sentences with *was, were, wasn't,* or *weren't.*

	Here	Absent
Carlos Delgado		✓
Luisa Flores	✓	
Min Jung Lee	✓ late	
Eun Young Lim		✓ sick
Sonia Lopez		✓ sick
Dora Moreno	✓	
Emilio Vargas		✓

1. Carlos ___*wasn't*___ in class yesterday.

2. Luisa and Min Jung _____ there, but Min Jung _____ late.

3. Eun Young and Sonia _____ there. They _____ both home sick.

4. Dora _____ there, but Emilio _____.

B **WRITE.** Look at the pictures. Write two sentences about each picture.

Last week

Yesterday

1. ___The teacher was sick last week.___ 3. _____

2. _____ 4. _____

PAIRS. Look at the pictures again. Talk about the differences. Use *was, were, wasn't,* and *weren't.*

A: *Last week the teacher was sick.*
B: *Right. And yesterday she wasn't sick.*

Can you…talk about the past? ☐

Read about walking for your health

Reading

1 BEFORE YOU READ

A **CLASS.** Do you walk every day? Do you walk a lot? Do you think walking is good for you?

B Look at the pictures. Which words complete the sentence? Circle the correct answers.

When you walk a lot, _____.

a.

you lose weight

b.

you get sick

c.

you have more energy

d.

You're in excellent health. No problems.

you prevent health problems

e.

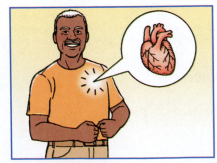

your heart gets strong

f.

your bones get strong

CD4 T34

Listen. Read the article.

Walk Your Way to Good Health!

It's free. It's easy. It's good for you. And guess what? You already do it every day! What is it? Walking!

Alan and Sue walk a lot. They walk 10,000 steps every day.

When you walk every day:

- You lose weight.
- Your bones get strong.
- Your heart gets strong.
- You prevent health problems like heart disease.
- You have a lot of energy.

For good health, you should walk 10,000 steps a day (about five miles).

Most people walk 4,000 steps a day. These 4,000 steps are part of your daily routine. You walk from the kitchen to the bedroom. You walk to your car or to the bus stop. You walk from the entrance of the school to your classroom. So you only need 6,000 more steps a day. You can add those steps to your daily routine:

- Don't take the elevator. Take the stairs.
- Walk when you talk on the phone.
- Get off the bus one stop early and walk the rest of the way.
- Don't park near the place you're going.

It's easy. So what are you waiting for? Start walking!

A **Read the article again: What is the main idea?**

a. Most people walk 4,000 steps a day.　　b. Walking is good for your health.

B **Read the sentences. Circle *True* or *False*.**

1. People should walk 10,000 steps a day.　　True　　False
2. Most people walk 6,000 steps a day.　　True　　False
3. To walk more, you need to go to the gym.　　True　　False

Show what you know!

NETWORK. Do you need to walk more? What can you do? Make a list. Find a partner. Look at your partner's goals. Check with your partner every week during your break. Ask, *Are you meeting your goals?*

Listening and Speaking

1 | **BEFORE YOU LISTEN**

CLASS. Talk about it. What do you do for a toothache? a backache? the flu?

2 | **LISTEN**

A Read the chart. Are your answers from *Before You Listen* in the chart?

ON THE AIR — What Does the Doctor Say?

Problem	Advice	The doctor says . . .	
		Do	**Don't**
☐ A toothache 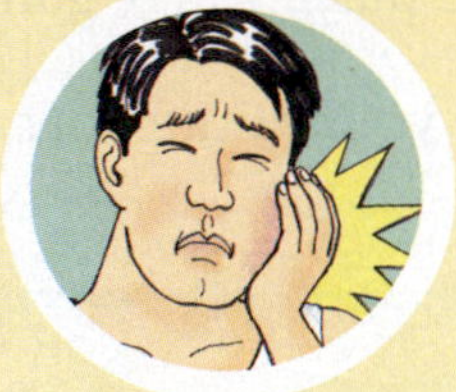	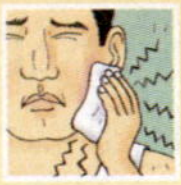 Put heat on it.	☐	☐
	 Eat a piece of onion.	☐	☐
	 Drink lime juice.	☐	☐
☐ A backache 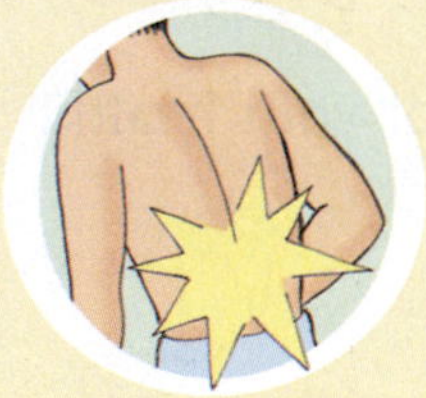	 Use an ice pack.	☐	☐
	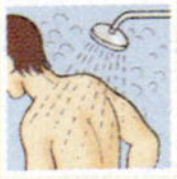 Take a hot shower.	☐	☐
	 Use a heating pad.	☐	☐
☐ The flu 	 Stay in bed.	☐	☐
	 Drink a lot.	☐	☐
	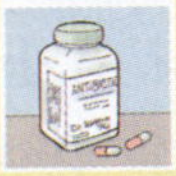 Take antibiotics.	☐	☐

Important: You should see a doctor or nurse if you don't feel better soon.

CD4 T35

B Listen to the radio show. Number the problems in the chart on page 220 in the order you hear them.

CD4 T35

C Listen again. What does the doctor say? Check (✓) *Do* or *Don't* for each problem on the chart on page 220.

3 CONVERSATION

A Look at the pictures. Clara has a sore throat. What does her friend Peter suggest? Do you think it is a good suggestion?

CD4 T36

B Listen and read the conversation. Then listen and repeat.

Clara: I have **a sore throat**.

Peter: I'm sorry to hear that. Maybe you should **drink tea and honey**.

Clara: That's a good idea.

Peter: But call the doctor if you don't feel better soon. You really shouldn't wait too long.

4 PRACTICE

A **PAIRS.** Practice the conversation. Then make new conversations. Use the information from the chart on page 220.

B **ROLE PLAY. GROUPS OF 3.** Make your own conversations. Use different problems and suggestions.

Grammar

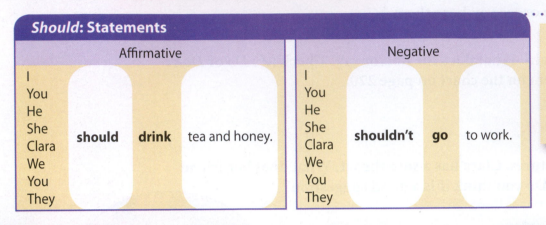

Should: Statements

Affirmative			
I You He She Clara We You They	should	drink	tea and honey.

Negative			
I You He She Clara We You They	shouldn't	go	to work.

Grammar Watch

Use the base form of the verb after *should* or *shouldn't*.

Contractions
shouldn't = should not

PRACTICE

A Complete the sentences about some people's problems. Underline the correct word. Choose affirmative for one sentence and negative for the other.

1. Agnes has a bad back. She **should / <u>shouldn't</u>** lift heavy things.

   She **should / shouldn't** ask a nurse about back exercises.

2. Ben has a stomachache. He **should / shouldn't** drink a lot of tea.

   He **should / shouldn't** eat fries.

3. Hassan has a sore throat and a cough. He **should / shouldn't** talk too much.

   He **should /shouldn't** take medicine.

4. Lan's ankle hurts. She **should / shouldn't** walk. She **should / shouldn't** put ice on it.

B **GROUPS OF 3.** Read the labels. What do they mean? Talk about them.

A: *What does this mean: "Take medication on an empty stomach"?*
B: *It means you shouldn't take it with food.*
C: *Right. You should take it before or after you eat.*

a. 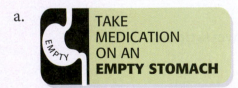 TAKE MEDICATION ON AN **EMPTY STOMACH**

b.  **P.M.**

c.  **DO NOT** REFRIGERATE

d.  TAKE MEDICATION **WITH FOOD**

e.  **DO NOT** DRINK MILK or EAT DAIRY PRODUCTS WHILE TAKING THIS MEDICATION

1 GRAMMAR

Complete the conversation between Ernesto and Mei-Yu. Use the words in the box. Use capital letters when necessary.

> does   feels   has   have   hurts   should   was   was   ~~weren't~~

Ernesto: You ___weren't___ here last week.

Mei-Yu: No, I _____ home. My son _____ sick with the flu.

Ernesto: Oh, I'm so sorry to hear that. _____ he feel better now?

Mei-Yu: Not really. He still _____ a bad headache, and his throat _____.

Ernesto: Hmm. Maybe you _____ take him to the doctor.

Mei-Yu: We _____ an appointment for tomorrow.

Ernesto: Well, I hope he _____ better soon.

Mei-Yu: Thanks.

2 WRITING

STEP 1. GROUPS OF 3. Read the problems. Make suggestions.

Problem 1 Bobby, a 10-year-old boy, has a stomachache every morning before school. What should his parents do?	**Problem 2** Sara has a backache. Her friend tells her to exercise. Is this a good suggestion? Sara isn't sure. What should she do?	**Problem 3** Ted has a bad sore throat. He wants to go to work. His wife thinks he should stay home. What should he do?

A: *OK, Problem 1. What should Bobby's parents do?*
B: *Hmm. Maybe they should talk to his teacher. Maybe there's a problem at school.*
C: *Or, maybe they should take him to the doctor.*

STEP 2. Write one suggestion for each problem.

Problem 1. _____

Problem 2. _____

Problem 3. _____

3 ACT IT OUT · What do you say?

CD4 T37

STEP 1. Listen to the conversation.

STEP 2. PAIRS. Student A, you are a doctor. Student B, you are a patient.

Student A:	**Student B:**
• Ask the patient, "What's the matter?" • Give the patient instructions. • Give the patient advice.	• Choose a health problem. Answer the doctor's questions. • Follow the doctor's instructions. • Thank the doctor.

4 READ AND REACT · Problem-solving

STEP 1. Read about Genet's problem.

Genet is a cashier. She works full-time, Monday to Friday. She has a seven-year-old son, Solomon. Solomon is in the second grade. He is usually at school all day from Monday to Friday. Today, Solomon is sick. He doesn't have a fever, but he has a stuffy nose and a sore throat. He has a headache. He feels terrible. He wants to stay home. But who can take care of him? Genet can't miss work.

STEP 2. PAIRS. Talk about it. What is Genet's problem? What can Genet do? Here are some ideas.

- She can send her son to school.
- She can stay home with her son.
- She can ask a neighbor to stay with her son.
- She can _____.

5 CONNECT

For your Goal-setting Activity, go to page 252.
For your Team Project, go to page 271.

Which goals can you check off? Go back to page 205.

Help
Wanted

Preview

**Look at the picture.
What do you see?**

UNIT GOALS

- ☐ Respond to a Help Wanted sign

- ☐ Talk about job skills

- ☐ Read want ads

- ☐ Talk about hours you can work

- ☐ Ask about job skills

- ☐ Use correct body language at a job interview

- ☐ Talk about work experience

- ☐ Complete a job application

1   WHAT DO YOU KNOW?

A   **CLASS.** Look at the pictures. Which job duties can you name?

> Number 1 is "answer the phone."

CD4 T38

B   🔘 Listen and point to the pictures. Then listen and repeat.

2   PRACTICE

A   **PAIRS.** Student A, point to a picture. Ask, "What is he/she doing?" Student B, answer.

A: *What is he doing?*
B: *He's using a computer.*

B   **WORD PLAY. TWO TEAMS.** Play Charades.

- Team 1, go first. Student A on Team 1, act out a job duty.
- Team 1, guess the duty. You have one minute. You get one point for a correct guess.
- Student A on Team 2, you're next.
- Teams take turns. The team with the most points wins.

C   **WRITE.** What do you do at work or at home every day? Write one of your duties. Look at the list on page 227 or use your own ideas.

At work, _I drive a truck_____.

OR

At home, _I take care of my children_____.

At _____, _____.

2

3

4

6

7

8

10

Job Duties

1. answer the phone
2. take messages
3. use a computer
4. make copies
5. drive a truck
6. lift heavy boxes
7. deliver packages
8. supervise workers
9. fix things
10. take care of grounds
11. clean floors
12. help people

Show what you know!

STEP 1. CLASS. Walk around the room. Ask about your classmates' duties. Complete the chart.

Paul: *Min-Ji, what do you do every day?*

Min-Ji: *At work, I drive a truck. What about you?*

Paul: *At home, I . . .*

Name	Duty	Place
Min-Ji	drives a truck	at work

STEP 2. Report to the class.

Min-Ji drives a truck at work.

Listening and Speaking

1   BEFORE YOU LISTEN

CLASS. Look at the picture of Dino's Diner. What do you see?

2   LISTEN

A Look at the picture. Assefa is in Dino's Diner. Guess: Why is he there?

a. He wants a hamburger.
b. He works there.
c. He wants a job.

CD4 T39

B Listen to the conversation. Was your guess in Exercise A correct? Listen again. Complete the sentences.

1. Assefa is a _____.

a.   b.   c.

2. He makes great _____.

a.   b.   c.

CD4 T40

C Listen to the whole conversation. Read the sentences. Circle *True* or *False*.

1. Dino gives Assefa a job.   True   False

2. Assefa is starting his new job tomorrow.   True   False

3. Assefa answers Dino's phone.   True   False

3 CONVERSATION

CD4 T41

A 💿 Listen. Then listen and repeat.

He can **make ham**burgers.　　He **can't** make **piz**za.

CD4 T42

B 💿 Listen to the sentences. Check (✓) the word you hear.

1. ☐ can　☐ can't　　2. ☐ can　☐ can't　　3. ☐ can　☐ can't

CD4 T43

C 💿 Listen and read the conversation. Then listen and repeat.

Assefa: I noticed the Help Wanted sign.
I'd like to apply for a job.

Dino: OK. Which job?

Assefa: Well, I'm a cook. I can make great hamburgers.

Dino: Can you make pizza?

Assefa: No. I can't make pizza, but I can learn.

4 PRACTICE

A **PAIRS.** Practice the conversation. Then make new conversations. Use the information in the boxes.

A: I noticed the Help Wanted sign. I'd like to apply for a job.

B: OK. Which job?

A: Well, I'm _____ . I can _____ .

B: Can you _____ ?

A: No. I can't _____ , but I can learn.

B **ROLE PLAY. PAIRS.** Make your own conversations. Use different jobs and skills.

a sales assistant

use a cash register　　take returns

an office assistant

use a computer　　take inventory

a carpenter

make cabinets　　fix furniture

Grammar

Can: Statements

Affirmative			
I You He Assefa She We You They	can	make use	hamburgers. a computer.

Negative			
I You He Assefa She We You They	can't	make use	pizza. a cash register.

···· Grammar Watch

Use the base form of the verb after *can* or *can't*.

Contractions
can't = can not

1 PRACTICE

A **Read Olga's job skills. Complete the sentences with *can* or *can't*.**

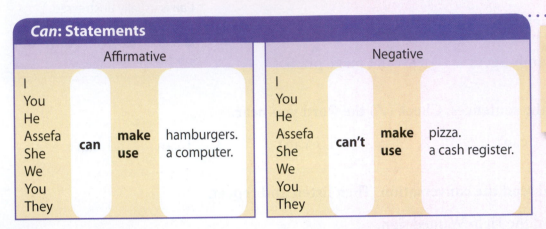

Name: _Olga Popova_

Office Jobs 4U

Check the skills you have.

☐ use a computer	✔ make copies	☐ work with numbers
✔ answer phones	☐ write reports	✔ help customers
✔ take messages	✔ organize things	☐ deliver mail

1. Olga ____*can't*____ use a computer, but she _____ answer phones.

2. She _____ take messages, but she _____ write reports.

3. She _____ work with numbers, but she _____ organize things.

4. She _____ deliver mail, but she _____ make copies.

5. She _____ help customers.

B **GROUPS OF 3. Look at the job skills in Exercise A. What can you do? What can't you do? Tell your partner.**

A: *I can use a computer. What about you?*
B: *I can use a computer, too.*
C: *I can't use a computer, but I can . . . .*

A: *I can't write reports.*
B: *I can't write reports, either.*
C: *I can write reports, but I can't . . .*

Look at the pictures. Complete the sentences with *can* or *can't* and the verbs in the box.

cook	drive	~~make~~
speak	take	take care of

1.

He ___can't make___ furniture.

2.

She _____ a taxi.

3.

How are you?

OK, thanks.

They _____ English.

4.

We _____.

5.

I _____ messages.

6.

He _____ children.

Show what you know! Talk about job skills

PAIRS. Look at the picture. What can the people do? What can't they do?

A: *The man in the green shirt can't fix the light.*
B: *Right. The woman in the red shirt can use a cash register.*

We're open until 9.

Customer Service

Sorry. No.

Do you speak Spanish?

Can you... talk about job skills? ☐

Read want ads

Life Skills

1 READ WANT ADS

A **PAIRS.** Read the information. Talk about it.
Do you work? Do you work full-time or part-time?

A: *I work full-time in a factory. What about you?*
B: *I have two part-time jobs.*

B Want ads are one way people find out about
job openings. Look at the want ads. Find the
abbreviations for these words. Write the
abbreviations.

1. full-time ___*FT*___

2. experience _____

3. necessary _____

4. hour _____

5. part-time _____

Full-time = 35–40 hours a week
Part-time = less than 35 hours
a week

HELP WANTED

A	**TRUCK DRIVER** FT. Exp. nec. $18/hr. FAX: Hanako (650) 555-2579
B	**CHILD-CARE WORKER** PT. M–F 9–3 $12/hr. Call Jasmine: (650) 555-3328.
C	**COOKS** Bill's Burgers No exp. nec. $7/hr. Evenings. Apply in person. 409 Market St.

2 PRACTICE

A **PAIRS.** Look at the want ads again. Complete the
sentences. Write the letter of the ad.

1. Job __*A*__ is full-time.

2. Job ____ pays $12 an hour.

3. Job ____ is evenings only.

4. You don't need experience for Job ____.

5. You need to go to the place to apply for Job ____.

6. You can call someone at the place for Job ____.

7. You can send a fax to the place for Job ____.

B **GROUPS OF 4.** Talk about it. What are some
other ways people find out about job openings?

C PAIRS. Read the information. Talk about it. Which shift do you work?

The **day shift** is usually from 7:00 A.M. to 3:00 P.M.
The **afternoon shift** is usually from 3:00 P.M. to 11:00 P.M. or 12:00 A.M.
The **night shift** is usually from 11:00 P.M. to 7:00 A.M.

D NETWORK. Find classmates with the same work shift as you. Form a group.
Ask the people in your group, *Do you like your shift? Why?*

CD4 T44

E Two friends are talking about a job opening. Look at the want ads.
Listen to the conversation. Which ad are they talking about?

HELP WANTED

SALES ASSISTANT	STOCK CLERKS	NURSE'S ASSISTANT
To work afternoon shift in busy store. FT. $10/hr. Call Tom: 323-555-4179	PT., all shifts available. No exp. nec. From $7/hr. Fax: 915-555-2286	Greenville General Hospital FT. M-F, 11 P.M. to 7 A.M. $12/hr. Apply in person. 5200 River St.
A	**B**	**C**

F PAIRS. Look at the ads again. Answer the question.

How much money does the nurse's assistant make in one week? _____

G WRITE. Write a want ad for a job you want.
Include the hours, pay, and experience required.

H PAIRS. Talk about your want ads. Why do you want this job?

Antonio: *I want a job as a security guard. The pay is good, and I can work the day or night shift. What about you, Tamar?*
Tamar: *I want a job as . . .*

I Report to the class.

Antonio wants a job as a security guard.

HELP WANTED

Can you...read want ads? ☐

Talk about hours you can work

Listening and Speaking

1 BEFORE YOU LISTEN

READ. Look at the picture of the clothing store Imagine. Read the information. Answer the questions.

It's a busy day! It's Wednesday, and there is a big sale at Imagine. There are a lot of customers in the store. All of the salespeople are working hard. They are helping customers, working the cash registers, and taking returns. Right now, the elevator is out of order. People need to take the escalator. So the salespeople are giving directions, too.

1. Why are there a lot of people at Imagine today?
   a. It's the weekend.   b. There's a big sale.

2. Why are the salespeople giving directions?
   a. The elevator isn't working.   b. The store is very big.

2 LISTEN

A Look at the picture again. Guess: Who is the woman?

a. a customer   b. an employee

CD4 T45

B Listen to the conversation. Was your guess in Exercise A correct?

Listen again. Which questions does the woman ask the man? Check (✓) the correct questions.

☐ Can you work this Saturday?   ☐ Can you work this evening?
☐ Can you work from 2:00 to 6:00?   ☐ Can you work from 2:00 to 7:00?

CD4 T46

C Listen to the whole conversation. Answer the questions.

1. Who is the man?
   a. a new sales assistant   b. an elevator repair person

2. Who does the woman think the man is?
   a. a new sales assistant   b. an elevator repair person

3. What does the woman want the man to do?
   a. work her shift on Saturday b. fix the elevator on Saturday

3 CONVERSATION

CD4 T47

A Listen. Then listen and repeat.

A: Can you start tomorrow?

B: Yes, I **can**.

A: Can you work Saturday?

B: No, I **can't**.

CD4 T48

B Listen and read the conversation. Then listen and repeat.

Dana: Hi, I'm Dana.

Sam: Hi, I'm Sam. Wow. This store is really busy.

Dana: I know. Listen, I need a favor. Can you work this Saturday?

Sam: Uh, well, yes, I can.

Dana: Oh, great, thanks, because I can't. Can you work from 2:00 to 7:00?

Sam: Um, yes. I guess so.

4 PRACTICE

A PAIRS. Practice the conversation. Then make new conversations. Use the words in the boxes.

A: This _____ is really busy.

B: I know. Listen, I need a favor.

Can you work _____ ?

A: Uh, well, yes, I can.

B: Oh, great, thanks, because I can't.

Can you work from _____ ?

A: Um, yes. I guess so.

restaurant	tomorrow	6:00–11:00
hospital	Monday	8:00–3:00
hotel	June 11	4:00–10:00

B ROLE PLAY. PAIRS. Make your own conversations. Ask someone you work with to change shifts with you.

A: *Listen, I need a favor. Can you work _____?*

B: *_____? Yes, I can.*

A: *Oh, great. And can you work _____?*

B: *_____? Sure.*

A: *Thanks!*

Grammar

Can: Yes/no questions and short answers

Can	you he she Sam they	work use	this Saturday? a computer?		Yes,	I he she he they	can.	No,	I he she he they	can't.

> Remember: Use a comma (,) after *Yes* or *No* in short answers.

1   **PRACTICE**

A   **WRITE.**   Write questions with *can.*
Use the words in parentheses. Give short answers.

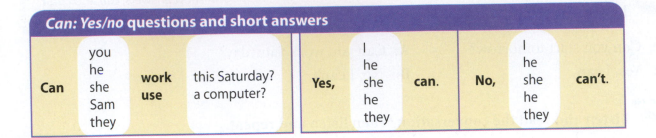

Can you work nights?

1. **A:** _Can you work nights?_ _____
                    (you / work nights)
   B: _Yes, I can._   I'm free every night.

2. **A:** _____
                    (you / work weekends)
   B: _____ I can only work weekdays. I'm busy on weekends.

3. **A:** _____
                    (you / come to work early tomorrow)
   B: _____ What time should I come in?

4. **A:** _____
                    (she / start tomorrow)
   B: _____ She can be here at 9:00.

5. **A:** _____
                    (your sister / fix the car)
   B: _____ She's good with cars.

6. **A:** _____
                    (Bill / drive a truck)
   B: _____ He doesn't have a driver's license.

B   CD4 T49   **Listen and check your answers.**

C   **PAIRS.**   Practice the conversations in Exercise A.

A Look at the want ad. Write job interview questions with *can*. Ask about a job applicant's skills and work hours.

1. Can you answer phones?

2. _____

3. _____

4. _____

5. _____

> **HELP WANTED**
>
> Office assistant. Answer phones, use a computer, organize files, write reports. Full-time.

B **PAIRS.** Student A, ask the questions in Exercise A. Student B, give true answers and add information.

A: *Can you answer phones?*
B: *Yes, I can. I can take messages, too.*

C **WRITE.** In your notebook, write five sentences about your skills. Use skills from Exercise A or other skills.

Show what you know! Ask about job skills

STEP 1. Think of a job. Write the name of the job. _____

STEP 2. GROUPS OF 5. Student A, say, "Guess my job." Other students, ask *yes/no* questions with *can* about Student A's job skills. You can ask ten questions.

A: *Guess my job.*
B: *Can you use a cash register?*
A: *No, I can't.*
C: *Can you drive a truck?*
A: *No, I can't.*
D: *Can you make furniture?*
A: *Yes, I can.*
E: *Are you a carpenter?*
A: *Yes, I am.*
B: *OK, my turn. Guess my job.*

Can you...ask about job skills? ☐

Reading

1 BEFORE YOU READ

A Read the paragraph. Then complete the sentence.

When you meet someone for the first time, you form an opinion about that person. For example, you think, "This person is helpful" or "This person is fun." This is your *first impression*.

A first impression is your opinion about a person you meet for the _____ time.

B PAIRS. Talk about it. Think about someone at work or school. What was your first impression of this person?

A: *I work with Camilo. My first impression was, "He's really friendly."*
B: *Simone is in my computer class. . . .*

C A person's *body language* is one thing that helps you form an impression. Your body language is important in a job interview. Look at the pictures. Read the sentences. Then practice the body language.

a
They're shaking hands firmly.

b
They're making eye contact.

c
She has her hands on her lap.

d
He's leaning forward.

e
She's smiling.

f
He's standing about three feet away.

2 READ

CD4 T50

🔲 **Listen. Read the article.**

MAKING A GOOD FIRST IMPRESSION

You have a job interview. How can you make a good first impression? Your words are important, but your body language is important too. Here are some tips.

When you meet the interviewer, shake hands firmly. Stand about three feet away. Make eye contact and smile. You may feel stressed, but try to look relaxed.

A good job interview starts with good body language.

When you sit down, stay relaxed and look friendly. Sit up in your chair and lean forward a little. This shows you are listening to the interviewer. Put your hands on your lap. Don't touch your face or hair.

When you leave the interview, shake hands with the interviewer again. Smile and make eye contact. And don't forget: Thank the interviewer. Practice all these tips before you go to your interview. The right body language can help you get the job. Good luck!

3 CHECK YOUR UNDERSTANDING

A **CLASS.** Read the article again. What is the main idea?

B **PAIRS.** Give each other tips on good body language for a job interview. Use your own words.

    A: *First, you should shake hands and smile.*
    B: *Right. And you should also . . .*

C **CLASS.** Talk about it. What are some other ways to make a good first impression in a job interview?

Show what you know!

PAIRS. Role play a job interview. Use good body language!

Listening and Speaking

1 LISTEN

A Look at the picture of Bao Tran and Hanh Le in the *Greenville Reporter*.

Guess: Why are they in the newspaper?

B CD4 T51 Listen to the Greenville News Radio show *Meet Your Neighbors*.
Was your guess in Exercise A correct?

C CD4 T51 Listen again. Complete the sentences.
Choose the correct words from the box.

a hospital	people's homes
a restaurant	a hotel

1. Bao was a cook in _____.

2. Hanh was a cook in _____.

D Complete the newspaper article. Use words from the radio interview
with Bao and Hanh.

ON THE AIR

Greenville Reporter

People in the News

Meet Bao Tran and Hanh Le. They are the owners of *Saigon*,
Greenville's first Vietnamese _____. Many people here
know Bao and Hanh. Bao was a _____, a waiter, and
a _____ at the Greenville Café for _____ years,
and Hanh worked in many people's homes as a cook. Bao and
Hanh were also _____ at the Greenville Adult School.
Their first teacher, Emily Reed, says: "They were very good
_____, but they were *great* _____. Our class
parties were always wonderful because of Bao and Hanh's _____. I'm sure their
restaurant will be a big success." Everyone in Greenville wishes the couple lots of luck.

Bao Tran (left) and Hanh Le

E **PAIRS.** Compare answers.

2 CONVERSATION

A When a person is successful at something, we say "Congratulations!"
Read the conversation in Exercise B. Why does Ayantu say
"Congratulations!" to Ivan?

CD4 T52

B Listen and read the conversation. Then listen and repeat.

Ayantu: Congratulations! This place looks great!
Ivan: Thanks.
Ayantu: So, is this your first café?
Ivan: Yes, it is. But I worked in a café before.
Ayantu: Oh. What did you do?
Ivan: I was a waiter.
Ayantu: How long were you there?
Ivan: Two years.

3 PRACTICE

A **PAIRS.** Practice the conversation. Then make new conversations. Use the information in the boxes.

A: Congratulations! This place looks great!
B: Thanks.
A: So, is this your first _____?
B: Yes, it is. But I worked in a _____ before.
A: Oh. What did you do?
B: I was a _____.
A: How long were you there?
B: _____ years.

B **ROLE PLAY. PAIRS.** Make your own conversations. Use different stores, jobs, and times.

hair salon

hair stylist

grocery store

cashier

clothing store

sales assistant

three

four

five

Grammar

Past of *be*: Questions and answers

Were	you they	successful?	Yes,	I	was.	No,	I	wasn't.
				we	were.		we	weren't.
				they	were.		they	weren't.
Was	he Bao she it			he	was.		he	wasn't.
				she	was.		she	wasn't.
				it	was.		it	wasn't.
How long were	you	at your last job?	Five years. From 2003 to 2008.					

PRACTICE

Grammar Watch

Contractions
wasn't = was not
weren't = were not

A **WRITE.** Write questions. Use *was* or *were*.

1. What / your last job   _What was your last job?_____

2. the job / full-time   _____

3. How long / you / there   _____

4. you / happy there   _____

CD4 T53

B ⊙ Listen and check your answers.

C **PAIRS.** Student A, you are a manager. Student B, you are a job applicant. Student A, interview the job applicant. Ask the questions in Exercise A. Student B, look at the job application. Answer the manager's questions.

A: *What was your last job?*
B: *I was a cashier.*

JOB HISTORY:

Company: ___Sam's Department Store___   Address: ___3 Main Street___

Phone Number: ___(760) 555-1279___   ___Riverside, California 93501___

Job: ___Cashier (full-time)___   Dates Worked: From ___2001___ To ___2007___

Reason for Leaving: ___store closed___

---

1 GRAMMAR

Eun-Young Lim is interviewing for a job as a sales assistant at Imagine. Complete the parts of the interview with *was*, *were*, *can*, and *can't*.

1. **Manager:** So, I see you _____were_____ a sales assistant at Creative Clothing in Smithfield. How long _____ you there?

   Eun-Young: Three years. I _____ there from 2003 to 2006. Then my family moved.

2. **Manager:** So, _____ you speak Korean? We have a lot of Korean customers.

   Eun-Young: Yes, I _____ speak Korean, English, and a little Spanish.

   I _____ a cashier in a Mexican restaurant for six months.

3. **Manager:** Our store is always busy on weekends. _____ you work weekends?

   Eun-Young: Well, I can work Saturdays, but I _____ work Sundays.

   Manager: That's OK. When can you start?

   Eun-Young: I _____ start next weekend.

2 WRITING

STEP 1. Complete the information about a job you had. Use true or made-up information.

Company: _____

Job: _____ Dates Worked: From _____ To _____

Reason for Leaving: _____

STEP 2. Write three sentences about the job in Step 1.

I was a sales assistant at Creative Clothing in Smithfield. I was there for three years.
I left because my family moved.

_____

_____

_____

_____

3 LIFE SKILLS WRITING   Complete a job application. See page 264.

4 ACT IT OUT — What do you say?

STEP 1. CD4 T54 🔊 Listen to the job interview.

STEP 2. Choose a place and a job. Make a list of the skills you need for this job. Student A, you are the manager. Interview Student B for the job. Ask about Student B's skills and experience. Ask when Student B can work.

HELP WANTED!
Cooks, Waiters

HELP WANTED!
Sales Assistants, Stock Clerks

HELP WANTED!
Office Assistants

5 READ AND REACT — Problem-solving

STEP 1. Read about Jin-Su's problem.

Jin-Su is a supervisor in a large store. He finds new employees for the store. He interviews people for cashier jobs and sales jobs. Jin-Su's manager thinks Jin-Su is a good supervisor, because he always finds good employees.

Jin-Su's younger cousin Min-Ji needs a job. Min-Ji wants to work as a cashier. She asks Jin-Su, "Can I work at your store?" Jin-Su wants to help Min-Ji. But he doesn't think she is a good worker. She is always late, and she isn't very organized.

STEP 2. PAIRS. Talk about it. What is Jin-Su's problem? What can he do? Here are some ideas.

- He can say, "There are no job openings now."
- He can give Min-Ji a job.
- He can help Min-Ji find a different job.
- He can _____.

6 CONNECT

For your Goal-setting Activity, go to page 252.
For your Team Project, go to page 272.

Which goals can you check off? Go back to page 225.

Persistence Activities

Unit 1   Name Game

GROUPS OF 5.   **Play the Name Game.**

Diana: My name is Diana.

Luis: This is Diana. My name is Luis.

Olga: This is Diana. This is Luis. My name is Olga.

Tran: This is Diana. Excuse me. What's your name again, please?

Luis: Luis.

Tran: OK, thanks. This is Diana. This is Luis. This is Olga. My name is Tran.

Laila: This is Diana. This is Luis. This is Olga. This is Tran. My name is Laila.

Unit 2   Goal Setting: Why Learn English?

A Complete the sentence. Check (✓) all the boxes that are true for you.

I want to learn English to _____.

☐ get a job

☐ get more education

☐ help my children
  with school

☐ get a new job

☐ become a U.S. citizen

☐ talk to doctors and my
  children's teachers

B **PAIRS.** Talk about your answers in Exercise A.

A: *I want to learn English to _____.*
B: *That's interesting. I want to . . .*

C **CLASS.** Tell the class your goals.

Unit 3   School Supplies

A **GROUPS OF 3.** What do students bring to class? Make a list of ten things.

School Supplies

a pencil _____   _____

_____   _____

_____   _____

_____   _____

For help, look at the pictures of classroom objects on pages 46–47.

B **SAME GROUPS.** Take turns. Ask, *Are you ready for school today?*

A: *Are you ready for school today?*
B: *Yes. I have a pencil, a . . . .*
What about you? Are you ready for school today?
C: *Yes. I have a pencil, a . . . .*

C Before you come to class next time, check that you have your supplies. Use the list.

Unit 4   My Friends and Family

A Think about your classmates, friends, neighbors, co-workers, and family. In your notebook, write the names of people you want to speak English to.

Classmates	Friends	Neighbors	Co-workers	Family
Sonia	Bo	Mr. Smith	Alice	Ricardo
Mai		Sally	Joe	Pablo

B Choose two or three people from your list. In your notebook, write your goals for speaking to each person in English. Use the ideas below or your own ideas.

> *I want to talk to Sonia in English about my family.*
> *I want to say hello to Alice in English.*
> *I want to read to Ricardo in English.*

C Which goals will you do this week? Circle your goals for this week.

D **PAIRS.** Tell your partner your goals for this week. Check with each other next week. Did you complete your goals?

This week, I want to talk to . . . . What about you?

Unit 5 Class Jobs

A **CLASS.** Look at the list of class jobs. These assistants help the teacher. Are there other jobs in your class? Write them in the list.

Job	Job Duty
Assistant 1	Write today's date on the board.
Assistant 2	Erase the board.
Assistant 3	Give out supplies.
Assistant 4	Take attendance.
Assistant 5	Collect supplies.
Assistant 6	_____

B **CLASS.** Choose assistants to help your teacher. Write the students' names in the list. Change assistants every week.

Unit 6 My Vocabulary Learning Strategies

A **CLASS.** Look at the Learning Strategies on pages 7, 27, 47, 67, 87, and 107.

B Which strategies do you use to learn vocabulary? Check (✓) the strategies.

☐ Write personal sentences   ☐ Use your language

☐ Use pictures   ☐ Make word groups

☐ Make labels   ☐ Other: _____

C **GROUPS OF 5.** Talk about it. Which strategies do you use?

A: *I use my language, and I use pictures. What about you?*
B: *I . . .*

D Write your vocabulary goal for this week.

I want to learn _____ new words this week.
                   (number)

I will use _____ to help me remember the new words.
           (title of Learning Strategy)

E **SAME GROUPS.** Tell your group your goal. Check with each other next week. Did you complete your goals?

Unit 7   Daily Planner

A When do you study or practice English? Write a daily planner. Use the planner below as a model. Make one planner for every day of the week.

Day: Monday	
Activity	Time
Go to English class	8:30 A.M.–11:30 A.M.
Use English at work	1:00 P.M.–5:00 P.M.
Listen to music in English	5:00 P.M.–5:30 P.M.
Do my homework	8:30 P.M.–9:00 P.M.

B GROUPS OF 3. Show your planners to your group.

(Note: For the Unit 8 Activity, you will need to bring tea and cookies or other refreshments.)

Unit 8   Getting-to-Know-You Tea

A CLASS. Bring tea and cookies to class. Take some of the tea and cookies. Sit with a classmate you don't know.

B PAIRS. Take turns. Ask and answer the questions below.

Lin: *What's your name?*
Mario: *My name is Mario. What's your name?*

- What's your name?
- Where are you from?
- Tell me about your family.
- What do you do?
- What do you like to do on the weekend?
- What kind of food do you like?
- What's your favorite holiday?
- What are your interests and special skills?

C Report to the class. Say one new thing you learned about your partner.

On the weekend, Mario cooks for his family.

Unit 9   Important Dates in School

A **CLASS.** **What dates are important in school from now to the end of the term? Look at the events in the box for some ideas. Make a list of important dates and events in the next month.**

> Tests   School holidays   Last day of class   Registration for next semester

B **Make a calendar. Write the important events on the calendar.**

November

S	M	T	W	T	F	S
		1 Election Day	2	3	4	5 Test
6	7	8	9	10	11 Veterans Day – School closed	12
13	14	15	16	17	18	19
20	21 Thanksgiving Party	22	23	24	25 Thanksgiving – School closed	26
27	28	29	30			

C **GROUPS OF 5.** **Plan ahead. Are there any events on the calendar you need to prepare for? Are there any events next month you need to prepare for? What do you need to do? Say two or three things for each event.**

A: *We have a test on November fifth.*
B: *Right. We need to study!*
C: *And we need to get a lot of sleep . . .*

Unit 10 Things I Read in English

A CLASS. Think about things you read in English in your community. Read the chart. Can you think of other things you read in English in your community?

Activity	Always	Sometimes	Never
I read signs in English on store windows.			
I read signs in English on doors.			
I read traffic signs in English.			
I read street signs in English.			
I read ads in English.			
I read food labels in English.			
I read menus in English.			
I read signs on buses in English.			

B Which activities do *you* do? How often? For each activity in the chart, check (✓) *always*, *sometimes*, or *never*.

C GROUPS OF 3. Talk about your answers in Exercise B.

A: *I sometimes read signs in English on store windows. What about you?*
B: *I never read signs in English on store windows. What about you?*
C: *I sometimes read signs in English on store windows. I . . .*

D What do you want to read in English? Write one goal for next week. Check with each other in two weeks. Did you complete your goal?

Next week, I will _____ in English.

E SAME GROUPS. Talk about your goals.

Unit 11 Individual Barriers, Group Support

A **CLASS.** *Barriers* are things that keep you from your goals. Think about your goals for studying English. What are some barriers? Make a list. Use ideas from the box or your own ideas.

> My husband needs the car.   The baby-sitter can't come.
> I'm tired after work.   The school parking lot isn't safe.

B Copy the list of barriers your class made in Exercise A. Which barriers in Exercise A are true for you? Check (✓) them. Circle one of the barriers you checked.

C **NETWORK.** Find classmates with the same barrier you circled. Make a group.

D **GROUPS.** What can you do to overcome your barrier? Make a list of ideas.

Call a classmate. Find out what I missed.

Unit 12   Now I Can

A Look at the first page of each unit. Read the Unit Goals. Which goals did you check off? Choose one goal that you are proud of from each page. Write the goals in a chart in your notebook.

Unit #	Now I Can . . .
1	Now I can talk about school.
2	Now I can introduce someone.

B Report to the class. Tell the class one goal that you can do now.

Now I can write a personal check!

C **CLASS.** Stand up and clap for everyone. CONGRATULATIONS ON YOUR SUCCESS!

Life Skills Writing

Unit 1

1 BEFORE YOU WRITE

A Read the form. Find *Print*, and *Ink*. What do they mean?

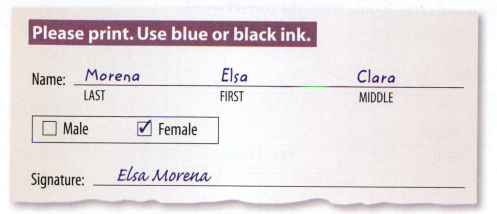

B Read the form again. Match the words with the examples in the box.

a. ![]   b. *Clara*   c. ![]   d. *Elsa Morena*

1. signature __d__   2. middle name ___   3. male ___   4. female ___

2 WRITE

Complete the form. Use your own information.

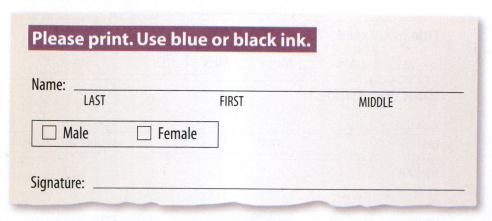

Can you...complete a form with your personal information? ☐

Unit 2

Read the form. Then read the sentences. One word in each sentence is not correct. Find the word and cross it out. Write the correct word.

Title (please check)

☑ Mr.   ☐ Ms.   ☐ Mrs.   ☐ Miss   ☐ Dr.

Name (please print)

Nowak	Alex	M.
LAST	FIRST	MIDDLE INITIAL

Phone

(312) 555-1313	(312) 555-8976	(779) 555-0123
HOME	WORK	CELL

                             Mr.
1. Alex's title is ~~Dr.~~

2. Alex's middle name is Nowak.

3. Alex is a female.

4. Alex's cell phone number is (312) 555-8976.

5. Alex's work phone number is (779) 555-0123.

Complete the form. Use true or made-up information.

Title (please check)

☐ Mr.   ☐ Ms.   ☐ Mrs.   ☐ Miss   ☐ Dr.

Name (please print)

LAST	FIRST	MIDDLE INITIAL

Phone

HOME	WORK	CELL

Can you...complete a form at work?   ☐

Unit 3

1 BEFORE YOU WRITE

A Read the school registration form. Find *M*, *F*, and *Subject*. What do they mean?

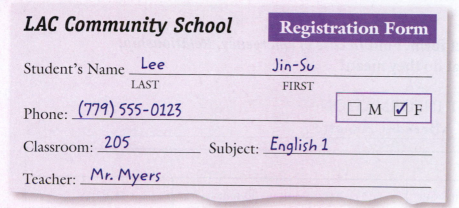

LAC Community School   **Registration Form**

Student's Name __Lee_____ __Jin-Su_____
                    LAST   FIRST

Phone: __(779) 555-0123_____   ☐ M ☑ F

Classroom: __205_____ Subject: __English 1_____

Teacher: __Mr. Myers_____

B Read the form again. Then underline the correct words.

1. The student's **first name** / <u>**last name**</u> is Lee.

2. The student's **phone number** / **classroom number** is 205.

3. The student is **a man** / **a woman**.

4. The student is in **English 1** / **English 2**.

5. The teacher's name is **Mr. Myers** / **Mr. Lee**.

2 WRITE

Complete the school registration form. Use your own information.

LAC Community School   **Registration Form**

Student's Name _____
                    LAST   FIRST

Phone: _____   ☐ M ☐ F

Classroom: _____ Subject: _____

Teacher: _____

Can you...complete a school registration form? ☐

Unit 4

A We fill out emergency contact forms at work, at home, and at school. Why is this important?

B Read the emergency contact form. Find *In case of emergency, Relationship, Daytime,* and *Evening.* What do they mean?

EMERGENCY CONTACT INFORMATION

STUDENT'S NAME (LAST, FIRST) __Bernard, Annette__

IN CASE OF EMERGENCY, CALL:

NAME	RELATIONSHIP	DAYTIME	EVENING	OTHER
Miriam Bernard	mother	(305) 555-1925	(305) 555-8877	Cell (786) 555-4343
Claude Bernard	father	(305) 555-7846	same as above	—

C Read the form again. Then read the sentences. Circle *True* or *False.*

1. The student's name is Bernard Annette. True (False)
2. Her mother is Miriam Bernard. True False
3. Her father's evening phone number is (305) 555-8877. True False

Complete the emergency contact form for yourself. Use true or made-up information.

EMERGENCY CONTACT INFORMATION

STUDENT'S NAME (LAST, FIRST) _____

IN CASE OF EMERGENCY, CALL:

NAME	RELATIONSHIP	DAYTIME	EVENING	OTHER

Can you...complete an emergency contact form? ☐

Unit 5

1 BEFORE YOU WRITE

A Read the check. Find *Pay to the order of, In the amount of,* and *Memo.*
What do they mean?

```
Zofia Kowalska                                              1243
17100 Collins St.
Encino, CA 91316                    DATE  6/9/10

PAY TO THE
ORDER OF ___Imagine_____     $ | 44.50 |
IN THE
AMOUNT OF ___Forty-Four 50/100_____ DOLLARS
FIRST SAVINGS BANK
CA
MEMO  Gift for Ivan            Zofia Kowalska

122213311:  5556665656  1243
```

B Read the check again. Answer the questions.

1. Who is the check from? _____
2. Who is the check to? _____
3. What is the date on the check? _____
4. How much money is the check for? _____
5. What does the check pay for? _____
6. Find Zofia's signature. Circle it.

2 WRITE

You're buying work clothes from the store Clothes World. The total is $39.75.
Write a check. Use today's date.

```
                                                           101

                                    DATE _____

PAY TO THE
ORDER OF _____     $ | ____ |
IN THE
AMOUNT OF _____ DOLLARS
FIRST SAVINGS BANK
CA
MEMO _____      _____

122213311:  5556665656  101
```

Can you...write a personal check? ☐

Unit 6

Read the envelope. Then read the sentences. Underline the correct words.

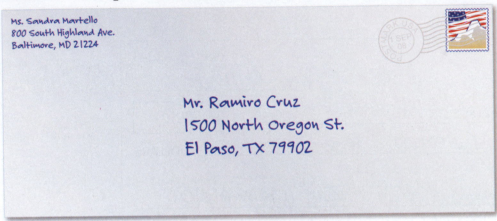

Ms. Sandra Martello
800 South Highland Ave.
Baltimore, MD 21224

Mr. Ramiro Cruz
1500 North Oregon St.
El Paso, TX 79902

1. The letter is from **Sandra Martello** / **Ramiro Cruz**.

2. The letter is to **Sandra Martello** / **Ramiro Cruz**.

3. Sandra Martello lives on **South Highland Avenue** / **North Oregon Street**.

4. Sandra Martello lives in the city of **Maryland** / **Baltimore**.

5. Ramiro Cruz lives in the state of **Texas** / **Maryland**.

6. Ramiro Cruz's zip code is **El Paso** / **79902**.

2 **WRITE**

You are writing a letter to a friend or to your teacher at the school address. Address the envelope. Use true or made-up information.

*Can you…*address an envelope? ☐

Unit 7

Look at the note. Then answer the questions.

To: Cristina Ramos
From: David Lambert
Date: June 1, 2010
Subject: Vacation request

Memorandum

I would like to take my vacation from June 20 to 24.
Please let me know if this is approved.

Thank you.

1. Who is the note from? _David Lambert_____

2. Who is the note to? _____

3. Guess: What is their relationship? _____

4. What is the reason for the note? _____

5. What do you think? What is going to happen next? _____

2 WRITE

Write a note to your manager. Ask for permission to take a vacation or time off from work. Use true or made-up information.

To:
From:
Date:
Subject:

Memorandum

Can you...write a note to your manager about vacation time? ☐

Unit 8

Look at the note. Then answer the questions.

1. Who is the note from? _Barbara_

2. Who is the note to? _____

3. What do you think their relationship is?

    _____

4. How much rice do they need? _____

5. How much coffee do they need? _____

6. How many tomatoes do they need? _____

> 10/24
>
> Sam,
>
> Please get these things
> from the store:
>
> 2 lbs. rice
>
> 1 gal. milk
>
> 1 lb. coffee
>
> 8 apples
>
> 4 large tomatoes
>
> Thanks!
>
> Barbara

2 WRITE

**Write a note to someone in your house. Make a list of six things
you need from the store. Use true or made-up information.**

Can you...write a note about things you need from the store? ☐

Unit 9

Read the postcard. Then answer the questions.

Jan. 22, 2010

Hi Wilma!
How are you? I'm writing from
Denver! It's snowing here.
It's really pretty. But it's cold!

See you soon!

Juanita

Wilma Flores
167 S. 4th Ave.
Yuma, AZ 85364

1. Who is the postcard from? _Juanita_____

2. Who is the postcard to? _____

3. Where is Juanita right now? _____

4. How is the weather in Denver? _____

5. Where does Wilma live? _____

2 WRITE

**Write a postcard to a
friend. Tell your friend
about the weather.**

_____
_____
_____
_____

Can you... write a postcard? ☐

Unit 10

Read the e-mail. Then answer the questions.

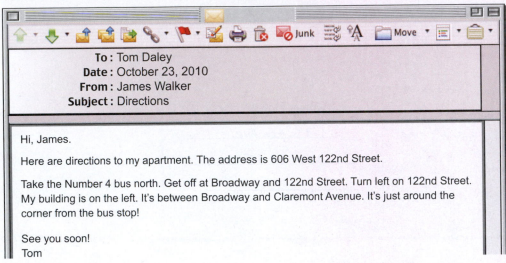

To : Tom Daley
Date : October 23, 2010
From : James Walker
Subject : Directions

Hi, James.

Here are directions to my apartment. The address is 606 West 122nd Street.

Take the Number 4 bus north. Get off at Broadway and 122nd Street. Turn left on 122nd Street. My building is on the left. It's between Broadway and Claremont Avenue. It's just around the corner from the bus stop!

See you soon!
Tom

1. What is Tom's address? <u>His address is 606 West 122nd Street.</u>

2. What bus does James take? _____

3. Where does he get off? _____

4. Where is Tom's building? _____

Write an e-mail to a friend. Give your friend directions to your home. Use true or made-up information.

To :
Date :
From :
Subject :

Can you… write directions to your home? ☐

Unit 11

A Read the form. Find the illnesses and conditions. Discuss the meanings.

PATIENT HEALTH QUESTIONNAIRE

Name _Blanca Gomes_   Date of Birth _8/21/69_   ☐ M ☑ F

Address _621 Arizona Ave., El Paso, TX 79902_   Phone _(915) 555-3538_

Please check illnesses or conditions you have now or had in the past	Childhood	☑ Measles ☑ Mumps ☑ Chicken Pox	Adult	☑ Asthma ☐ High Blood Pressure ☐ HIV/AIDS	☐ Diabetes ☐ Tuberculosis ☐ Heart Disease

Are you allergic to any medicine? Please list: _Penicillin_

Are you currently taking any medication? Please list: _Asthma medication_

B Read the form again. Answer the questions.

1. What illnesses did Ms. Gomes have as a child? _measles, mumps, and chicken pox_

2. What illnesses does she have now? _____

3. What medicine does she take? _____

4. What medicine is she allergic to? _____

2 WRITE

Complete the form for yourself. Use true or made-up information.

PATIENT HEALTH QUESTIONNAIRE

Name _____   Date of Birth _____   ☐ M ☐ F

Address _____   Phone _____

Please check illnesses or conditions you have now or had in the past	Childhood	☐ Measles ☐ Mumps ☐ Chicken Pox	Adult	☐ Asthma ☐ High Blood Pressure ☐ HIV/AIDS	☐ Diabetes ☐ Tuberculosis ☐ Heart Disease

Are you allergic to any medicine? Please list: _____

Are you currently taking any medication? Please list: _____

Can you... complete a medical history form? ☐

Unit 12

Read the job application form. Find *Over 18 years of age*, *Last attended*, and *Most recent*. What do they mean?

Review the job applications on pages 242 and 243. Then complete this job application. Use true or made-up information.

Green's Department Store

Personal Information

Last Name _____ First Name _____

Home Address _____
                                      City   State   Zip

Home Phone _____ E-mail _____

Job applying for _____ When can you start? _____

Are you over 18 years of age? _____ If not, date of birth _____

Please list all the times you are available to work (from 6 A.M. to 12 A.M.)

SUN _____ M _____ T _____ W _____ TH _____ F _____ SAT _____

Education

Last school attended _____ Date last attended _____
                        (name of school)

Job History (list most recent first)

Company _____ Phone Number _____

Address _____

Job _____ Dates worked from _____ to _____

Reason for leaving _____

Company _____ Phone Number _____

Address _____

Job _____ Dates worked from _____ to _____

Reason for leaving _____

Can you…complete a job application? ☐

Team Projects

Unit 1　Meet Your Classmates　<u>MAKE A POSTER</u>

TEAM OF 4　Captain, Co-captain, Assistant, Spokesperson

GET READY　**Captain:** Ask your teammates, "Where are you from?"
Assistant: Write your teammates' answers in the chart.
Add the Captain's answer
Co-captain: Watch the time. You have five minutes.

First Name	Last Name	Country

CREATE　**Co-captain:** Get the materials. Then watch the time. You have ten minutes.
Team: Create your poster.

REPORT　**Spokesperson:** Tell the class about your poster.

Materials
• large paper
• markers
• digital camera or cell phone with camera

Meet Your Classmates

Dora is from Peru.

Dawit is from Ethiopia.

Sen is from Vietnam.

Arturo is from El Salvador.

Unit 2   **Where People Work**   <u>MAKE A VENN DIAGRAM</u>

Materials
- large paper
- markers

TEAM OF 4   Captain, Co-captain, Assistant, Spokesperson

GET READY   **Team:** Choose two workplaces from the box.

Captain: Ask your teammates, "What jobs are in these workplaces?"

a construction site	a hospital	a hotel	an office
a restaurant	a school	a service station	a store

Workplace 1: _____	**Workplace 2:** _____

CREATE   **Co-captain:** Get the materials. Then watch the time.
You have eight minutes.
Team: Create your Venn diagram.

<u>JOBS IN A HOTEL</u>
housekeeper
driver

<u>JOBS IN BOTH</u>
office assistant
landscaper
security guard
cook

<u>JOBS IN A SCHOOL</u>
teacher
principal
librarian
nurse

REPORT   **Spokesperson:** Tell the class about your Venn diagram.

Unit 3 Our School <u>MAKE A BOOKLET</u>

TEAMS OF 4 Captain, Co-captain, Assistant, Spokesperson

Captain: Ask your teammates, "What do new students need to know about your school?" Ask about the important people and their titles. Ask about the important places and the room numbers.

Assistant: Write your teammates' answers in the charts.

Co-captain: Watch the time. You have five minutes.

Important People	Job Titles

Important Places	Room Numbers

CREATE **Co-captain:** Get the materials. Then watch the time. You have ten minutes.
Team: Create your booklet. Draw a map of your school in the booklet.

REPORT **Spokesperson:** Tell the class about your booklet.

Unit 4 Holidays <u>MAKE A CALENDAR</u>

CLASS

GET READY Create a calendar for the year. Use one piece of paper for each month. Put it at the front of the room.

CREATE Write holidays on the calendar. Include U.S. holidays and holidays from your countries.

REPORT Take turns. Tell the class about one holiday. Begin with January 1.

Unit 5   Where We Shop MAKE A BAR GRAPH

TEAMS OF 4 Captain, Co-captain, Assistant, Spokesperson

Materials
• large paper
• colored markers

GET READY **Captain:** Ask your teammates about places they shop
for clothes. Ask *yes/no* questions about the places in the chart.
For example, ask, "Do you shop in department stores?"
(**Team:** You can answer *yes* for more than one place.)
Co-Captain: Watch the time. You have five minutes.
Assistant: Complete the chart with your teammates' names and *yes* or *no*.
Add the Captain's Answer.

Name	In Department Stores	In Small Clothing Stores	In Thrift Stores	On the Internet	In Other Places

CREATE **Co-captain:** Get the materials. Then watch the time. You have ten minutes.
Team: Create your bar graph.

REPORT **Spokesperson:** Tell the class about your bar graph.

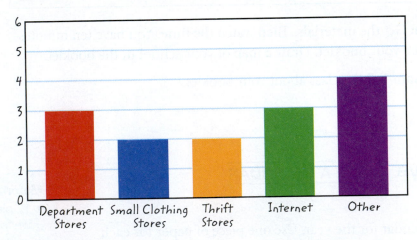

Unit 6: Your Dream House <u>MAKE A FLOOR PLAN</u>

Materials
- large paper
- markers

TEAMS OF 4 Captain, Co-captain, Assistant, Spokesperson

GET READY **Captain:** Ask your teammates, "What does your dream house look like?"
Team: Decide together. How many floors does your dream house have? Which rooms are on each floor?
Assistant: Write your teammates' answers.
Co-captain: Watch the time. You have five minutes.

> *1st floor: kitchen, dining room, living room, laundry room*

CREATE **Co-captain:** Get the materials. Then watch the time. You have ten minutes.
Team: Create the floor plan for your dream house. (Hint: See page 113 for an example of a floor plan.)

REPORT **Spokesperson:** Tell the class about your floor plan.

Unit 7 A Day in the Life of . . . <u>MAKE A MAGAZINE</u>

Materials
- 1 piece of white paper
- pen or small marker
- pictures of a famous person (optional)
- stapler and staples

TEAMS OF 4 Captain, Co-captain, Assistant, Spokesperson

GET READY **Team:** Choose a famous person.
Captain: Ask your teammates, "Imagine: What does this person do all day?"
Assistant: Complete the chart.
Co-captain: Watch the time. You have five minutes.

Person: _____					
Morning		**Afternoon**		**Evening**	
Activity	Time	Activity	Time	Activity	Time

CREATE **Co-captain:** Get the materials. Then watch the time. You have ten minutes.
Team: Create a magazine page for your famous person.

REPORT **Spokesperson:** Tell the class about your famous person's day.

COLLECT **Class:** Collect the magazine pages from each group. Staple them together to make a magazine of *People in the News*.

Unit 8　What's for Lunch or Dinner?　MAKE A MENU

TEAMS OF 4　Captain, Co-captain, Assistant, Spokesperson

GET READY　You are opening an American restaurant.
Captain: Ask your teammates, "What's the name of your restaurant? What's on the lunch or dinner menu?"
Assistant: Write your teammates' answers in the chart.
Co-captain: Watch the time. You have five minutes.

Materials
- 2 pieces of white paper
- pen or small marker
- stapler and staples

Restaurant Name: _____		Menu for: _____	
Main Courses	**Sides**	**Desserts**	**Drinks**

CREATE　**Co-captain:** Get the materials. Then watch the time. You have ten minutes.
Team: Create your menu.

REPORT　**Spokesperson:** Tell the class about your menu.

Unit 9　How's the Weather?　GIVE A WEATHER REPORT

Materials
- large paper
- markers

TEAMS OF 4　Captain, Co-captain, Assistant, Spokesperson

GET READY　Your teacher will give each team a month.
Captain: Ask your teammates, "What's the weather here like in _____?"
(month)
Assistant: Write your teammates' answers in the chart.
Co-captain: Watch the time. You have five minutes.

Month: _____		
	Temperatures	**Kind of Weather**
High		
Low		

CREATE　**Co-captain:** Get the materials. Then watch the time. You have ten minutes.
Team: Create your weather report.

REPORT　**Spokesperson:** Give your group's weather report. The class guesses the month.

Unit 10 Our Community <u>MAKE A BOOKLET</u>

Materials
- 1 piece of white paper
- pen or small marker
- stapler and staples

TEAMS OF 4 Captain, Co-captain, Assistant, Spokesperson

GET READY **Team:** Choose a kind of place from the box below.
Captain: Ask your teammates, "What _____
(kind of place)

in our city do you like? Where are they? Why do you like them?"
Assistant: Write your teammates' answers in the chart.
Co-captain: Watch the time. You have five minutes.

| famous places | museums | parks | places for children |
| places to relax | places for sports | restaurants | stores |

Kind of Place _____		
Name of Place	**Location**	**Why It's Good**

CREATE **Co-captain:** Get the materials. Then watch the time. You have ten minutes.
Team: Create a booklet page for your places.

REPORT **Spokesperson:** Tell the class about the places on your page.

Unit 11 Staying Healthy <u>MAKE A POSTER</u>

Materials
- large paper
- markers

TEAMS OF 4 Captain, Co-captain, Assistant, Spokesperson

GET READY **Captain:** Ask your teammates, "What habits are good for your health (healthy)? What habits are not good for your health (unhealthy)?"
Assistant: Write your teammates' answers in the chart.
Co-captain: Watch the time. You have five minutes.

Healthy Habits	Unhealthy Habits

CREATE **Co-captain:** Get the materials. Then watch the time. You have ten minutes.
Team: Create your poster.

REPORT **Spokesperson:** Tell the class about your poster.

Unit 12   Skills You Need   MAKE A POSTER

Materials
• large paper
• markers

TEAMS OF 4   Captain, Co-captain, Assistant, Spokesperson

GET READY   **Team:** Think of three jobs. Brainstorm with your teammates.
Captain: Ask your teammates, "What skills do you need for those jobs?"
Assistant: Write your teammates' answers in the chart.
Co-captain: Watch the time. You have five minutes.

Job 1: _____
Skills

Job 2: _____
Skills

Job 3: _____
Skills

CREATE   **Co-captain:** Get the materials. Then watch the time. You have ten minutes.
Team: Create your poster.

REPORT   **Spokesperson:** Tell the class about your poster.

Grammar Reference

Unit 2, Lesson 3, page 31

Some irregular plural nouns

child	**children**	person	**people**
man	**men**	foot	**feet**
woman	**women**	tooth	**teeth**

Unit 2, Lesson 9, page 42

Spelling rules for simple present tense: Third-person singular (*he, she, it*)

1. Add **-s** for most verbs: *work—work**s**   play—play**s***
2. Add **-es** for words that end in **-ch, -s, -sh, -x,** or **-z** : *watch—watches   relax—relax**es***
3. Change the **y** to **i** and add **-es** when the base form ends in a consonant **+y**: *study—stud**ies***
4. Add **-s** when the base form ends in a **vowel + y**: *play—play**s**   enjoy—enjoy**s***
5. Some verbs have **irregular forms**: *do—**does**   have—**has**   go—**goes***

Unit 7, Lesson 3, page 130

Prepositions of time

at 9:00

before 9:00

after 9:00

on Monday

for two days

(*in* + month)

in May

(*in* + year)

in 2012

(*on* + date)

on May 2

Unit 8, Lesson 3, page 150

Some common non-count nouns

Food: beef, bread, butter, cabbage, cake, cereal, chicken, chocolate, fish, ice cream, lettuce, oil, pizza, rice, salmon, shrimp, soup, yogurt

Drinks: coffee, juice, milk, soda, tea, water

School Subjects: art, English, history, math, music, science

Activities: basketball, homework, laundry, soccer

Others: air-conditioning, chalk, electricity, furniture, hair, information, luggage, money, news, paper, transportation, weather

Remember: Non-count nouns are singular. Example: *Pizza is my favorite food.*

Spelling rules for plural count nouns

Add *-s* to most nouns	book—books
Add *-es* to most nouns that end in *-ch*, *-s*, *-sh*, *-x*, or a consonant + *o*.	watch—watch**es** box—box**es** guess—guess**es** potato—potato**es** dish—dish**es**
Change *y* to *i* and add *-es* to nouns that end in a consonant + *y*.	baby—bab**ies** city—cit**ies**
Change *f* to *v* and add *-s* to nouns that end in *-fe*. Change *f* to *v* and add *-es* to nouns that ends in *-f*.	knife—kni**ves** wife—wi**ves** loaf—loa**ves** shelf shel**ves**

Unit 9, Lesson 3, page 170

Spelling rules for present continuous

1. Add *-ing* to the base form: *cook—cooking   eat—eating*
2. For verbs that end in *e*, drop the final *e* and add *-ing*: *take—taking   make—making*
3. For one-syllable verbs that end in a consonant, a vowel, and a consonant, double the final consonant and add *-ing*. Do not double the final consonant if it is a *w, x,* or *y*: *get—getting play—playing*

Unit 10, Lesson 3, page 190

Prepositions of place

in Los Angeles	*across from* the bank
on First Street	*around* the corner
at 231 First Street	*next to* the supermarket
down the block	*near* the corner
between First *and* Second Streets	*in/at* school

Word List

UNIT 1

Countries

Brazil, 7
Canada, 7
China, 7
El Salvador, 7
England, 7
Ethiopia, 7
Haiti, 7
Korea, 7

Mexico, 7
Peru, 7
Poland, 7
Russia, 7
Somalia, 7
the United States, 7
Vietnam, 7

absent, 12
boring, 18
easy, 18
first name, 10
for work, 16
friendly, 19
good, 18
great, 18
hard, 18

helpful, 19
Interesting, 18
last name, 10
late, 12
shake hands, 8
smart, 19
title, 11
to be safe, 16
to be with family, 16

UNIT 2

accountant, 27
actor, 34
area code, 32
artist, 27
assembly line worker, 41
athlete, 37
bank,
caregiver, 41
carpenter, 41
cashier, 27
child-care center, 32
child-care worker, 27

clean, 38
construction site, 41
cook (n), 27
cook (v), 38
doctor, 27
driver, 27
electrician, 27
factory, 41
gardener, 27
good with children, 39
good with numbers, 39
homemaker, 27

hospital, 32
housekeeper, 27
nurse, 27
nursing home, 41
office, 32
office assistant, 27
organized, 38
painter, 27
pay the bills, 38
phone number, 32
restaurant, 32

sales assistant, 27
security guard, 40
singer, 37
stock clerk, 41
store, 41
take care of
 children, 38
uniform, 40
use a computer, 38
waiter, 27
waitress, 27

UNIT 3

across from, 49
backpack, 47
board, 47
book, 47
borrow, 48
bring, 48
cafeteria, 59
CD, 47
cell phone, 47
chair, 47
computer, 47
computer lab, 59

computer lab assistant, 60
custodian, 60
desk, 47
dictionary, 47
DVD, 54
elevator, 59
eraser, 47
folder, 47
for a short time, 52
hall, 59
interrupt, 51
keyboard, 54

librarian, 60
library, 59
marker, 47
monitor, 54
mouse, 54
next to, 50
notebook, 47
office, 59
on the left, 59
on the right, 59
piece of chalk, 47
piece of paper, 47

principal, 60
set study goals, 52
stairs, 59
study habits, 52
teacher, 48
three-ring binder, 47
throw out, 52
turn off, 50

UNIT 4

aunt, 69
average height, 74
average weight, 74
beard, 74
birthday, 79
blended family, 72
boy, 80
brother, 67
calendar, 78
children, 67
cousin, 69
date, 78
date of birth, 79
daughter, 67
divorced, 72

family tree, 67
father, 67
girl, 80
grandfather, 67
grandmother, 67
half-sister, 72
heavy, 74
husband, 67
kids, 80
long hair, 74
looks like, 70
month, 78
mother, 67
mustache, 74
parents, 67

remarried, 72
short, 74
short hair, 76
sister, 67
son , 67
stepbrother, 72
stepfather, 72
stepmother, 72
stepsister, 72
tall, 74
thin, 74
uncle, 69
wife, 67

Days
Sunday, 78
Monday, 78
Tuesday, 78
Wednesday, 78
Thursday, 78
Friday, 78
Saturday, 78

Months
January, 78
February, 78
March, 78
April, 78
May, 78
June, 78
July, 78
August, 78
September, 78
October, 78
November, 78
December, 78

UNIT 5

beige, 87
bill, 98
black, 87
blouse, 87
blue, 87
broken, 100
brown, 87
cash, 92
change, 93
coin, 92
credit card, 101
dime, 92
dress, 87

extra large, 94
extra small, 94
fit, 100
gift, 88
government, 99
gray, 87
green, 87
handbag, 89
jacket, 87
jeans, 87
large, 94
look good, 100
match, 100

medium, 94
money, 92
need, 88
nickel, 92
orange, 87
pants, 87
penny, 92
personal check, 93
pink, 87
president, 98
price, 93
price tag, 93
purple, 87

quarter, 92
receipt, 93
red, 87
return
  something, 100
shirt, 87
shoes, 87
size, 94
skirt, 87
small, 94
sneakers, 87
socks, 87
sweater, 87

T-shirt, 87
tax, 93
wallet, 89
want, 88
watch, 88
white, 87
work, 100
yellow, 87
zipper, 100

UNIT 6

address, 118
air-conditioning, 119
apartment, 112
appliances, 114
avenue, 118
bathroom, 107
bathtub, 107
bed, 107
bedroom, 107
boulevard, 118
building, 115
chair, 107
cheap, 108
closet, 107
coffee table, 115
dark, 108
dining room, 107

downstairs, 111
dresser, 107
east, 120
expensive, 108
fire, 112
floor lamp, 115
furnished, 114
furniture, 114
garage, 109
goes off, 112
included, 119
kitchen, 107
lamp, 107
large, 108
laundry room, 109
living room, 107
microwave, 107

neighbor, 112
new, 108
north, 120
old, 108
one-bedroom
    apartment, 110
parking, 119
refrigerator, 107
rent, 108
road, 118
shower, 107
sink, 107
small, 108
sofa, 107
smoke, 112
smoke alarm, 112
south, 120

stove, 107
street, 118
studio, 115
sunny, 108
table, 107
table lamp, 115
two-bedroom apartment, 115
unfurnished, 114
upstairs, 111
utilities, 119
toilet, 107
wake up, 112
west, 120
yard, 109

UNIT 7

A.M., 126
always, 136
baby-sit, 129
bored, 141
busy, 128
check e-mail, 127
cook dinner, 127
clean, 134
do my homework, 135
do puzzles, 140
do the laundry, 135
eat breakfast, 127
eat dinner, 127
eat lunch, 127
employee, 133
excited, 141

exercise, 127
free, 134
free time, 138
go dancing, 135
go food shopping, 134
go running, 140
go swimming, 135
go to the beach, 135
go to the mall, 128
go to the park, 128
get dressed, 127
get home, 127
get up, 127
go to sleep, 127
go to work, 127
happy, 141

knit, 140
never, 136
P.M., 126
play basketball, 135
play cards, 135
play soccer, 128
play video games, 135
read the mail, 127
read the newspaper, 127
read the paper, 135
relax, 141
relaxed, 141
ride my bike, 135
sad, 141
see a movie, 128
sometimes, 136

spend time with someone, 134
stressed, 141
take a (computer) class, 129
take a hot bath, 140
take a long walk, 140
take a shower, 127
time in, 133
time out, 133
time sheet, 133
usually, 136
visit someone, 129
wash the dishes, 127
watch TV, 127
weekend, 134
work on my car, 135

UNIT 8

apple pie, 154
apples, 147
baked potato, 154
bananas, 147
beans, 147
beef, 147
bottle of water, 154
bread, 147
butter, 147
cabbage, 147
cabinets, 152
cake, 149
calories, 159
cereal, 147
cheese, 147
chef's salad, 154
chicken, 147
coffee, 154

cookies, 149
counter, 152
cucumbers, 161
cup, 154
dairy, 147
dessert, 155
eggs, 147
expiration date, 153
fat, 158
fish, 147
freezer, 152
fried, 160
fries, 154
fruit, 146
fruit cup, 154
grains, 147
grams (g), 159

green beans, 158
green salad, 154
grilled, 160
hamburger, 148
hungry, 148
ice cream, 154
iced tea, 154
keep (food), 152
lettuce, 147
meat, 146
menu, 155
milk, 147
milligrams (mg), 159
net weight, 159
oils, 147
olives, 161
onions, 147

oranges, 147
ounce (oz.), 157
pancakes, 149
pasta, 149
pepperoni pizza, 154
pizza, 148
pound (lb.), 157
red peppers, 161
rice, 147
roast beef, 161
salmon, 161
sandwich, 154
scrambled eggs, 149
sell by, 152
serving size, 159
shrimp, 161

soda, 154
sodium, 159
steak, 149
steamed, 160
sugar, 158
taco, 148
tomatoes, 161
tomato soup, 154
turkey, 161
use by, 152
vegetable oil, 147
vegetables, 146
yogurt, 147

UNIT 9

batteries, 173
boots, 180
candles, 173
cloudy, 167
cold, 167
cool, 167
drugstore, 175
ear muffs, 180
earthquake, 172
emergency, 172

fall, 167
first aid kit, 173
flashlight, 173
flood, 172
foggy, 169
gas station, 175
gloves, 180
grocery store, 175
hat, 180
heat wave, 172

hot, 167
humid, 169
hurricane, 172
light clothes, 180
matches, 173
medicine, 173
radio, 173
raincoat, 180
rainy, 167
scarf, 180

shorts, 180
small talk, 178
snowstorm, 172
snowy, 167
spring, 167
summer, 167
sun block, 180
sunglasses, 180
sunny, 167
thunderstorm, 172

tornado, 172
turn on, 175
umbrella, 180
warm, 167
weather report, 181
wild fire, 172
windy, 169
winter, 167

UNIT 10

around the corner from, 190
ATM, 187
bank, 187
baseball game, 200
bike, 191
bus, 191
bus stop, 187
car, 191
chocolate, 197

coffee shop, 187
concert, 200
courthouse, 189
DMV, 189
down the block from, 190
department store, 187
drugstore, 187
due date, 198
exact change, 194

fare, 194
fire station, 187
gas station, 187
get off/on, 194
grand opening, 200
hair salon, 187
laundromat, 187
library card, 198
near, 190
park, 187

parking lot, 187
police station, 187
post office, 187
public library, 198
subway, 191
supermarket, 187
taxi, 191
tissues, 197
train, 191
yard sale, 200

UNIT 11

alcoholic beverage, 213
ankle, 207
antibiotics, 220
arm, 207
back, 207
backache, 220
bones, 218
chest, 207
clap, 207
cold, 209
cough, 209
day before yesterday, 215
ear, 207
earache, 209
elbow, 207
eye, 207
face, 207
feel sick, 208

feel well, 208
feet, 207
fever, 209
flu, 209
foot, 207
get sick, 218
get strong, 218
hand, 207
have energy, 218
head, 207
headache, 208
heart, 218
heating pad, 220
hurts, 208
ice pack, 220
knee, 207
last night, 214

leg, 207
lie down, 212
look straight ahead, 212
lose weight, 218
make a fist, 212
mouth, 207
neck, 207
nod, 207
nose, 207
Open your mouth and say *Ahh*, 212
orally, 213
out of reach, 213
prevent health problems, 218
roll up your sleeve, 212
shake, 207

shoulder, 207
sit on the table, 212
sore throat, 208
step, 212
step on the scale, 212
stomach, 207
stomachache, 208
stuffy nose, 209
tablet, 213
take a deep breath, 212
teeth, 207
throat, 208
tooth, 207
toothache, 208
touch, 207
wrist, 207
yesterday, 215

UNIT 12

afternoon shift, 233
answer the phone, 227
body language, 238
clean floors, 227
day shift, 233
deliver packages, 227
drive a truck, 227
experience, 232
firmly, 238

first impression, 238
fix furniture, 229
fix things, 227
full-time, 232
hair stylist, 241
help people, 227
lap, 238
lean forward, 238
lift heavy boxes, 227

make cabinets, 229
make copies, 227
make eye contact, 238
night shift, 233
part-time, 232
smile, 238
stand three feet away, 238
supervise workers, 227
take care of grounds, 227

take inventory, 229
take messages, 227
take returns, 229
use a cash register, 227
use a computer, 227
want ad, 232

Audio Script

PRE-UNIT

Page 2, Use the Alphabet, Exercise C

1. A   2. F   3. y   4. B   5. Q   6. Z   7. H   8. J

Page 2, Use the Alphabet, Exercise D

1. A   2. E   3. I   4. O   5. U

Page 2, Use Numbers, Exercise C

1. 5   2. 70   3. 9   4. 50   5. 2
6. 8   7. 10   8. 90   9. 40   10. 6

UNIT 1

Page 8, Listen, Exercise B

Luisa: Hi, I'm Luisa Flores.
Ilya: Hi, I'm Ilya Petrov.
Luisa: Nice to meet you.
Ilya: Nice to meet you, too.

Page 8, Listen, Exercise C

Luisa: Hi, I'm Luisa Flores.
Ilya : Hi, I'm Ilya Petrov.
Luisa: Nice to meet you.
Ilya : Nice to meet you, too.
Luisa: Where are you from, Ilya?
Ilya: I'm from Russia. What about you?
Luisa: I'm from Peru.

Page 11, Practice, Exercise B

1.
A: Your name, please?
B: Michael Chen.
A: Can you spell your first name, please?
B: Sure. M-I-C-H-A-E-L.
A: M-I-C-H-A-E-L. OK, Mr. Chen. You want to take English classes, right?

2.
A: Your name, please?
B: Darya Kotova.
A: Can you spell your last name, please?
B: Sure. K-O-T-O-V-A.
A: K-O-T-O-V-A. OK, Miss Kotova. You want to take English classes, right?

3.
A: Your name, please?
B: Ana Lopez.
A: Can you spell your last name, please?
B: Sure. L-O-P-E-Z.
A: L-O-P-E-Z. OK, Ms. Lopez. You want to take computer classes, right?

Page 12, Listen, Exercise B

Luisa: Who's that?
Sen: That's Ilya.
Luisa: No, that's not Ilya.
Sen: Oh, you're right. That's Nikolai.
Luisa: Nikolai? Where's he from?
Sen: He's from Russia.

Page 12, Listen, Exercise C

Luisa: Who's that?
Sen: That's Ilya.
Luisa: No, that's not Ilya.
Sen: Oh, you're right. That's Nikolai.
Luisa: Nikolai? Where's he from?
Sen: He's from Russia.
Luisa: So, where's Ilya?
Sen: I don't know. I guess he's absent.
Ilya: I'm not absent. I'm here! Sorry I'm late.

Page 13, Conversation, Exercise B

1. She's a student.
2. He's in level 1.
3. He's late.

Page 18, Listen, Exercise B

Min Jung: Hi! So, what class are you in?
Ilya: We're in level 1.
Min Jung: Oh. How is it?
Kamaria: It's good. The teacher is great.
Min Jung: What about the students?
Ilya: They're great, too.

Page 18, Listen, Exercise C

Min Jung: Hi! So, what class are you in?
Ilya: We're in level 1.
Min Jung: Oh. How is it?
Kamaria: It's good. The teacher is great.
Min Jung: What about the students?
Ilya: They're great, too. There's just one problem.
Min Jung: Oh? What's the problem?
Ilya: English is *hard*.

UNIT 2

Page 28, Listen, Exercise B

Gabriela: So, what do you do?
Pierre: I'm a gardener. And I'm a student at Greenville Adult School.
Gabriela: Really? I'm a student there, too. And I'm an artist.
Pierre: Oh, that's interesting.

Page 28, Listen, Exercise C

Gabriela: So, what do you do?
Pierre: I'm a gardener. And I'm a student at Greenville Adult School.
Gabriela: Really? I'm a student there, too. And I'm an artist.
Pierre: Oh, that's interesting. I think Emilio is an artist, too.
Gabriela: No, he's not.
Pierre: Yes, he is. He's a painter.
Gabriela: Right, but he's a *house* painter, not an artist!

Page 31, Practice, Exercise B

nurses
gardeners
cashiers
waitresses
drivers

Page 32, Practice, Exercise A

1. five, one, two
2. seven, one, four
3. three, oh, five
4. seven, oh, eight
5. nine, one, nine
6. seven, eight, six

Page 33, Give Phone Numbers

1.
Hi, Than. This is Mr. Fernandez at Center Hospital. I'm calling about the gardener job. Please call me back at 562-555-1349. That's 562-555-1349.

2.
Hi, Maya. This is Grace Simms at Grace's Office Supplies. I'm calling about the cashier job. Please call me back. My number is 408-555-7821. That's 408-555-7821.

3.
Hi, Nara. This is Jin Heng Wu at Riverside Child Care. I'm calling about the child-care worker job. Please call me back at 773-555-9602. That's 773-555-9602.

4.
Hi, Juan. This is Ms. Rodriguez at Carla's Restaurant. I'm calling about the waiter job. Please call me back at 339-555-8851. That's 339-555-8851.

Page 34, Listen, Exercise B

Claudia: Who's that? Is she a teacher?
Ilya: No, she's not. She's a student. And she's a cashier at Al's Restaurant.
Claudia: Oh, that's interesting. And what do you do?
Ilya: I'm a cook.

Page 34, Listen, Exercise C

Claudia: Who's that? Is she a teacher?
Ilya: No, she's not. She's a student. And she's a cashier at Al's Restaurant.
Claudia: Oh, that's interesting. And what do you do?
Ilya: I'm a cook.
Claudia: A cook! I'm a cook, too.
Ilya: Really?
Claudia: Yes. I'm a cook, a waitress, a child-care worker, and a doctor.
Ilya: *Four* jobs?!
Claudia: Yes! I'm a homemaker!

Page 35, Conversation, Exercise B

1. Is she a teacher?
2. She's a student.
3. What do you do?
4. Are you a doctor?

Page 40, Listen, Exercises B and C

Dora: What do you do?
Miriam: I'm a nurse.
Dora: Really? Where do you work?
Miriam: I work at a school on Main Street. I'm a school nurse.
Dora: Oh. That's interesting.

Page 40, Listen, Exercise D

Dora: What do you do?
Miriam: I'm a nurse.
Dora: Really? Where do you work?
Miriam: I work at a school on Main Street. I'm a school nurse.
Dora: Oh. That's interesting. What about you, Pierre?
Pierre: I work at a school, too.
Dora: Oh. Are you a teacher?
Pierre: No. I'm a student.
Miriam: That's not a job, Pierre!
Pierre: Oh, yes it is. It's a *hard* job!

Page 44, Act It Out, Step 1

Paula: Minh, this is Sahra. Sahra, this is Minh.
Minh: Nice to meet you, Sahra.
Sahra: Nice to meet you, too, Minh. What do you do?
Minh: I'm a stock clerk. What about you?
Sahra: I'm a driver.
Minh: Oh. That's interesting. Where do you work?
Sahra: I work at Holiday Hotel. And you? Where do you work?
Minh: I work at a store—Gil's Supermarket.

UNIT 3

Page 48, Listen, Exercises A and B

Ms. Reed: OK, everyone. Are you ready for the test? Put away your books. Take out a piece of paper.
Aram: Chan, can I borrow a pencil?
Chan: Sure, Aram.

Page 48, Listen, Exercise C

Ms. Reed: OK, everyone. Get ready for the test. Don't look at your books. Take out your notebooks.
Aram: Chan, can I borrow a pencil?
Chan: Sure, Aram.
Ms. Reed: Uh-oh. Please turn off your cell phones, everyone.
Aram: Uhmm, Ms. Reed?
Ms. Reed: Yes?
Aram: I think that's *your* cell phone.
Ms. Reed: Oh!

Page 54, Listen, Exercise B

Carlos: What's this called in English?
Mei-Yu: It's a mouse.
Carlos: And these? What are these called?
Mei-Yu: They're CDs.

Page 54, Listen, Exercise C

Carlos: What's this called in English?
Mei-Yu: It's a mouse.
Carlos: And these? What are these called?
Mei-Yu: They're CDs.
Carlos: Nope. You're wrong.
Mei-Yu: What? I'm not wrong. That's a mouse and those are CDs.
Carlos: No, they're not. This is a *picture* of a mouse and that's *picture* of CDs.
Mei-Yu: Very funny.

Page 58, Practice, Exercise B

1.
A: What page are we on?
B: Nineteen.

2.
A: How many of your classmates work?
B: Twelve.

3.
A: How many students are here today?
B: Thirty-five.

4.
A: Which room is the office?
B: Room fifty-nine.

5.
A: How many desks are in the classroom?
B: Forty.

6.
A: How many dictionaries are in the classroom?
B: Thirty.

7.
A: How many students in our class are from China?
B: Seventeen.

8.
A: How many students are in level 1?
B: Eighty-two.

Page 60, Listen, Exercise B

Ken: Excuse me. Is the computer lab open?
Berta: Sorry. I don't know. Ask him.
Ken: Oh, OK. But . . . Who is he?
Berta: He's the computer lab assistant!

Page 60, Listen, Exercise C

Ken: Excuse me. Is the computer lab open?
Berta: Sorry. I don't know. Ask him.
Ken: Oh, OK. But . . . Who is he?
Berta: He's the computer lab assistant!

UNIT 4

Page 68, Listen, Exercise B

Sen: That's a great photo. Who's that?
Dora: My father.
Sen: Oh, he looks nice.
Dora: Thanks.

Page 68, Listen, Exercise C

Sen: That's a great photo. Who's that?
Dora: My father.
Sen: Oh, he looks nice.
Dora: Thanks.
Sen: And is that your sister? She looks like you.
Dora: Thanks, but that's not my sister. That's my daughter!

Page 74, Listen, Exercises A and B

Zofia: Is your family here in this country?
Ernesto: My brother is here. He's a carpenter.
Zofia: Oh. What's he like?
Ernesto: He's great. He's a lot of fun.
Zofia: Does he look like you?
Ernesto: No. He's tall and thin and he has long hair.

Page 74, Listen, Exercise C

Zofia: Is your family here in this country?
Ernesto: My brother is here. He's a carpenter.
Zofia: Oh. What's he like?
Ernesto: He's great. He's a lot of fun.
Zofia: Does he look like you?
Ernesto: No. He's tall and thin and he has long hair. Here's a picture of him.
Zofia: Oh. He has a beard and a mustache, too.
Ernesto: He has one more thing, too.
Zofia: Oh, yeah? What's that?
Ernesto: He has a wife.
Zofia: Oh.

Page 78, Practice, Exercise C

1. January twenty-first
2. January fifth
3. January seventeenth
4. January eighth
5. January twenty-fourth
6. January eleventh
7. January thirtieth
8. January ninth

Page 79, Practice, Exercise F

1.
A: What's your date of birth?
B: It's March fourteenth, nineteen seventy-seven.
2.
A: When was your son born?
B: October second, two thousand and one.
3.
A: What's your sister's date of birth?
B: It's May twenty-eighth, nineteen eighty-eight.
4.
A: When was your daughter born?
B: August thirty-first, nineteen ninety-five.
5.
A: When was your father born?
B: December seventeenth, nineteen fifty-nine.
6.
A: What's your brother's date of birth?
B: It's September second, nineteen sixty-two.

Page 80, Listen, Exercise B

Assefa: Hi, Zofia. Where are you?
Zofia: I'm at my friend's house. I'm babysitting for her kids.
Assefa: Oh. How old are they?
Zofia: Well, her son is eleven. He's in the fifth grade. And her daughter is six. She's in the first grade.

Page 80, Listen, Exercise C

Assefa: Hi, Zofia. Where are you?
Zofia: I'm at my friend's house. I'm babysitting for her kids.
Assefa: Oh. How old are they?
Zofia: Well, her son is eleven. He's in the fifth grade. And her daughter is six. She's in the first grade.
Assefa: What are they like?
Zofia: Well, Kevin's great.
Assefa: Oh. And what about her daughter?
Zofia: Terry? She's really friendly, but my friend calls her "Terry the terrible."
Assefa: Why?
Zofia: I really don't know.

UNIT 5

Page 88, Listen, Exercises A and B

Zofia: I need a gift for my brother Robert. It's his birthday next week.

Carlos: How about clothes?

Zofia: Well, he *needs* clothes, but he *wants* a backpack!

Page 88, Listen, Exercise C

Zofia: I need a gift for my brother Robert. It's his birthday next week.

Carlos: How about clothes?

Zofia: Well, he *needs* clothes, but he *wants* a backpack!

Carlos: Then get two backpacks!

Zofia: Two?

Carlos: Yes. My birthday is next month and I want a backpack, too!

Page 93, Practice, Exercise A

1. **Customer:** Excuse me. How much is this blouse?
   Assistant: It's $11.95.

2. **Customer:** Excuse me. How much are these shoes?
   Assistant: They're $34.99.

3. **Customer:** Excuse me. How much is this watch?
   Assistant: It's $23.50.

4. **Customer:** Excuse me. How much are these pants?
   Assistant: They're $13.49.

Page 94, Listen, Exercise B

Assefa: Do you have this sweater in a large?

Assistant: No, I'm sorry. We don't.

Assefa: Too bad. It's for my sister and she needs a large.

Page 94, Listen, Exercise C

Assefa: Do you have this sweater in a large?

Assistant: No, I'm sorry. We don't.

Assefa: Too bad. It's for my sister and she needs a large.

Assistant: What about this sweater? Does she like blue?

Assefa: Yes, she does.

Assistant: Well, here you go.

Assefa: Great. Thanks.

Page 100, Listen, Exercises B and C

Matt: Good morning! This is Matt Spencer, and you're listening to *Shopping Time* on Greenville News Radio. Today's question is: Why do people return clothes? Right now, I'm in the popular clothing store Imagine. Many people are in line here at the customer service desk. Let's find out why they're here . . . Hello, Ma'am.

Woman 1: Hi.

Matt: Ma'am, can you tell us why you're here today?

Woman 1: Well, I need to return this shirt.

Matt: And why do you need to return it?

Woman 1: My husband doesn't like it. I need to get him a different gift!

Matt: Oh, too bad. It looks like a nice shirt to me! But I guess I'm not your husband. OK, how about over here—sir? What are you returning, and what's the problem?

Man 1: I'm returning these pants. They don't match my shirt.

Matt: Oh, no? So, you need a different color.

Man 1: Right. I want beige pants instead.

Matt: All right. Now, the next person in line is a young woman . . . Miss?

Woman 2: Uh, yeah?

Matt: What are *you* here for today?

Woman 2: I'm returning these pants. They don't fit. They're too big!

Matt: Ahh. Well, that's a good reason. OK, let's ask one more person . . . Sir? I see you're returning a jacket. What's the problem with it?

Man 2: The zipper doesn't work.

Matt: It doesn't work? You mean, it's broken?

Man 2: Yeah. I need a new one.

Matt: OK, well, good luck with that. . . . And that's all we have time for today! Join me tomorrow, for a discussion of the question: What's the best toy? We'll talk to Susan Ianello, the president of Good for You Toys . . .

UNIT 6

Page 108, Listen, Exercise B

Dan: Oh, wow! This house looks great!

Emily: Really?

Dan: Yes. There are two bedrooms and a large kitchen.

Emily: What about a dining room?

Dan: Well, no. There's no dining room.

Page 108, Listen, Exercise C

Dan: Oh, wow! This house looks great!

Emily: Really?

Dan: Yes. There are two bedrooms and a large kitchen.

Emily: What about a dining room?

Dan: Well, no. There's no dining room.

Emily: That's OK. The kitchen's large. How's the rent?

Dan: Not bad. It's pretty cheap. There *is* one problem, though.

Emily: Oh? What's that?

Dan: It's not in the United States. It's in Canada!

Page 114, Listen, Exercise B

Amy: Excuse me. Is there an apartment for rent in this building?

Manager: Yes, there is. There's a one-bedroom apartment on the second floor.

Amy: Oh, great. Is it furnished?

Manager: Well, yes and no. There's a dresser, but no beds.

Lei: Oh. Well, are there appliances?

Manager: Uh, yes and no. There's a stove, but no refrigerator.

Page 114, Listen, Exercise C

Amy: Excuse me. Is there an apartment for rent in this building?

Manager: Yes, there is. There's a one-bedroom apartment on the second floor.

Amy: Oh, great. Is it furnished?

Manager: Well, yes and no. There's a dresser, but no beds.

Lei: Oh. Well, are there appliances?

Manager: Uh, yes and no. There's a stove, but no refrigerator. So? Are you interested?

Amy: Well, yes.

Lei: And no!

Page 120, Listen, Exercise B

Thank you for calling Joe's Furniture Store. We're located at 231 Fifth Avenue in Riverside.

For store hours, please press 1. For directions, press 2.

For directions from the north, press 1.
For directions from the south, press 2.

Page 120, Listen, Exercise C

Thank you for calling Joe's Furniture Store. We're located at 231 Fifth Avenue in Riverside.

For store hours, please press 1. For directions, press 2.

For directions from the north, press 1.
For directions from the south, press 2.

You're coming from the south. Go north on 12th Street. Turn left on Fifth Avenue. Continue on Fifth Avenue for one block. Joe's is on the left, across from the hospital. Once again, go north on 12th street. Turn left on Fifth Avenue. Go one block. You can't miss it. So, hurry into Joe's and save!

UNIT 7

Page 128, Listen, Exercise B

Gloria: Are you free tomorrow? How about a movie?

Sen: Sorry, I'm busy. I work on Saturdays.

Gloria: Oh. Well, when do you get home?

Sen: At 8:00.

Page 128, Listen, Exercise C

Gloria: Are you free tomorrow? How about a movie?

Sen: Sorry, I'm busy. I work on Saturdays.

Gloria: Oh. Well, when do you get home?

Sen: At 8:00.

Gloria: That's not a problem.

Sen: No? What time is the movie?

Gloria: What do you mean?

Sen: What time does the movie start?

Gloria: It starts when we want. It's a DVD!

Page 134, Listen, Exercise B

Mei-Yu: Gee, I'm so glad it's Friday!

Ernesto: Me, too. What do you usually do on the weekend?

Mei-Yu: Well, I always clean the house on Saturdays, and I always spend time with my family on Sundays. What about you?

Ernesto: I usually shop for food on Saturdays, and I sometimes go to the park on Sundays.

Page 134, Listen, Exercise C

Mei-Yu: Gee, I'm so glad it's Friday!

Ernesto: Me, too. What do you usually do on the weekend?

Mei-Yu: Well, I always clean the house on Saturdays, and I always spend time with my family on Sundays. What about you?

Ernesto: I usually shop for food on Saturdays, and I sometimes go to the park on Sundays.

Mei-Yu: I love the weekend.

Ernesto: Yeah, especially Sunday.

Mei-Yu: Right. Saturday is for cleaning and shopping, and Sunday is for fun.

Ernesto: Exactly. In our house, we call Sunday "fun day."

Page 140, Listen, Exercises B and C

Hello. This is Sue Miller with *Life Styles*. Our program today is about relaxing. So, how often do *you* relax? Many people say: "Relax? I never relax." What about *you*?

How often do you take a long hot bath?

How often do you go running?

How often do you listen to music?

How often do you take a long walk?

Sometimes? Never? That's not good.

We're all busy, but we need to relax—and not just sometimes. You need to relax every day. It helps you study better, it helps you work better, and it helps you be a better parent.

Well, that's all for today. . . .

Thank you for listening to *Life Styles*. This is Sue Miller saying *relax* and good-bye from Greenville News Radio.

UNIT 8

Page 148, Listen, Exercise B

Marius: Wow, I'm hungry!
Gabriela: Yeah, me, too. What do you want for lunch?
Marius: Pizza! I love pizza! What about you?
Gabriela: I don't really like pizza, but I *love* tacos!

Page 148, Listen, Exercise C

Marius: Wow, I'm hungry!
Gabriela: Yeah, me, too. What do you want for lunch?
Marius: Pizza! I love pizza! What about you?
Gabriela: I don't really like pizza, but I *love* tacos! And look! There's a taco place over there!
Marius: Sounds good! But wait a minute. It's not time for lunch!
Gabriela: No?
Marius: No. It's only 10:30!
Gabriela: So, forget about lunch. Let's have pizza and tacos for breakfast!

Page 154, Listen, Exercise B

Waiter: Can I help you?
Greg: Yes, I'd like a hamburger and a soda.
Waiter: Is that a large soda or a small soda?
Greg: Large, please.
Waiter: OK, a large soda . . . Anything else?
Greg: Yes. A small order of fries.

Page 154, Listen, Exercise C

Waiter: Can I help you?
Greg: Yes, I'd like a hamburger and a soda.
Waiter: Is that a large soda or a small soda?
Greg: Large, please.
Waiter: OK, a large soda . . . Anything else?
Greg: Yes. A small order of fries.
Liz: A hamburger, fries, and a soda? You know, that's not very healthy! What about vegetables?
Greg: Well, there's lettuce on the hamburger.
Liz: OK . . . And what about fruit?
Greg: You're right! I need fruit. I know . . . I'll have a piece of apple pie, too.

Page 157, Compare Food Prices, Exercise B

1.
A: How much is the chicken?
B: It's three twenty-nine a pound.

2.
A: How much are the bananas?
B: They're ninety-nine cents a pound.

3.
A: How much is the yogurt?
B: It's three eighty-five.

4.
A: How much are the apples?
B: They're one ninety-nine a pound.

5.
A: How much are the onions?
B: They're eighty-nine cents a pound.

6.
A: How much is the bread?
B: It's two fifty-nine.

Page 160, Listen Exercises A and B

Hannah: Good morning. This is Hannah Charles with Greenville News Radio. You're listening to *The Food Show*. Do you have questions about food? Well, call and ask. Now here's our first caller . . .
Greg: Hi Hannah. I'm Greg Johnson. My wife says that I don't eat healthy food. She says, "Eat more fruit and vegetables." But I'm a meat and potatoes man.
Hannah: OK, Mr. Meat and Potatoes. Tell me, do you like chicken?
Greg: Sure. I eat a lot of chicken.
Hannah: And do you like grilled chicken or fried chicken?
Greg: I like grilled chicken *and* fried chicken.

Hannah: OK. Now, let me ask you a question. How many calories are there in a piece of fried chicken?

Greg: Hmm. I don't know.

Hannah: 250 calories.

Greg: 250 calories!

Hannah: That's right, but in a piece of grilled chicken there are only about 100 calories. So, the choice is easy. The next time you have chicken, eat grilled chicken, not fried.

Greg: OK. That's not so hard.

Hannah: Now another question. This is about potatoes. How much fat is there in an order of fries? Do you know?

Greg: A lot?

Hannah: You're right. There are 15 grams of fat in a small order of fries. But there's no fat in a plain baked potato. That's 15 grams in the fries and no grams in the baked! But remember, no butter! So, the next time you have potatoes, think baked, not fried.

Greg: Wow. I don't believe it!

Hannah: Yes. And one more thing, listen to your wife! . . . She's right. Those vegetables and fruit *are* good for you. Thanks a lot for calling *The Food Show*. We have time for one more call.

Page 163, Grammar

A: This omelet is really good. What's in it?

B: Eggs and cheese. Oh, and there's salt, but not much.

A: Eggs? How many eggs?

B: Three.

A: And how much cheese?

B: Just one slice.

A: What do you cook it in? Do you use butter or oil?

B: I use oil, but it's good with butter, too.

UNIT 9

Page 168, Listen, Exercises B and C

David: Hello?

Laura: Hi! It's me. How are you?

David: Fine, thanks. Where are you?

Laura: I'm in Tampa. I'm visiting family, but they're at work now.

David: Tampa! That's great! How's the weather there?

Laura: Well, it's cold and rainy.

Page 168, Listen, Exercise D

David: Hello?

Laura: Hi! It's me. How are you?

David: Fine, thanks. Where are you?

Laura: I'm in Tampa. I'm visiting family, but they're at work now.

David: Tampa! That's great! How's the weather there?

Laura: Well, it's cold and rainy.

David: Oh, that's too bad. It's beautiful here in Green Bay. It's not warm, but it's sunny.

Laura: Don't tell me that! Here I am in Tampa, and I'm just sitting in the living room and watching the rain!

Page 174, Listen, Exercise B

Dan: Are you watching the news?

Emily: No, I'm not. I'm reading a magazine.

Dan: Well, turn on the TV. A big storm is coming.

Emily: Really?

Dan: Yes. In fact, I'm coming home early. I'm at the supermarket now.

Page 174, Listen, Exercise C

Dan: Are you watching the news?

Emily: No, I'm not. I'm reading a magazine.

Dan: Well, turn on the TV. A big storm is coming.

Emily: Really?

Dan: Yes. In fact, I'm coming home early. I'm at the supermarket now.

Emily: Oh, good. Are you getting water?

Dan: Yes. I'm getting water, food, and a lot of batteries.

Emily: Great. Get matches, too.

Dan: OK. Do we need anything else?

Emily: Yes. We need good weather!

Page 181, Listen, Exercises A and B

Good morning. This is *Weather Watch* on Greenville News Radio. Here's the weather report for cities across the country.

It's cloudy and very hot in Los Angeles. The temperature is already 90 degrees. Wear light clothes and drink lots of water if you go outside.

It's a beautiful day in Atlanta! It's warm and very sunny now with a temperature of 75 degrees. So, go outside, take your sunglasses, and enjoy the nice weather!

It's raining in New York City, and the temperature is 62 degrees. Take your umbrella if you go out.

It's very windy in Chicago. The temperature is only 38 degrees. So, don't forget your scarf and gloves. It's pretty cold out there!

UNIT 10

Page 188, Listen, Exercise B

Berta: Excuse me. Can you help me? I'm looking for Foodsmart.
Mail Carrier: Sure. It's on Seventh between Hill and Oak.
Berta: Sorry?
Mail Carrier: It's on Seventh Avenue between Hill Street and Oak Street.
Berta: Thanks.

Page 188, Listen, Exercise C

Berta: Excuse me. Can you help me? I'm looking for Foodsmart.
Mail Carrier: Sure. It's on Seventh between Hill and Oak.
Berta: Sorry?
Mail Carrier: It's on Seventh Avenue between Hill Street and Oak Street.
Berta: Thanks. Uh… is that near here?
Mail Carrier: Yes. It's just around the corner.
Berta: They're having a grand opening. I guess there are a lot of people there.
Mail Carrier: No, not really. Only one or two workers.
Berta: Really? I don't understand.
Mail Carrier: Today is October 7. The grand opening is *tomorrow*, October 8!

Page 192, Practice

Conversation 1
A: Don't turn left here.
B: Oh, thanks. I'll turn at the next street.

Conversation 2
A: Be careful. There's a school near here.
B: You're right. I'll drive slowly. A lot of kids cross here.

Conversation 3
A: Be careful. There's a railroad crossing.
B: I know. Do you see a train?
A: Not right now, but be careful anyway.

Page 194, Listen, Exercise B

Tina: Excuse me. How do you get to Adams College?
Officer: Take the Number 4 bus, and get off at Second Street. It's not far from there.
Tina: Thanks. Oh, and how much does the bus cost?
Officer: Two dollars, but you need exact change.

Page 194, Listen, Exercise C

Driver: Second Street.
Matt: OK. Here we are at Second Street. Now what?
Tina: There's a woman. Let's ask her.
Matt: Excuse me. We want to go to Adams College. How do we get there?
Woman: It's easy! Study, study, study!

Pages 200–201, Listen, Exercises A and B

Welcome back to Greenville News Radio. It's time for our *Weekend Watch*.

What are your plans for this weekend? Are you looking for something to do? Well, here's what's happening in our community.

Foodsmart is having its grand opening on Saturday, October 8. They're giving away samples at 3:00. There'll be lots of food and drinks at this free event.

Saturday night, Greenville's very own Zeebees are singing at the community college. The concert begins at 8:00. Tickets are on sale now for five dollars.

There's a baseball game Sunday afternoon at one o' clock. Greenville High is playing Lincoln High in Greenville Park. Free with a student ID.

And also on Sunday there's a community yard sale at the Community Center across from the fire station. People are selling old toys, furniture, and clothes. The sale is from 10 A.M. to 4 P.M. Get there early. It doesn't cost just to look!

This is Simon Chan. Have a great weekend!

UNIT 11

Page 207, Show What You Know, Step 1

1. Touch your nose.
2. Clap your hands.
3. Close your eyes.
4. Shake your head.
5. Touch your arm.
6. Point to your chest.
7. Nod your head.
8. Point to your knee.

Page 208, Listen, Exercise B

Assistant: Good morning. Greenville Elementary.
Mrs. Lee: Hello. This is Terry Lee. I'm calling about my son Alex.
Assistant: Is that Alex Lee?
Mrs. Lee: Yes. He's sick today. He has a sore throat and a headache.
Assistant: I'm sorry to hear that. What class is he in?
Mrs. Lee: He's in Ms. Wong's class.

Page 208, Listen, Exercise C

Assistant: Good morning. Greenville Elementary.
Mrs. Lee: Hello. This is Terry Lee. I'm calling about my son Alex.
Assistant: Is that Alex Lee?
Mrs. Lee: Yes. He's sick today. He has a sore throat and a headache.
Assistant: I'm sorry to hear that. What class is he in?
Mrs. Lee: He's in Ms. Wong's class.

Assistant:	OK. Thank you for calling. I'll tell Ms. Wong. I hope he feels better soon.
Daughter 1:	Mom, my throat hurts!
Son:	Mom, my head hurts!
Daughter 2:	Mommy, my stomach hurts!
Mrs. Lee:	Uh-oh. Can I call you back?

Page 213, Practice, Exercise A

Pain Away!

Pain Reliever. Fever reducer.

Directions: Take 2 tablets orally every 6 hours.
Warnings:
• Do not take more than 8 tablets per day.
• Take with food or milk.
• Do not drink alcoholic beverages.
• Do not give to children under twelve.
• Keep out of reach of children.

Page 214, Listen, Exercise B

Tuan: You weren't here yesterday.
Luisa: I know. My daughter was home sick. She had a bad cold.
Tuan: Oh, too bad. How is she now?
Luisa: A lot better, thanks. She's back at school.

Page 214, Listen, Exercise C

Tuan: You weren't here yesterday.
Luisa: I know. My daughter was home sick. She had a bad cold.
Tuan: Oh, too bad. How is she now?
Luisa: A lot better, thanks. She's back in school.
Tuan: Great. And what about your other kids?
Luisa: Well, they were sick *last* week, but they're OK now.
Tuan: That's good. Well, take care, Luisa, and have a good day.
Luisa: Oh, thanks, Tuan. I'll try.

Page 215, Conversation, Exercise B

1. Marie wasn't here yesterday morning.
2. The students were in class.
3. The teacher was absent.
4. We weren't at work.

Page 221, Listen, Exercises B and C

Dr. Garcia:	Good evening. This is Dr. Elias Garcia with Greenville News Radio. You're listening to *Ask the Doctor*. I'm here to answer your health questions. . . . Our first call today is from Carl Gold. Carl?
Carl:	Yes. Hello, Dr. Garcia. Here's my problem. I exercise. I know it's good to exercise but I get these terrible backaches. what should I do?

	Should I use an ice pack?
Dr. Garcia:	Yes, ice is good if your backache is from exercising. But only when you first feel the pain. Later, heat is better. You should take a long hot shower.
Carl:	A hot shower?
Dr. Garcia:	Yes. And you should use a heating pad, too.
Carl:	OK, great. Thank you, Dr. Garcia.
Dr. Garcia:	You're welcome. Hello, this is *Ask the Doctor*. Who's speaking?
Jon:	Hello, Dr. Garacia. My name is Jon Kerins. I have a terrible toothache. What should I do? Should I put heat on it?
Dr. Garcia:	Oh, no. You shouldn't put heat on a toothache. Heat might feel good, but it isn't good for you. Here's what you should do: You should eat a small piece of onion.
Jon:	Onion?
Dr. Garcia:	Yes! Believe it or not, onion helps the pain. Also, you should drink lime juice regularly —it helps prevent toothaches.
Jon:	Wow. Lime juice. OK, thank you, Dr. Garcia.
Dr. Garcia:	Thanks for calling. And now we have time for one more call. . . . Hello?
Dana:	Hi, I'm Dana Jones. My husband, my son, and I all have the flu. What should we do?
Dr. Garcia:	Gee, I'm really sorry to hear that. There's not much you can do. You should stay in bed and drink a lot of fluids.
Dana:	You mean, like water?
Dr. Garcia:	Yes, water, or tea, or even juice. You should drink as much as you can.
Dana:	What about antibiotics?
Dr. Garcia:	Unfortunately, antibiotics don't help the flu. You shouldn't take them.
Dana:	OK. Well, thanks.
Dr. Garcia:	I hope you all feel better soon. And that's all the time we have for today. . . .

UNIT 12

Page 228, Listen, Exercise B

Assefa: I noticed the "Help Wanted" sign. I'd like to apply for a job.
Dino: OK. Which job?
Assefa: Well, I'm a cook. I can make great hamburgers.
Dino: Can you make pizza?
Assefa: No, I can't make pizza, but I can learn.

Page 228, Listen, Exercise C

Assefa: I noticed the "Help Wanted" sign. I'd like to apply for a job.

Dino: OK. Which job?

Assefa: Well, I'm a cook. I can make great hamburgers.

Dino: Can you make pizza?

Assefa: No, I can't make pizza, but I can learn.

Dino: Good. As you can see, this place is really busy. The phone never stops.

Assefa: Well, I can answer the phone, too.

Dino: Great. Can you start now? Can you answer the phone?

Assefa: Sure. Dino's Diner. Can I help you?

Page 233, Practice, Exercise E

A: Hey, you're looking for a job, right?

B: That's right. Why?

A: Well, here's one in the paper. It says "no experience necessary."

B: Really? What's the schedule like?

A: Well, it's only part-time, but you can work any shift.

B: Oh, that's great. And how much do they pay?

A: Seven dollars an hour.

B: Hmmm. I guess that's not bad. How can I apply?

Page 234, Listen, Exercise B

Dana: Hi, I'm Dana.

Sam: Hi. I'm Sam. Wow. This store is really busy.

Dana: I know! Listen, I need a favor. Can you work this Saturday?

Sam: Uh, well, yes, I can.

Dana: Oh, great, thanks, because I can't. Can you work from 2:00 to 7:00?

Sam: Un, yes. I guess so.

Page 234, Listen, Exercise C

Dana: Hi, I'm Dana.

Sam: Hi. I'm Sam. Wow. This store is really busy.

Dana: I know! Listen, I need a favor. Can you work this Saturday?

Sam: Uh, well, yes, I can.

Dana: Oh, great, thanks, because I can't. Can you work from 2:00 to 7:00?

Sam: Um, yes. I guess so. . . . but, I don't understand. Why are you asking me all these questions?

Dana: Well, you're the new sales assistant, right?

Sam: No . . . I'm the elevator repair guy. I'm here to fix the elevator.

Page 240, Listen, Exercises B and C

Tina: Good afternoon. This is Tina Martins. You're listening to *Meet Your Neighbors*. Today I'm in Saigon, Greenville's first Vietnamese restaurant, and I'm talking with Bao Tran and Hanh Le. Hello. And congratulations! Your restaurant looks great.

Hanh: Thank you.

Bao: Thanks, Tina.

Tina: So, Bao, is this your first restaurant?

Bao: Yes, it is. But I worked in a restaurant before.

Tina: Oh. Was that here in Greenville?

Bao: Yes. The Greenville Café.

Tina: How long were you there?

Bao: Eight years.

Tina: And what did you do? Were you a cook?

Bao: Oh, I did a lot of things. I was a cashier, a waiter, *and* a cook.

Tina: Wow. So you really know the restaurant business.

Bao: Yes, I think so.

Tina: Hanh, were you in the restaurant business, too?

Hanh: No. I worked in people's homes. I took care of children and I cooked for the families.

Tina: That's interesting. When did you two come to this country?

Hanh: Twelve years ago.

Tina: Well, your English is great.

Hanh: Thanks. We were students at the Greenville Adult School. We also cooked at the school!

Tina: Really!?

Bao: Yes, we cooked for class parties.

Hahn: Right. We were good students, but we were *great* cooks! Just ask our teacher, Ms. Reed!

Hahn: Actually, Bao and I always loved to cook. And now we can cook for everyone here in Greenville. We want everyone here to visit us.

Bao: Yes. We're right across the street from the new Foodsmart. And we're open every day from noon to 11 P.M.

Tina: Well, it's almost noon now, and there are people waiting to get in. So business looks good, and the food smells delicious. For those of you listening today, make a reservation for Saigon at 555-8776. And thank you for listening to *Meet Your Neighbors*.

Page 244, Act It Out, Step 1

Angela: Hi, Miguel. I'm Angela Miller. Thanks for coming in today.

Miguel: Thank *you*. It's nice to meet you.

Angela: You can have a seat here. Now, as you know, we're looking for office assistants. I see you have some experience with that?

Miguel: Yes, I do. I worked for Newtown Auto Supplies.

Angela: How long were you there?

Miguel: Three years. And then my family moved here, to Greenville.

Angela: I see. And what are your skills? Can you use a computer?

Miguel: Yes, I can. I can also answer phones, make copies . . . And I can take inventory, too.

Index

Map of the United States and Canada

U. S. Postal Abbreviations

Alabama	AL	Montana	MT
Alaska	AK	Nebraska	NE
Arizona	AZ	Nevada	NV
Arkansas	AR	New Hampshire	NH
California	CA	New Jersey	NJ
Colorado	CO	New Mexico	NM
Connecticut	CT	New York	NY
Delaware	DE	North Carolina	NC
District of Columbia	DC	North Dakota	ND
Florida	FL	Ohio	OH
Georgia	GA	Oklahoma	OK
Hawaii	HI	Oregon	OR
Idaho	ID	Pennsylvania	PA
Illinois	IL	Rhode Island	RI
Indiana	IN	South Carolina	SC
Iowa	IA	South Dakota	SD
Kansas	KS	Tennessee	TN
Kentucky	KY	Texas	TX
Louisiana	LA	Utah	UT
Maine	ME	Vermont	VT
Maryland	MD	Virginia	VA
Massachusetts	MA	Washington	WA
Michigan	MI	West Virginia	WV
Minnesota	MN	Wisconsin	WI
Mississippi	MS	Wyoming	WY
Missouri	MO		

Canadian Postal Abbreviations

Alberta	AB	Nova Scotia	NS
British Columbia	BC	Nunavut	NU
Manitoba	MB	Prince Edward Island	PE
New Brunswick	NB	Quebec	QC
Newfoundland and Labrador	NL	Saskatchewan	SK
Northwest Territories	NT	Yukon	YT

ARCTIC OCEAN

Barents Sea

EUROPE

Black Sea

Mediterranean Sea

TUNISIA

LIBYA

EGYPT

A F R I C A

NIGER

CHAD

SUDAN

ERITREA

CENTRAL AFRICAN REPUBLIC

ETHIOPIA

GERIA

AMEROON

DEMOCRATIC REPUBLIC OF CONGO

CONGO

UGANDA

KENYA

RWANDA
BURUNDI
MALAWI
COMOROS

TANZANIA

ANGOLA

ZAMBIA

ZIMBABWE

NAMIBIA

BOTSWANA

REPUBLIC OF SOUTH AFRICA

MOZAMBIQUE

SWAZILAND

LESOTHO

MADAGASCAR

SOMALIA

MAURITIUS

REUNION (FRANCE)

INDIAN OCEAN

RUSSIA

A S I A

KAZAKHSTAN

MONGOLIA

GEORGIA

Caspian Sea

UZBEKISTAN

KYRGYZSTAN

ARMENIA

AZERBAIJAN

TURKMENISTAN

TAJIKISTAN

TURKEY

CYPRUS
LEBANON
ISRAEL

SYRIA

IRAQ

IRAN

AFGHANISTAN

CHINA

JORDAN

KUWAIT

BAHRAIN

QATAR

SAUDI ARABIA

UNITED ARAB EMIRATES

PAKISTAN

NEPAL

BHUTAN

YEMEN

OMAN

Arabian Sea

INDIA

MYANMAR BURMA

LAOS

DJIBOUTI

SOCOTRA (YEMEN)

BANGLADESH

THAILAND

VIETNAM

CAMBODIA

SRI LANKA

NORTH KOREA

Sea of Japan

SOUTH KOREA

JAPAN

East China Sea

TAIWAN

PHILIPPINES

South China Sea

BRUNEI

MALAYSIA

SINGAPORE

I N D O N E S I A

EAST TIMOR

PACIFIC OCEAN

Sea of Okhotsk

Bering Sea

WAKE ISLAND (US)

NORTHERN MARIANA ISLANDS

GUAM

YAP

PALAU

FEDERATED STATES OF MICRONESIA

MARSHALL ISLANDS

NAURU

SOLOMON ISLANDS

TUVALU

PAPUA NEW GUINEA

Coral Sea

VANUATU

FIJI

NEW CALEDONIA

AUSTRALIA

TASMANIA (Australia)

NEW ZEALAND

ATLANTIC OCEAN

ICELAND

FAROE ISLANDS

SHETLAND ISLANDS

SCOTLAND

UNITED KINGDOM

NORTHERN IRELAND

REPUBLIC OF IRELAND

ENGLAND

E U R O P E

NORWAY

SWEDEN

Gulf of Bothnia

FINLAND

North Sea

DENMARK

NETHERLANDS
LUXEMBURG
BELGIUM

Baltic Sea

ESTONIA

LATVIA

LITHUANIA

RUSSIA

BELARUS

POLAND

GERMANY

LIECHTENSTEIN

CZECH REPUBLIC

SLOVAKIA

UKRAINE

G. Gascogne

FRANCE

AUSTRIA

SLOVENIA

HUNGARY

MOLDOVA

ROMANIA

CROATIA

BOSNIA-H.

SERBIA & MONTENEGRO

MONACO

ANDORRA

PORTUGAL

SPAIN

SWITZERLAND

ITALY

MACEDONIA

ALBANIA

BULGARIA

GREECE

TURKEY

MALTA

Credits